An Introduction to
Politics, State and Society

An Introduction to Politics, State and Society

James W. McAuley

SAGE Publications
London • Thousand Oaks • New Delhi

SAGE Publications Ltd
6 Bonhill Street
London EC2A 4PU

SAGE Publications Inc
2455 Teller Road
Thousand Oaks, California 91320

SAGE Publications India Pvt Ltd
B-42, Panchsheel Enclave
Post Box 4109
New Delhi – 100 017

British Library Cataloguing in Publication data

A catalogue record for this book is available from the British Library

ISBN 978 0 8039 7932 1

Library of Congress Control Number 2002112351

Typeset by Mayhew Typesetting, Rhayader, Powys

In memory of my father,
Isaac McAuley (1918–2002)

Contents

Acknowledgements

This book has taken me much longer to produce than expected. Such delay has created obvious problems, not least of which is the stretching of deadlines, and sometimes others' patience, to the limits. I wish to begin, therefore, by thanking all of those concerned in the production of the book at Sage for their help and especially Lucy Robinson for her support and goodwill throughout the project.

In my case the sluggishness of creation provides me with an additional quandary. Those who know me best often make it obvious that my memory is far from my strongest feature (as far as I remember that's the way they put it!). So any attempt by me to recall in detail all those who have provided assistance and guidance throughout the extended gestation of this script would no doubt prove futile. I do, however, wish to offer an expression of my gratitude to those many friends who have provided me with succor, guidance, support and much more.

I also wish also to record here my appreciation and indebtedness to my family for all that they have done and the love and strength they have furnished.

To all those others at the University of Huddersfield and far beyond, who have provided intellectual sustenance, leadership, encouragement, food and drink, constructive criticism, time, late night debate, last-minute goals, music and comfort during the time I have spent writing this book – thank you, and long may it continue.

Finally, I want to thank all of the students who over the years have taken the various manifestations of my political sociology courses for their inspiration and help, but most of all their indulgence.

Introduction: Politics, State and Society

Key concepts and issues	Key theorists and writers
• Defining politics and the political	• Louis Althusser
• Political ideologies	• Ronald Inglehart
• Political legitimacy	• Steven Lukes
• Political cultures	• Chantal Mouffe
• Political power	

Areas in social life where political struggles take place (known as 'sites of power') are not just limited to the actions of those in government, or violent armed struggles between revolutionary groups, but instead politics is a wide category existing at both a macro and micro level. Sites of power in contemporary life can be anything from power in interpersonal communication, gender relations in a family, the ability of a professional group to have their 'professional' status recognized in law, up to and including the actions in the House of Commons of those elected to run the country. (Kidd et al., 1998b: 529)

Introduction

All of us live in a social world dramatically altered and recreated in recent decades. It is a world still undergoing rapid economic, social and political change in lifestyle, in gender roles, in the running of the state, and in the very definition of society in a globalized world. How, for example, are we to best understand such climactic transformations as those involving the collapse of the Soviet bloc and end of the Cold War, the startling speed of technological change, the effects of globalization and the turn towards religious fundamentalist, ethic, regionalist, environmentalist and consumerist politics?

In addressing such issues, many social scientists, media commentators, journalists and leading politicians constantly tell us that the old social theories and established political explanations have little meaning or validity. Further, it is argued that the whole realm of politics has lost its capacity to inspire, and that political leaders have lost their ability to guide and influence society. Rather, public debates and discourses are dominated by arguments about declining moral values, individual lifestyles, consumption and the new politics of environmentalism, anti-corporate protests or other contemporary counter-cultures.

Beyond this we are increasingly seen as subject to irrepressible social and political forces of change, such as globalization, which are dissolving national boundaries and the power of individual nation-states. The major industrial processes are now post-Fordist and the intellectual thrust of society post-modern. What is being experienced is a fundamental restructuring of both economic and social relations. In the developed world, societies are overtly multicultural, the nature of the family has been transformed and old elites have been dissolved. It is a new world of freedom for individual choice and individual expression.

More broadly, the collectivism of the past, expressed through a commitment to full employment, rising living standards and the generous provisions of welfare, which provided key organizational and analytical principles throughout the West, has faded. The time of social democracy, dominant in the postwar period has, it is further claimed, now passed. In its place is a new set of social relations focused around individualism. Indeed, some even argue that the terms 'Right' and 'Left' are no longer meaningful in understanding or structuring contemporary politics and society.

But how realistic are the claims and arguments sketched out above and rather more straightforwardly what does it all mean? In trying to analyse and answer these questions this book seeks to introduce, explore and develop a fuller understanding of some of the central theories and issues in political sociology and to apply these to a series of substantive case studies. In doing so we will also consider how social divisions are embodied in the understandings and definitions of 'politics' and the relationship of the individual to the major institutional settings of power and policy-making.

One of the underlying themes of this book concerns the relationships between politics, the social structure and how individuals become and remain engaged with politics. Several further strands emerge in the book. These include, first, the rapid transformations in contemporary social structures and their impact on social and political life. Secondly, the role of human agency and its significance to social and political action and contemporary social and political movements. Thirdly, considerations of contemporary cultural and social dislocations, and the consequences of these processes for some of the major contested areas of political life and political structures.

To do this the book will explore the discourses of and connections between various political ideas and concepts and a range of political groupings, social and political movements and organizations. In particular, it will consider the complex and diverse ways in which divisions of class, ethnicity, gender, sexuality and other social identities still interact to shape life chances, experiences, identities and politics and how these are expressed through political thinking, movements, organization and processes. To begin with, however, we first need to discuss briefly what is understood by the term 'politics'.

Politics and society

For many, the question 'what is politics?' merits a straightforward and probably rather brief answer. There are certain areas of our lives that to many are obviously 'political'. Recent examples of the political include, the government's responses to the conflicts in the Balkans, party political broadcasts on television and the giant political billboard advertising that have become features of our everyday lives. There are also debates in parliament, Prime Minister's question time and of course the politics involved in corralling votes in local and more often general elections, such as those that resulted in the Labour 'landslide' election victories of 1997 and 2001.

Yet, despite the consequences that such a result may have on many peoples lives, it is important to recognize that politics can be, indeed should be, understood as so much more. To have real meaning, the notion of politics must be understood in much wider terms. The realization of such an idea has a strong personal resonance. I can still remember when I first seriously considered the idea that politics was more than putting a 'cross' in a box every four or five years. The precipitant was not any major event on the world stage. It was not even events in the highly politicized arena of my native Belfast, where I spent all of my youth, which invoked such a notion. Rather, it was one of the great loves in my life, music, that opened up this horizon to someone, who in retrospect, largely understood politics through the great set pieces of Unionism and Nationalism, which characterized so much of Northern Irish politics. In particular, for this author, it was the wave of highly politicized music in the mid- to late 1970s that opened horizons of the possibility of politics. The following is a vivid example, from one of my favourite groups of the time, the Tom Robinson Band, of a broader understanding of what politics can be about. Their album, *Power in the Darkness*, carried part of the following interview with the band's leader from *New Musical Express*, as part of its sleeve notes:

> Politics isn't party political broadcasts and general election, it's yer kid sister who can't get an abortion, yer best mate getting paki-bashed, or sent down for possessing one joint of marijuana. . . . I got no illusions about the political left any more than the right: just a shrew idea which of the two side's gonna stomp on us first. All of us – you, me, rock 'n' rollers, punks, longhairs, dope smokers, squatters, students, unmarried mothers, prisoners, gays, the jobless, immigrants, gypsies . . . to stand aside is to take sides.

The political, therefore, is an adjective that can be applied to a whole range of activities. Or at least it should be. What do those people mean who say that 'there's a political dimension to everything we do'? Partly, this may be a result of the coming together of several lines of contemporary political thought. These may include, for example, the feminist argument that the 'personal is the political', or draw upon the Marxist tradition, used to produce a critique of all aspects of social life, or it may make reference to Foucault's important notion that power is everywhere. All of these viewpoints guide us towards a fuller understanding of the political world.

If we try to restrict politics to formal political exchanges we are in danger of leaving out something important, excluding something vital and dynamic, namely the social dimensions to politics. What this book seeks to develop is a view of politics that encloses and involves many areas of social life, such as social class, ethnicity, gender, identity and so on. To do this it is necessary to distinguish between what can be called politics and what is best termed 'the political'. Mouffe puts it as follows:

> The political designates the potential antagonisms inherent in human rela-
> tions and can manifest itself in many different social relations. Politics, for its
> part, indicates the ensemble of discourses, institutions and practices which
> aim at establishing an order; at organising human coexistence, in a context
> that is always conflictual because of the presence of the political. (Mouffe,
> 1993b: 8)

The main subject matter of this book is, therefore, what Mouffe terms 'the political'. Indeed, one of the features this book seeks to highlight is that this notion of the political is not a separate area of human activity. Rather, it is an aspect of broader social relationships, and certainly not something that is, or should be, confined to political organizations, institutions or government. The central links to be made are those of the book's title, connections between society, the state and the political.

Following on from this, it is also necessary to ask what is understood by the term 'society'? Clearly this is not a question that can be quickly answered. Indeed, it could easily provide the entire subject matter for the book. There are, however, two main senses in which the term 'society' is normally used.

First, and at its broadest, it can refer to the totality of human relationships. It is that system of interrelationships and structures that connects individuals. Secondly, in a more narrow sense, it can be used to make reference to a self-perpetuating grouping, which possesses its own distinctive and identifiable culture and institutions. It is probably most useful at this stage to think of a society as a social system, which can be distinguished by identifiable structural, cultural and political characteristics.

This includes an identifiable group of people, living in a clearly demarcated territory, subject to a system of political authority and understandings. It is this interpretation that finds most meaning in this book. The notion of society remains central to sociological analysis, if only because it is at this level that many of the most important elements of social life are organized.

A political culture is that system of attitudes, values and knowledge that is widely shared within a society. It is learned and transmitted from generation to generation (see below). Indeed, as Inglehart (1977a, 1977b, 1980) and Inglehart and Rabier (1986) point out, different societies can be characterized by those specific political cultural attitudes that are relatively enduring. This political culture approach suggests that both political socialization and subjective orientations shape people's responses to their situations. Central to these responses are how people interpret their own circumstances and how they construct their understandings of the broader social dimensions of politics.

As we shall see these perspectives can vary dramatically, cross-culturally and within sub-cultures, nations and states. Further, these variations in subjective orientations reflect different socialization patterns and are therefore difficult to undo or change. Thus, political orientations and actions are due not only to external circumstances, but also to enduring differences in processes and patterns of cultural learning.

This attempt to link macro variables with micro ones and to locate theoretical issues with actual events will be explored throughout the book. Politics and the struggle for power manifests and operates at different levels in society. Sociology involves the conceptualization and theorization of how power operates and is distributed in society. It also seeks to identify the key sources of power. This varies depending upon how power is understood but includes the ideological, economic, military and the political, dispersed through structures of class, gender, ethnicity, patriarchy, sexual orientation and so on.

The individual and politics

In every society individuals become acquainted with a political system in ways that often structure their reaction to political events and their perception of what politics is about. People, in this sense, have, at some level, to 'learn' what political issues and politics are. Most people live their lives sticking to their own political ideology, their own set of values, of understandings and beliefs. This is, of course, usually inconsistent over time, made up of a mixture of self-interest, self-evident 'truths', inconsistent or partially understood ideology, personalized reference points, life history experiences and interactions with other 'politically' motivated individuals, organizations and groups.

One important starting point is the consideration of just how in any given society individuals learn what is, and what is not, political. Likewise, people must also come to understand what is, and what is not, of political relevance and importance at any particular time. It is possible to illustrate this, if we take the following two examples, separated by distance, but occurring at roughly the same time.

The first reflects the experience of David Roediger as a boy growing up in the USA in the 1960s, the second that of John Boyd as a young Protestant living in Northern Ireland in the late 1950s. Here, Roediger recalls an incident of his youth:

When I was ten, it suddenly became possible to hit Little League pitching and, after my first (and only) five-hit game, the league's best player asked if I'd go to the carnival with him. This was a sign of acceptance, but as we walked to the fairgrounds the stakes increased. My new friend produced a long knife that he was not supposed to have and I was not supposed to know he had. 'This', he told me conspiratorially, 'is a nigger gigger.' Neither of us knew if this meant that the knife was for attacking blacks or of a sort used by them. Neither of us knew any blacks. None lived in the small German-American quarrying and farming town in which we were growing up. . . . Even in an all-white town race was never absent. I learned absolutely no lore of my German ancestry and no more than a few meaningless snatches of Irish songs, but missed little of racist folklore. (Roediger, 1991: 3)

Boyd (1985: 176) also recounts part of his early socialization in a pre-dominately working-class, Protestant area of Belfast, at more or less the same time, '"Fight for Billy", "Fight for Billy", "Fight for the Cock o' the North!"'. That was one of our best songs, and we used to shout it at the top of our voices as we paraded along the smelly back entrys in defiance of the Catholics who were preparing to attack us.' He continues, 'That none of us had ever seen a Catholic or knew anything about the "Cock of the North" didn't matter in the least. Somewhere near us there was a big fight going on and we Protestants wanted to be on the winning side.'

Both patterns of socialization into racism and sectarianism (admirably resisted by both authors) clearly show the strength and development of strong common communal values and how each community's ignorance of the other's life patterns gave rise to a distinctive worldview. The social construction of 'the Other' was central to both sets of experiences in determining perceptions and understandings of politics. Moreover, both examples illustrate the construction of common reactions to political phenomena. Further, the reproduction of the dominant ideological views on display bore little, or no, overlap with concrete everyday experiences.

Political ideology

Culture, understood in its broadest sociological sense, consists of sets of shared meanings and values transmitted from one generation to the next. One aspect of culture vital to our understanding of politics is the concept of 'ideology'. The definition of ideology is complex and contested. Most broadly, it concerns how individuals interpret and understand the world in which they live. These understandings involve relationships between individual political psychologies and social structures. Ideology mediates between and overlaps these core areas.

Such relationships are far from direct or uncontested. One problem is that the term 'ideology' has often been used in many different ways, so as to accumulate many different meanings and responses. It may therefore be useful to outline some starting points. What is the extent to which ideology is at work in all societies most of the time and how is to be recognized? This will be another theme upon which we shall touch throughout the book.

First, for example, it is possible to consider ideology as having distinctly limited parameters, as another way of expressing 'rigid thinking'. Hence in recent times, when Margaret Thatcher, Neil Kinnock, John Major, John Smith, Tony Blair, William Hague and Iain Duncan Smith have clashed at Westminster during Prime Minister's Question Time, they have often accused each other being overly 'ideological', or that each other's policy proposal is ideologically driven. What they usually mean in using the term in this highly negative way is that the person (or group) taking an opposing perspective is seen as having approached the issue in a limited way, through the filter of a fixed set of ideas. Each political opponent therefore believes that the other is incapable of seeing the 'truth' of the argument.

Central to the self-image that Tony Blair has sought to create since becoming leader has been the claim that the contemporary Labour Party has shed the ideological baggage of its past. This, in everyday speech, fits with what most people understand by the term, namely, a constricted and fixed worldview. What is in place is now called 'New Labour', supposedly capable of representing the new attitudes and economic realities and post-ideological in its construction (see, Brivati and Bale, 1997; D. Coates and Lawler, 2000; K. Coates, 1996; Gould, 1999).

We will deal with the politics of New Labour in later chapters, but for the meantime there are at least two major problems with this everyday understanding of ideology. First, every statement about the world is deeply embedded in a set of 'commonsense' assumptions. So, one person's inflexible, rigid worldview is for another merely a series of self-evident truths.

Secondly, it is important to introduce the classic Marxist notion of ideology as 'false consciousness'. We will encounter this notion at several points throughout the book. In broad terms, for the moment, Marx defined 'class consciousness' as a form of social condition whereby members of social classes would become 'aware' of themselves and their common conditions as a class. The idea of false consciousness refers to a lack of such awareness. One of the major consequences of this is that it results in a completely distorted view of reality, and in particular of the existence of the exploitation upon which the class system is based.

So far the definitions of ideology we have encountered could be read merely as a matter of cognition and political ideas. Many modern commentators, however, have followed Althusser (1971, 1977, 1984) in stressing the idea of ideology as a lived experience. In this sense ideology is seen as deeply rooted in peoples' commonsense beliefs about the nature of the society in which they live and how the world 'works'. As Eagleton (1991: 18) explains, ideology for Althusser is a particular organization of signifying practices that go to constitute human beings as social subjects, and which produces the lived relations by which such subjects are connected to the dominant relations of production in society. There are also problems with Althusser's account, some of which we will encounter in Chapter 2. He is, however, surely correct when he tries to widen the scope to consider those ways in which ideology pervades everyday life.

Central to further understanding this aspect of politics are the works of Gramsci (1968, 1971). From within a Gramscian framework, ideology is understood in terms of sets of ideas, meanings and practices, which, although represented as universal truths, are actually supporting the power of particular social groups. The process of producing these maps of meanings, maintaining and reproducing such ideas as authoritarian and dominant, is what Gramsci calls 'hegemony'. For those adopting a Gramscian perspective, ideology is not something that is separate from the practical activities of life. Rather, it is a material phenomenon embedded in everyday social and political relationships. Such ideologies provide people with the rules of behaviour.

The notion of hegemony refers to the position when a 'bloc' of ruling-class factions finds itself in a position to exercise social authority and leadership over subordinate factions. One way to exert such authority, of course, is through force or coercion. More importantly from a Gramscian viewpoint, however, is the ability of the dominant grouping to ensure its position through the construction of consent. In particular, the ruling faction must be able to present its own narrow interests as common to, and in the interests of, the vast majority. Hegemony is therefore understood as the strategies by which the perspectives of the dominant group, around, for example, class, sexuality, ethnicity or national identity, are so conferred (see Chapter 2).

This position is, however, far from stable. Hegemony can never be static. It is constructed through a whole series of discourses and social practices. It is consistently contested and must be constantly re-won and restructured. This understanding also allows for the formation of social forces to construct counter-hegemony to challenge dominant discourses and forms of organization. In the early part of the twenty-first century, for example, British nationality and sovereigntry is an ideological matter, particularly manifest in debates over the United Kingdom's place in Europe and the ways in which 'Britishness' is represented, both internally and to the rest of the world.

Importantly, of course, for a large part Britishness is just this, a representation. This can be seen in the disparate populist images, which are projected as symbolizing Britishness. These may include calendar photographs or biscuit box covers reproducing Constable's and Turner's pictures of 'rural England', Coronation mugs, the Queen's Christmas Day speech on television and radio at 3 p.m., or Kenneth Moore's famous portrayal of Douglas Bader in the film, *Reach for the Sky*. Others may refer to cultural reference points such as the last night of the Proms, the singing of 'Abide with Me' before the FA Cup Final, pop music, an afternoon pint of bitter in the country pub, a game of village cricket or even the Archers on BBC Radio 4.

Such representations of Britishness, which would be recognized throughout the world, are also, of course, more often merely a presentation of Englishness. For many, Englishness and Britishness remain synonymous. Indeed, if we reduce populist notions of Britishness to its essence, we find predominantly English historical myths, values and institutions. Further, England remains dominant, not just ideologically, but also in terms of population, economic and political power. After all, it is within England, and more specifically London, that we still find all of Britain's major financial institutions and the seats of the monarchy and political power.

As Paxman (1999: vii) demonstrates, however, for others the traditional images of Englishness are now most often met with amusement and that, 'the conventions that defined the English are dead'. What then, if anything, may replace these conventions and representations? Some such as Hall (2000) or Parekh (2000) argue that in order to develop a common feeling of belonging in the new millennium, the British need to redefine national identity in a way that is more encompassing and acceptable to all of its citizens. This will no doubt involve a continuing divorce of Britishness from Englishness.

In ideological terms this is no little task, given the strength of existing constructs. Politically, it has to some extent already been recognized and found expression through the political devolution of Scotland, Wales and, to a lesser extent, Northern Ireland (Bogdanor, 2001). Another core ideological manifestation of this is the tendency for many to equate Englishness with 'whiteness'. As the Runnymede Trust Report on *The Future of Multi-Ethnic Britain* (2000) argues, while whiteness nowhere features as an explicit condition of being British, it is widely understood that Englishness, and therefore by extension Britishness, is racially coded. Hall encapsulates this directly in the following:

> That great patriot Enoch Powell once remarked that 'the life of nations is lived largely in the imagination'. It is worth continuing to ask the awkward question, how is the nation imagined? What pops into the mind's eye, when people say 'Britain' or 'British'? By now, few people can imagine the British Olympic team without a black face. On the other hand, during the recent celebration of 'Britain's Finest Hour', it was not the faces of Asian and Caribbean World War II volunteers which automatically first came to mind. Where were they in the fly-past? (Hall, 2000)

Given rapidly changing social and political circumstances, it is no coincidence that for the first time in a century the English are beginning to question their own sense of identity and that the hegemonic construction of Englishness is being overtly contested. This is an issue we will explore more fully at various points throughout the book, and especially in Chapter 2, in terms of the ideological construction of political identity.

Political power

It is through the further study of various theories of ideology that it is possible to begin to understand how the interests of individuals and groups can be reinforced and strengthened, or rebutted and resisted by the promotion or relegation of 'ideas'. Power exists in many forms and on many levels. This book will examine power at various levels within our society, the state, and those directly involved in exercising power and determining who has power.

Hence, Giddens (1985) argues that power can be seen as a transforming capacity in all humans. It allows people to intervene in a variety of events throughout the world in order to alter them. However, in trying to develop a sociological concept of power, we must also recognize that the actions of human agents manifest in very different figurations of social relations. This leads us directly to consider the ultimate importance of the concept of power.

As Bottomore so insightfully explains, political sociology is concerned with power in its social context:

> By 'power' is meant here the ability of an individual or a social group to pursue a course of action (to make and implement decisions, and more broadly to determine the agenda for decision making) if necessary against the interests, and even against the opposition, of other individuals or groups. (Bottomore, 1979: 8)

Thus, Mann (1986) suggests that power emerges constantly in human societies. He further identifies four organizational sources of power as follows:

- Ideological Power, which emerges from the fact that humans seek to operate in terms of meanings, norms and rituals. It is ideologies that meet these needs. As such, ideological power can be 'transcendent', standing apart from society in a sacred way, such as religion, or 'immanent', dispersed through society by group cohesion and a sense of shared membership.
- Economic Power, which derives from production, distribution, exchange and consumption. It is best expressed through a class structure.
- Military Power from competition for physical survival. It produces direct control within a concentrated centre and the effect of indirect coercion on surrounding areas.
- Political Power, which comes from the control of a physical territory and its population by a centrally administered regulation, concentrated in the state.

This leads on to the discussion of other important issues concerning political organization. What are classes and status groups and how important are they to understanding power in society? How do modern capitalist democratic states seek to maintain internal unity? Put even more simply what holds such societies together? How should we explain the 'power of belief' in the state, and the continued importance of the power of ideology?

Much of the remainder of the book will, therefore, seek to develop these concepts and, in particular, the notion of social power and the relationships of power in the actions of human agents in a vast range of social relations. As Hay (1997) clearly demonstrates, while power is probably the most universal and fundamental of political concepts, it is still a highly contested one.

In this context, Lukes offers some perceptive thoughts, arguing that, at a basic level, power should be understood as the ability of 'bringing about of consequences' (1974: 634). In other words, power involves the production of causal effects. One of his central notions is the ability of core groups in society to control the political agenda. Moving past the notion of power as consisting of conscious actions which influence decisions and then through the idea of power as the ability to prevent decisions being made, Lukes arrives at the 'third dimension' of power.

This is the ability to influence others by shaping what they want (or at least think they want). This is power best understood as ideological indoctrination, to shape people's preferences, so that conflict largely remains concealed and dormant. It is about the ability of powerful groups to keep contentious issues from ever reaching the agenda for public debate.

We will encounter these different notions of power directly in several points in the book. It is possible to regard power simply as the ability of an individual, group or organization to force others in a particular way – hence, power as something that it is possible for individuals or groups to possess and as something observable and measurable. This conceptualization of power represents an extremely stagnant and rigid understanding of power.

It is possible, however, to regard power in a more complex manner, as something deeply embedded in social relationships. Power is something that is mobilized and mediated through an individual's or group's political position within the state, and in relationships between the state and society. Further, it is also important to understand political power in a more sophisticated manner as the ability to define the situation within particular parameters. In this sense politics is socially constructed around definitions of knowledge and the power to define particular understandings and institutions as more relevant and reasonable than others are. It is through such processes that powerful groups and the state construct dominant paradigms by which politics are interpreted and understood.

Given this, there are important questions to be asked concerning the contemporary powers and roles of the state. Throughout the 1980s and 1990s the primary dynamic throughout much of Europe and the USA was to move former state-dominated enterprises into the remit of private enterprise. It is almost impossible to over-estimate the historical and political impact of the New Right administrations vanguarded in the West by the political leaderships of Margaret Thatcher and Ronald Reagan. Their philosophy of neoliberalism was given further credence by the collapse of the Soviet bloc and the claims by some that history was at an end and liberal capitalism was to be forever more in the ascendancy.

Any review of the claim to widespread changes brought about by those administrations adhering to neoliberal philosophy, however, needs to be treated with some caution. The move towards the 'private' was never complete and never without resistance. In several European states, such as Austria, France, Germany, Italy, Spain, Sweden and Switzerland, government spending as a percentage of Gross Domestic Products (GDP) actually rose in the last two decades of the twentieth century.

As we shall see, however, neoliberal ideology remains strong throughout much of the developed world, particularly with the increased pace of the dynamic of transnational capital and processes of globalization. Indeed, the functions and roles of the contemporary state have to be understood against the backdrop of this wider process. In particular, globalization has set in train a wide range of debates surrounding tensions between the forces of global capitalism and sovereign states, and between those promoting neoliberal free markets and those who seek to resist it from below.

This brings us to further issues concerning the power of governments and how they seek to maintain, or reject, traditional roles and to discard or embrace new ones. The state is faced with a vast range of policy options and alternatives. The various directives of government reflect political beliefs and give priority to certain individuals and groups over others within state boundaries. Increasingly, however, much of the power of the state seems limited by the development of the politics of a new world economic order. Obviously much of this is unpredictable, but the possibilities may be better understood if we can develop a systematic understanding of the theoretical basis of how the state works and the concept of political power.

Political legitimacy

The ultimate goals of the book are to gain a clearer understanding of how power is distributed in society, and the various forms that politics can take. It also provides insights into why things happen as they do in the political arena and develops some ideas around the forces that develop to challenge the dominant forms of power and political organization. When we appreciate this understanding of power, we can begin to understand politics in much broader terms, as a much more social and collective activity. Politics can be seen to be something that operates at all levels of society and in all arenas of social behaviour. Traditional definitions of politics and the political have, for example, often excluded core groupings such as women and ethnic minorities, restricting them to a well-defined private arena.

The focus on established power also needs to consider how power and authority are challenged. Political power is seldom executed or expressed in any overt manner. Only rarely will the state unleash naked physical force, perhaps by way of its armed forces, in the open defence of its interests. Rather, there are various processes whereby the powerful can, and do, gain acceptance, and generate legitimacy for, their authority. For many, particularly those operating from within Marxist and neo-Marxist traditions, this function is central to understanding the role of ideology in society.

Thus, existing political structures and ideas are often represented as 'normal', and 'right', in a way that continued obligation to and support of these political values is also seen as natural. In nearly all societies there exist laws that compel, or at least seek strongly to direct, individuals to engage in, or refrain from, particular forms of behaviour. Further, in most societies, again albeit in various forms, a central concern of those people who exercise power over others is to claim legitimacy for their actions.

When we seek to identify the exercises of power that require justification, the most obvious candidate is the state and its law-making powers. Conventional political studies often concentrate on questions surrounding the relationships between state and citizens, legalization and the powers and formal checks on those in positions of authority. To do so, however, is to miss out on other important questions regarding the social basis of legitimacy in contemporary societies.

There are also many exercises of power within society that are not obviously by the state at all, although they may well be underpinned by the state. This point has been increasingly recognized by some feminists and others, for example, who have asked whether the family is not best understood as part of the public sphere, rather than the private.

This distinction between public and private, and the blurring between them, has become an increasing concern for those who seek to question the distributions of power, authority and advantage. We are forced to ask, if power is exclusively, or even mainly, held in legal rights and obligations, or does it also consist of, and exist in, patterns of expectations, understandings and beliefs that are embedded in ideologies and even perhaps in the language of politics itself?

Political cultures

Before developing some of these arguments, it is necessary to clarify further the starting point and to return to the concept of political cultures. People often talk about politics and the resolution of political differences and conflict through it, as if it involves negotiation within an agreed set of values and ideas held by everyone. This, of course, is far from the case. Rather, there are a series of competing understandings and interpretations of politics. What it is possible to talk about meaningfully is a dominant political culture that sets the framework within which politics is interpreted and understood. The classic starting point for the study of political culture in the United Kingdom remains that of Almond and Verba (1963). Here they claimed Britain had the ideal civic culture, which balanced values of citizen participation with trust in elites and responsiveness to the law.

Obviously, the political culture of the United Kingdom has radically altered since the position laid out by Almond and Verba in the early 1960s. This is especially true in terms of those who exercise most power, and in the variety of political sub-cultures and political identities that exist. The parameters and contours of this changing political culture will form the subject matter for much of this book. Indeed, there are those who would argue that long-standing notions of politics and society are now meaningless, given the relativity, dislocation, uncertainty, fragmentation, pluralism and multiculturalism of contemporary Western societies.

Such ideas rest on the concept of a break with modernity and the emergence of a new postmodern world. If this is so, then clearly it is of some significance. Postmodernism is seen to mark a discontinuity between the economy, society and politics which has, albeit in very different ways, been seen as marking a fundamental rupture with our interpretations of society and politics.

Issues, organization and structure of the book

From the above we can begin to distinguish the types of issue which set the parameters for the main themes of the book. Among these are the relationship between the individual and politics. Essential questions of 'who rules?' Who takes decisions in the capitalist democratic state and in whose interests do they take such decisions? How much validity is there in more recent postmodernist interpretations of society which highlight many people's disillusionment with contemporary politics? Or are contemporary politics in the United Kingdom, and beyond, still best understood in terms of capitalist power relations and the domination of powerful groups? Is it that powerful global forces and the resistance to them are a precursor to new form of politics?

Central to the arguments in this book is the belief that the fusion of sociology and politics can enrich the understanding of contemporary society, political events, and social and political change. It is this that the book seeks to undertake. One of the crucial ways in which individuals begin to understand what politics is about in our society remains through their interactions with state institutions.

The main task of the book is to introduce and expand upon some key concepts and topics in political sociology. Special attention is given to competing and contested notions of power and the state. The book also seeks to set these issues into a broader social context and provide a fuller understanding of the relationship between political cultures, political socialization, political action and wider social structural issues.

Broadly, this book takes an approach that is intended to show that politics cannot be properly understood in terms of institutions and issues cannot simply be derived directly from those setting the political agenda. Hence, the book introduces the importance of broader social relationships, and the links between society, social structure and power in defining and understanding politics.

To do this one key focus is the state. There are many lines of inquiry here. What roles do political elites and ordinary citizens have in the working of the state and how does it affect modern society? What is the relationship between states and the market in encouraging economic development? How does the development of a global civil society affect the traditional functioning of the nation-state?

The book addresses these and related questions through developing an understanding of both classical and contemporary sociological theory and case studies. Further, the book also seeks to provide a comprehensive analysis of the origins, nature, development and transformation of the state, examining the basis of and relationships between politics, the state and society in different settings.

Section I begins by addressing some major issues concerning theories of politics, power and the state. Hence, Chapter 1 presents an analysis of the major founding theories of politics and the state, including pluralism and elite theory, Marxist and feminist theories, the writings of Foucault and some of their variants.

Chapter 2 provides material on conflicting perspectives on legitimacy and power. This leads to a critical analysis of classical and contemporary theories of nationalism and a case study of nationalisms within the United Kingdom. It provides an examination of the nature and role of the state in the less-developed periphery, explicating neo-colonial variants within the United Kingdom.

In Section II, we consider some central issues of political change in society. One key issue for political sociology is the interrelationship of society and the state. This section highlights the interactive nature of that relationship. The context is that within which the state acts upon society and is itself the object of political action. As Chapter 2 indicates, some theories of power, such as pluralism and elitism, have concentrated on how the structure of society impinges on action by the state. Other theories of the state have concentrated on the effects of state action upon society. The main goal of the chapter is to accentuate and examine some major starting points to investigate issues of power and theories of the state.

In Chapter 3 we consider the effect of the New Right domination of both party and ideological dimensions of United Kingdom politics throughout the 1980s and part of the 1990s. Moreover, its legacy is still profoundly felt into the new millennium. Some of the specific aspects of political change surrounding welfare provision and the welfare state are considered in Chapter 4. This chapter is grounded in a discussion of contested theoretical approaches, although empirical and comparative issues are dealt with to some extent.

One set of questions examines how is it possible to best conceptualize the political and social basis of welfare states? Another series of issues involves evaluating the various available theoretical perspectives, such as Marxism, neoliberalism and feminism on the role of welfare states and social policy. Finally, consideration is given to the conflicting visions for the future directions for welfare states.

Chapter 5 considers the politics of Northern Ireland. It focuses mainly on the contemporary issues of political change surrounding the peace process and the search for a political settlement. This, however, is addressed in the context of broader political and historical changes. In particular, issues surrounding the politics of defining terrorism and political violence and the continuing conflictual nature of Northern Irish society are dealt with in some detail.

The far-reaching theme for Section III is the future of politics and the state. In Chapter 6 the contemporary relevance of class is discussed in detail. To begin we shall discuss competing perspectives on the relationship between the nature of the state, its class basis and the development of politics. There are those who argue that we are now in an era of 'post-class' politics and that class can no longer be regarded as a central organizing theme in society.

A fuller assessment of this perspective is crucial, especially given the changing patterns of social movements and collective action over the last 30 years. This part of the book, therefore, considers some of the major roles of social movements in political life, including why they originate, why people join them, the effects they have on ushering social and political change, and the cycles they experience.

Finally, Chapter 7 examines the possible nature of politics in the new millennium. The book concludes with a discussion on the relationship between class, state and power on a world scale and attempts to explain the politics of change as the outcome of social transformation effected through control of the state.

Overall, this book seeks to provide a concise and comprehensive guide to, and analysis of, the role of politics and the state in the United Kingdom. To do this the book engages with a wide variety of theoretical approaches which different writers have developed to explain social and political phenomena and the social and cultural bases of power and authority. In doing so, it hopes to make a positive contribution to political sociology and to those related disciplines devoted to the study of the state.

To begin with, let us consider some the most important ways in which the state has been understood, and some of the fundamental understandings that have been developed. One key starting point concerns debates surrounding the future form of the state. In particular there are intense political controversies concerning the continuance of social democracy and ideas that social inequalities can be alleviated by direct state intervention, as a central organizing principle in the United Kingdom and beyond. This dispute underpins much of the book and sets this discussion within the context of broader social and political processes, societal and global change.

DISCUSSION QUESTIONS

- **What is politics?**
- **What is political power and who holds it?**
- **How do people 'experience' politics?**
- **How are political values transmitted from generation to generation?**

Politics, Power, Political Legitimacy and the State

1

Founding Arguments: Theorizing Politics, Power and the State

Key concepts and issues	Key theorists and writers
• Defining the modern state • Elite theories of politics and the state • Pluralist theories of politics and the state • Marxist theories of politics and the state • Corporatist theories of politics and the state • Feminist theories of politics and the state • Foucault, politics and the state	• Valerie Bryson • Robert A. Dahl • Michel Foucault • David Held • Michael Mann • Karl Marx and Fredrick Engels • Keith Middlemas • Gaetano Mosca and Vilfredo Pareto • Nicos Poulantzas and Ralph Miliband • Shelia Rowbotham • Charles Tilly • Sylvia Walby

Although the study of the polity – of the structures, operation and processes of government and social decision meeting – is usually deemed to be within the purview of political science, sociologists have always maintained a keen interest in the issue. The study of the polity is more than the study of political parties and voting patterns. It includes the social decision-making process – a process that has an impact on every member of a society. (Knuttila, 1996: 231)

What is the state?

In recent years it has been impossible to give even a cursory look to any major book concerning politics or political sociology without being struck by the increased prominence of writings on the theories and structure of the state (see Dunleavy and O'Leary, 1987; Hay, 1996; Jessop, 1982; Jordan, 1985; Nash, 2000; Poggi, 1990; Schwarzmantel, 1994). Yet as we shall see, such writings are highly diverse and conflicting regarding the main features of the roles and functions of the state. Indeed, there is not even a universally agreed definition of the meaning of the concept.

One feature on which there has been agreement, however, is the importance of the state, which, by the nineteenth century, had become the key political actor in most developed countries. At its peak in the United Kingdom, the state promised to intervene directly to provide care and support for its citizens from cradle to grave. Over the past 30 years, however, the ideology, nature and forms of state intervention have changed dramatically.

Central developments have featured a 'hollowing out' of state powers, in a whole series of moves towards more regulatory and less interventionist roles for the state. This has taken place against a background of increasing privatization and market liberalization.

To begin to understand this it is necessary to outline the development and structure of the state. As a starting point, it is possible to conceive of the state in two main ways. First, as the apparatus of rule of government within a particular geographical area; and secondly, as the social system that is subject to a particular set of rules or domination. Although Hall and Ilkenberry (1989: 1) confirm that there is much disagreement, they suggest a composite definition of the state would include three main features. A set of institutions staffed by the state's own personnel, at the centre of a geographically bounded territory, where the state has a monopoly over rule-making.

Further, Hall (1984: 9–10) identifies the following traits of the modern state: that power is shared; that rights to participate in government are legally or constitutionally defined; that representation is wide; that power is fully secular; and that the boundaries of national sovereignty are clearly defined. While such definitions refer to 'ideal types', they still offer useful starting points when considering the contemporary state.

Despite the difficulties in reaching any agreement on a definition of the state, one thing is clear, that the state has a direct influence on all our lives. Importantly, through its key institutions, we as individuals often feel that we experience the modern state in a way that is very different from other institutions in our society. As opposed to the somewhat nebulous and sometimes shadowy concept of the state, the family, for example, is often seen as a much more direct part of our experience. We feel we know about it at first hand. We can all offer some 'commonsense' definition of what the family is, or at least what it should be. Most feel that they are in a position to comment on the relationships within the family, and the functions and roles it should perform. This is not so as far as the state is concerned. Most often the state is seen as highly abstracted, or at the commonsense level as something separated from everyday life, which sets about imposing its will from above through a detached and inaccessible bureaucracy.

While much of our experience of the state is indeed indirect, certainly compared with other institutions such as the family, the state profoundly influences our lives. If we continue to look at the family we see that its structure and experiences can be highly mediated by the state. For example, by supporting or downgrading particular welfare or health services, or by providing or not providing realistic levels of child benefit and childcare. The state, of course, also claims the right to monitor the family, to legitimate professional intervention if certain functions are not fulfilled. Further, the state still claims the role to legitimate marriage itself and the form the family takes.

We will encounter this again in Chapter 4. For the moment, however, it is important to point to how this notion of a normative family finds expression at different levels. At its most basic, for example, bigamy remains a criminal offence, enforceable by the law. Not all examples are so direct, however. Throughout the decade and a half of New Right administration in the 1980s and 1990s social policy regarding the family became central to the political agenda and has remained there ever since.

During this time, the Conservative administration consistently re-emphasized its commitment to free market principles, individual enterprise, a minimal state and increased personal responsibility. Throughout the last Conservative administration there was also a restatement of a belief in anti-state welfare policies, and a reduction in welfare provision by the state, even though tensions arose because many saw a clear conflict between these views and the claims to be 'pro-family'. In the most recent period, the post-1997 New Labour administration has promoted a slightly different notion of the family (see Chapter 4), but this too has been strengthened by a variety of forms of intervention directed by the state seeking to mould the family in a particular form.

The state may not necessarily take on an overt interventionist role to enforce its desires, however. Rather, it plays a crucial role in determining what is, and importantly, what is not, socially acceptable behaviour. There is, for example, a clear ideological position put forward by the state regarding the family. Getting married and having children is clearly still acceptable, and is supported by a strong social construction of what is 'normal' family relations, which is only rarely, if ever, referred to directly in legislation.

The state, however, still largely 'frowns' upon other forms of alternative living, such as gay couples, or single parents, particularly single mothers, that do not conform to the dominant construction and perceived prominence of the private nuclear family as the core of our society. The state can also sometimes, as in the case of homosexuality, directly use the force of law to support its views. More broadly, the social security system, tax system, financial benefits and agencies of social intervention remain structured by a dominant view, based on traditional morality, of the desired structure of the family in the contemporary United Kingdom.

Here, the state also seeks to identify ideologically what is and what is not political (see Chapter 2). This is done in part at least, by defining what is deemed legitimate and what illegitimate, what is legal and what illegal, those who are 'deserving' and 'undeserving'. Most crucially, it occurs by defining what is properly seen to be in the public domain and what in the private.

So, for example, despite much intervention by the state concerning the family and family law, the dominant view of the domestic domain of sexual politics, gender divisions, sexual violence and unpaid labour are that all should remain firmly located within the private. In particular the right to ownership and accumulation of private wealth and property is supported and promoted by the state. As Held (1984) points out, however, in our own society, the issue of private property is depoliticized, treated as if it were not a proper subject area for politics. By so defending the private and the right of individuals to accumulate private wealth the state has already taken sides. It does so with regularity, intervening directly in other highly politicized arenas surrounding gender, class, ethnicity and definitions of citizenship and conceptions of identity and nationhood.

Society without the state

There are, however, also societies within which the state is not highly developed. Indeed, there are even a few societies that it may be reasonable to refer to as 'stateless'. The Nuer of southern Sudan and the Jale of the highlands of New Guinea, are two examples of such societies. These are often based on hunter-gatherer economies and do not have the need to co-ordinate large numbers of people, or control the use of stored resources, within a fixed territory. They therefore tend not to depend on central organizations or have a recognizable state organization. Likewise, small-scale agrarian societies, while often operating within a fixed geographical location, rarely have clearly demarcated boundaries or a clear political organization.

That does not mean, however, that such societies are devoid of any mechanisms of political regulation. Indeed, far from it. If we consider other social structures within non-industrialized societies, for example, we can find larger groups, which often share a common language and culture, and which usually obtain food from cultivation and the herding of animals. Such societies are politically organized in a variety of ways. Family and kinship structures, custom and traditions, or the authority of religious leaders may all have important roles to play in dispute regulation and political structure. Village councils or groups of elders often take decisions on public matters and perhaps the monitoring of relations of kinship and descent.

Elsewhere, chiefdoms involve a ranking of people and a centralized authority. The chief is the inheritor of office, and performs a series of administrative roles: such as the distributor of resources, the arbiter of the legal system, and perhaps even religious functionary. Keesing (1981), studying the Polynesians of Hawaiian Islands, describes how in their political organization, the islands are divided into chiefdoms, each ruled by a 'paramount chief', whose authority combined secular powers and religious authority.

It is also possible to find examples of non-industrialized societies where the concept of the state is somewhat more highly developed. Here, people are

TABLE 1.1 FEATURES OF STATELESS AND STATE SOCIETIES

Stateless societies	State societies
Informal mechanisms of government	Political apparatus or governmental institutions differentiated from other organizations in the community
No clear boundaries to a society	Rule takes place over a specific population or territory
Disputes and decisions settled by family or kin groups, or by larger tribal structures headed by a chief with the support of a council	Legal system backed by a capacity to use force
Relationships and transactions significantly defined by custom	Institutional divisions within government (the executive, civil service and army, for example) are formally co-ordinated

Source: Held (1992)

recognized as being a citizen of a territorially defined political unit, and status derived from lineage becomes less meaningful. State organization, as it does exist, surrounds the authority of central control, the co-ordination and structuring of different social groups, for example, slaves, bureaucrats, priests and politicians. Thus, Roberts (1979: 137) suggests that where the state is partly developed, the features many non-industrialized societies share is the presence of a supreme authority, 'ruling over a defined territory, who is recognized as having power to make decisions in matters of government (touching at least defence and the public services), is able to enforce such decisions and generally maintain order within the state.'

All of these are examples of the state as a social phenomenon, constructed in differing forms under particular historical conditions. Held (1992: 73) further distinguishes some of the key features of stateless and state societies, as outlined in Table 1.1.

The state itself has, of course, changed its form over time. In Europe, the embryonic nation-state emerged from around the fifteenth century, and largely achieved a full-blown form by the nineteenth century. The nation-state that has emanated since then largely consists of a 'people' or 'peoples', expressing their right to self-determination, and within a 'sovereign' territory. Further, they claim the right to defend specific geographical boundaries against real or imaginary aggressors, irrespective of the persons who actually govern them. Moreover, within the modern nation-state, a government is seen to have authority over the area and is the ultimate power within it. The modern nation-state marks the replacement of absolutist rulers by a set of rules administered by a state-organized bureaucracy. It is in this that the state is seen to achieve legitimacy. Much of this will be dealt with in more detail in the next chapter when we consider directly issues of political legitimacy within the United Kingdom.

The rise of the modern state

In the meantime, however, it is important to recognize that the contemporary state is in no way 'natural', although some may project it as such. Nor does it mark a stage in an evolutionary cycle that inevitably follows on from tribes and chiefdoms as a form of political organization. Many recent debates, in defining the state, have concerned the relationship between state power and other forms and sources of social power. Therefore, equally important in defining the state itself is the definition of civil society and those areas of social life such as economics, cultural activities and political interaction which are organized by private arrangements outside the direct control of the state. Indeed, a key task for any developed state is how it can take charge of, or control, major aspects of civic society. However, as we shall see, this involves an extremely complex set of social processes and interaction that we shall examine in much more detail in the forthcoming pages.

So how have the major phenomena surrounding the modern state emerged? The state is relatively new in human terms, and the nation-state even more so. Its original form was primarily that of the ancient empire, the Assyrian, Egyptian, Minoan, Mycenean, Macedonian, being clear examples, or the city-state as demonstrated by the regimes in Babylon, Athens, Sparta and Rome.

The development of the state coincides with the development of other crucial social phenomena. These include written language, the growth of the centralized management of surplus economic production, in the shape of taxation and the use of organized 'legitimate' state forces to guard against internal threat and external enemies. Also important in the development of the above states was that they had a centralized belief system or ideology, usually in the form of a state religion. Their leaders were invested either with god-like status, or with the power of the gods as their agents. Often the earliest state managers were priests in states based on theodicy.

Another perspective can be found in the work of Mann. In *States, War and Capitalism* (1988) he provides evidence of how the relationship between the state and society dramatically changed with the onset of industrial capitalism. Prior to this the state has an approximately autonomous role about civil society. Afterwards, 'for most analytic purposes the State can be reduced to class structure'. Focusing on the different conditions necessary to create large-scale networks of social interaction, Mann argues that in agrarian societies, economic and infrastructure weaknesses make this impossible. However, the development of military organization was one means by which larger-scale interventions were made possible. So, for example, in both Rome and China it was the army that established the boundaries of the state, largely by erecting physical barriers. This made possible other key developments, such as a taxation system within the established borders.

Mann (1988) contrasts this with more modern conditions of communication, which have made it possible for economic relations to integrate large physical spaces. This has consequences for the form of state power. Modernity has realized the rise of statist regimes, which were as much concerned with coercion as production. While all empires have acquired territory through force, what have differed are patterns of consolidation following conquest. At certain phases economic means could not provide incorporation, only later did economic imperialism, within a military-protected border, take over.

Other important insights into the development of the modern state are provided by Tilly (1990). For him the state has historically performed three essential activities. These are, first, statemaking. That is the attacking of competitors and challengers within the territory claimed by the state. Secondly, warmaking through attacking rivals outside the territory already claimed by the state. Thirdly, protection, which takes the form of attacking and checking rivals of the rulers' principal allies, whether inside or outside the state's claimed territory.

There are, however, other crucial activities of the state. These are extraction, whereby the state draws from its subject population the means to carry out the process outlined above. Another key role is adjudication, the authoritative settlement of disputes among members of the subject population distribution. The state also intervenes in the allocation of goods among members of the subject population. Finally, the state demands control of the creation and transformation of goods and services by members of the subject population.

Importantly for Tilly, after the middle of the eighteenth century, states began direct intervention in local communities, households and productive enterprises. Rulers frequently sought to homogenize their populations, in linguistic, religious and ideological terms. This had many advantages, not least that a homogenous population meant that the masses were more likely to identify with their rulers, communications could run more efficiently, and an administrative innovation that worked in one segment was likely to work elsewhere as well. Furthermore, people who sensed a common origin were more likely to unite against external threats, whether real or perceived.

With the installation of direct rule also came those forms of surveillance that make local administrators responsible for the prediction and prevention of social movements and organizations that could threaten state power. The remit of the state thus expanded far beyond its military core, and in return for their loyalty its citizens began to make new demands on it, for protection, adjudication, production and distribution. As direct rule expanded throughout Europe, the welfare, culture and daily routines of ordinary Europeans increasingly came to depend on whichever state they happened to reside in. This was particularly so as states began to impose national languages, national educational systems, conscripted national military service, and so on.

Contemporary nation-states

Given the above, it can therefore be reasonably claimed that all modern states are nation-states, with distinct political apparatuses, holding supreme jurisdiction over a demarcated territorial area, backed by a claim to a monopoly of coercive power, and enjoying a minimum level of loyalty from its citizens.

A further defining characteristic of the nation-state is that most of those living within its boundaries and structured by its political system are citizens of that state, with rights and duties directly relevant to that state. Technically, of course, this is not the case in the United Kingdom, where those living within the boundaries of the state are not citizens, but subjects of the Monarchy. However, bar a very few cases, such as political exiles or refugees, everyone is today identified within a particular nation-state.

Finally, modern nation-states are often directly associated with the wider concept of 'nationalism'. The two are, however, by no means synonymous. We shall explore this more fully in the next chapter. Meanwhile, however, Giddens (1985) provides some useful initial distinctions. He suggests that on the one hand, nationalism may be primarily understood as a psychological phenomenon, with 'affiliations of individuals to a set of symbols and beliefs emphasising commonality amongst members of a political order'.

On the other hand, for Giddens a nation is a collectivity, existing within a demarcated territory, which is subject to a unitary administration, monitored both by internal state apparatuses and those of other states. The nation-state, which exists in a complex of other nation-states, 'is a set of institutional form of governance maintaining an administrative monopoly over a territory with demarcated boundaries (borders), its rule being sanctioned by law and direct control of the means of internal and external violence' (Giddens, 1985: 121).

Clearly, not only do people recognize the state, they also 'believe' in it and see it as having 'legitimate' roles in their everyday lives. Most accept its right, albeit sometimes reluctantly, to structure and restrain their day-to-day existence. The majority respects at least some of its institutions: the Monarchy; Parliament; the law courts; the police; and the military. Most are aware that they no longer live under the rule of all-powerful sovereigns, rather that they inhabit nation-states within which law and order and politics have become highly specialized endeavours. Politicians, for example, periodically offer themselves to gain popular support for the right to control public policy and the nation's strategy and resources. Police forces and the military are authorized by the state to use force to maintain internal order and protect state boundaries from external threat.

People also clearly internalize and accept psychologically the boundaries and parameters of the nation-state. Or they may seek to change the existing physical parameters of the state. In the United Kingdom the most contested boundary surrounds the six counties of Northern Ireland, which has given rise to much bloody conflict and the antagonism of the past 30 years. It is obvious here that national identity does not fit with the existing borders of the nation-state. This issue will be dealt with in some detail in Chapter 5. Fundamentally, however, the conflict revolves around two mutually exclusive senses of national identity. Nationalism need not, however, find such negative expression. Many are profoundly proud to be Irish or Welsh, Libyan, Argentinean, Afghan, and so on. The relationship between nationalism and the nation-state is not therefore a straightforward one. It will be explored further in later chapters.

Some of the above statements could easily give the impression that the state is a single actor with a highly unified set of goals and aims. This is, of course, far from the case. Any state is composed of many individuals, organizations and groups. What is of interest is how, and why, they combine to pursue collective goals. How is authority legitimized and maintained by a dominant group and what political forces exist to block them in their goals, or to challenge their position? To begin to answer some of these questions it is necessary to discuss further some of the central perspectives on power and the contemporary state. It is also intended to link this with a wider discussion, already highlighted, concerning where the boundaries of state and society fall, the connections between micro and macro, local and global levels of society, and how the conjunctions between them may be conceptualized and understood.

The examination in the following section will be necessarily brief, but it will begin by focusing on six fundamental sociological approaches, which can provide the tools to understand central notions of power, politics and the state in democratic capitalist societies. These approaches are: elitism; pluralism; Marxism; corporatism; feminism and Foucaultian perspectives.

Elite theory, politics and the state

Let us begin with one of the oldest sets of explanations regarding politics, elite theories that consider power to be concentrated in the hands of some select grouping. To try to outline its tenets simply, elite theory suggests that a single group, the ruling elite, take all the major decisions in determining the direction and organization of liberal democracies. Clearly, there may well be overlap here with other approaches, such as Marxism, and their concept of the concentration of economic and political power in a small elite, the ruling class. However, in elite theory the dominant group is not seen as deriving its power directly from the economy.

Indeed, as we shall see in this section, some of the more 'classical' works of elite theory were written from expressly anti-Marxist positions. They take as a common starting point the belief that the state is permeated at key decision-making levels by dominant social groups and that the state functions to serve the interests of this powerful minority.

This classical approach within elite theory can be traced back to the works of Pareto and Mosca, two late nineteenth-century Italian social scientists. For Mosca, the political ruling elite was made up of individuals whose 'natural aptitudes' best suited them for the task of leadership. The group's training, socialization, education and life experiences all supported this. Thus, he rejected the notion that the position of the elite was explicable in terms of economic relations. Rather, for Mosca the ruling group consists of all the separate ruling minorities in a society, a political elite, which is both a necessary and inevitable feature of society. As Mosca himself writes:

Among the constant facts and tendencies that are to be found in all political organisms, one is so obvious that it is apparent to the most casual eye. In all societies . . . two classes of people appear – a class that rules and a class that is ruled. The first class, always the less numerous, performs all the political functions, monopolises power and enjoys all the advantages that power brings, whereas the second, the more numerous class, is directed and controlled by the first, in a manner which is now more or less legal, now more or less arbitrary and violent. (Mosca, 1939: 50)

For Pareto, elites were not necessarily based on the qualities of the individuals involved. Rather, they were an inherent characteristic of organizations once they grew beyond a certain size. Important decision-making in large-scale organizations or complex societies simply cannot concern all of those involved. Rather, what inevitably happens is that decision-making is condensed in the hands of a small number. A further consequence of this is that the elite becomes self-perpetuating, with its own interests, not necessarily in harmony with those of the larger organization. Such an elite becomes entrenched and extremely difficult to replace. Hence, for Pareto, much social life was governed by underlying non-rational psychological forces, explicitly rejecting any notion that the dominant group in society results from economic structures.

Pareto thus divided elites into two major types: those who came to power using 'instincts of combination', and those who achieved it through 'persistence of aggregates'. The former tend to use 'ideas and imagination', the latter order and stability. This led to Pareto's now famous characterization between the ideal types of such group, the first as 'foxes' and the second as 'lions'. Importantly, to explain the political dynamics of society, Pareto further introduces the notion of the circulation of such elites. The foxes may replace the lions, gradually through stealth. Or the lions may replace the foxes, but if this takes place it is usually done quickly and involves physical force. The elites circulate because, once in power for some time, their inherent weaknesses are revealed. Thus, foxes may compromise and concede their dominant position too often, or the ruthlessness that lions use to maintain their position may become increasingly unacceptable to large numbers.

Another writer often included in classical elite theory is Michels. He, like both Pareto and Mosca, was in part at least responding to the works of Marx. Briefly, Michels suggests that it is the elites rather than the masses that exercise most power in society. Therefore, in order to understand any society one must concentrate any examination on powerful elites, the bases of their power, how they exercise it, and the purposes for which they exert power.

These principles led Michels to formulate the 'iron law of oligarchy'. This claims that once leaders gain delegated authority, the tendency is always for them to turn it to domination. Because leaders are in power, they always tend to appear superior. Any criticisms of the individual can seem to be, or may be represented, as an attack on the institutions and structures of power. Michels puts it as follows:

Organisation implies the tendency to oligarchy. In every organisation, whether it be a political party, a professional Union, or any other organisation of the kind, the aristocracy tendency manifests itself very clearly. The mechanism of the organisation, while conferring a solidity of structure, induces serious changes in the organised mass, completely inverting the respective positions of the leaders and the led. As a result of organisation, every party or professional Union becomes divided into a minority of directors and a majority of directed. (Michels, 1993: 113)

There is a further non-Marxist line of thought on the elite that emerges from the works of C. Wright Mills. Writing in the USA in the 1950s, he suggests that the elite is embedded in the structures of society and therefore highly institutionalized in the USA. A 'power elite' made all the most crucial judgements and remained in a position, 'to make decisions having major consequences' (Mills, 1956: 4). This elite consisted of three sets of leadership: first, corporate; secondly, military; and thirdly, political. While those who support a pluralist analysis may point to this as supporting their thesis, Mills would no doubt argue that such pluralism took place only at the 'middle level of power' and only to the agenda set by the ruling elite.

Here, Bottomore (1979) has also made important distinctions. On the one hand, he argues that there exists a political elite, made up of individuals who actually exercise power, and which includes members of the government, those in high administration, military leaders, leaders of 'powerful economic enterprises' and perhaps influential families. On the other hand, there can be identified a 'political class' comprising the political elite but supplemented by leaders of opposition parties, trade union leaders, leading businesspeople and politically active intellectuals. If we follow this definition, the political elite is seen to be composed of the bureaucratic, military, aristocratic and business elites while the political class will include elites from other areas of the social world.

In contemporary Britain, for example, Scott (1991, 1994, 1996a, 1996b) effectively demonstrates how British politics has been dominated by an alignment of the capitalist class with the entrepreneurial, professional and managerial classes. The capitalist class has remained dominant, disproportionately represented in all key areas of the state elite. Clearly, here it is possible to follow Bottomore to suggest that the basis for elite power may rest on a variety of sources. This idea will now be considered more fully, beginning with pluralist perspectives, many of which developed as a counter to the elite perspectives outlined above.

Pluralist theory, politics and the state

Stated bluntly, most pluralists believe that a concentration of power in any one individual or grouping is simply not possible in any complex society. Rather, it should be recognized that political power is both fragmented and widely dispersed. It is held by groups of people acting together to press particular causes and viewpoints. For this reason many pluralists do not even talk explicitly of the 'state' at all. More often they seek to substitute the term 'government' and express views in terms of 'political actors' and 'political demands' made to the administration. The pluralist view of politics in part draws on the notions of political power as outlined by Max Weber and Joseph Schumpeter.

From a Weberian perspective, while class interests tend to predominate in advanced capitalist democracies, ruling alliances are also determined by status groups and political alliances. So, for example, Weber, in *Economy and Society*, classically spoke of 'stratification by class, status and political parties' (1978: 926–39). Hence, classes, status groups and parties are all phenomena of the 'distribution of power'. However, whereas for Marxists the underlying mode of power is the economy, for Weberians it tends to be the bureaucracy (1978: 212–26, 956–1003; see also Chapter 6).

Schumpeter (1976) supports many of Weber's thoughts on political behaviour and argues strongly that there is a limit to mass political partici-pation. Hence, democracy was important as a means of generating respon-sible government, rather than as a form of providing power for the majority. Political representatives must always, therefore, be 'sensitive' to the demands of the electorate. Much of Schumpeter's concept of politics surrounded the notion of the politician as a 'dealer in votes'. Indeed, for Schumpeter, modern democracy is little more than a system through which rival political elites contend for power through organized elections. Importantly, like Weber, he regards politics as a distinct area of life, largely separate from the economy.

Pluralism also draws to some extent on another political tradition, that of liberalism, which upholds the individual as the core of 'moral worth'. Perhaps the best known exponent of such views is Adam Smith, and perhaps the best known of his views surround his insistence that the state play a minimal role in the social organization of society. Underlying this is the belief that political power is always open to abuse and there was a need to control all forms of power. Thus, the idea emerges of the limited state, restraining state action and limiting its activities. From a traditional liberal perspective a limited, restricted state is not a weak state, rather it exists to guarantee basic 'natural rights' of the individual. One of the key functions of the state, therefore, becomes the protection of the individual from arbitrary interference, whether from other individuals or the state itself. The state itself has to be controlled and constantly checked in case it infringes civil liberties.

Such a notion of pluralism cannot, however, always be reconciled with ideas of democracy. Indeed, the liberal state is by no means synonymous with participation by the masses, or government by the people. Many pluralists, for example, tend to argue that the direct political involvement of the entire population in the modern nation-state is impossible. Consequently, it is pluralism that offers the only practical form of democracy within com-plex social structures. Ensuring freedom of speech, and that any individual is free to join a group to promote a particular perspective through pressure group politics, means that no one individual or group can become dominant. Society is seen to operate best through compromise and politics through consensus.

While the term 'pluralism' is sometimes used to refer to a school of coherent political thought, this is by no means the case. However, in its modern form, pluralism is largely associated with the works of Robert A. Dahl (1961, 1966, 1982, 1989), whose views dominated pluralist thought throughout much of the 1960s and 1970s. He claims power describes a relationship, such as A's capacity for acting in such a manner to control B's responses (Dahl, 1956). Elsewhere, Dahl (1961) suggests power is a successful attempt by A to get B to do something he or she would not otherwise do. In this sense, Dahl's concept of power follows directly from Weber's, high-lighting a narrow range of observable conflictual aspects as the essence of political life.

Dahl's particularly concern was with the distribution of power in local communities in USA. Here, certainly according to the views of protagonists, political parties and pressure groups have both come to assume some measure of power. The ultimate outcomes, the eventual political decisions made, and their realizations, were all the results of compromises between these various foci of power. The basis for this is the belief that in any political system there should be a plurality of different centres and influences and that power should not be concentrated in the hands of any one person or group. The political system should be based on competing parties, a network of pressure groups and associations, and a separation of economic and political powers.

Importantly, economic leaders do not coincide or overlap with political leaders, As Dahl puts it in the context of his major study of 'New Haven':

> Economic notables, far from being a ruling group, are simply one of the many groups out of which individuals sporadically emerge to influence the policies and acts of city officials. Almost anything one might say about the influence of the economic notables could be said with equal justice of about half a dozen other groups in the New Haven community. (Dahl, 1961: 72)

There are clear implications here for pluralist analysis, which assumes competition on an equal basis between rival interest groups. For Dahl, all social and political power is 'non-cumulative'. The nature of political power and pluralist competition is strongly affected by this wider structure of power and wider social context. Most importantly, power is disaggregated. Compe-tition, in other words, is not on equal terms, and there is an unequal dis-tribution of resources. Some groups may have greater economic, social or political influence than others, and the state will be more responsive to them, but only in the narrow areas they represent.

At the heart of the pluralist argument is the belief that no group has the ability to dominate over a wide range of different interest areas and that there is no coherent or cohesive 'ruling group'. Power is diffuse in society, and there is no concentration within particular groupings. One reason why pluralists adopt this perspective is that their methodology tends to focus on visible 'decision-making' processes and on overt statements of interests by orderly groups and counter-statements by those organized in opposition.

In the context of New Haven, there were many conflicts to determine public policy, as different groups pressed for different sectional claims. However, this very process of barter and compromise ensures that policy decision-making was healthy and in the interests of the general population. Dahl concludes that it is not political parties, interest groups, social and economic elites, or politicians who govern. Rather, leaders and masses govern together. For pluralists this is central to an understanding of politics. To gain legitimacy for actions, leaders frequently surrounded their covert behaviour with democratic rituals. The distinction between the rituals of power and the realities of power is frequently an obscure one. First, some people influence decisions more directly than others do because they are closer to the stage when laws are vetoed. Secondly, the relationship between leaders and citizens in a pluralistic democracy is frequently reciprocal.

The members of the political stratum are a small group of individuals who are the main bearers of political thought and skills. They are politically dynamic and involved in an inter-community network of other political activists. The political stratum is not a static, stable grouping. Rather, it is easily penetrated because competitive elections give politicians a powerful motive for expanding their coalitions. The members of the stratum are affiliated with different political parties. However, although members of the stratum are directly and primarily involved in shaping political issues, they are also easily manipulated by politicians. Through reward and deprivation of political favours, the politician can manipulate support on certain issues.

For Dahl, even if a minority of leaders controls the policies of political associations, the policies of the leaders in local government would tend to reflect the preferences of the populace. Citizens have little direct influence on policies, but they may exert a large degree of indirect influence through elections. The state is seen as having a range of pressure groups each trying to influence government. Politics is therefore based on consensus, involving small, increment adjustments and fine-tuning by government to maintain the equilibrium in place between competing pressure groups. As Gray (1989: 305) suggests in the context of the United Kingdom, 'pluralists stress the democratic nature of politics . . . and see government as the voice of the people'.

A further key question within pluralism therefore surrounds the operation and maintenance of an equilibrium of power in society. Pluralists tend to talk of power as being in balance. So if there is a producers' group, then a consumers' group may organize around what it sees as oppositional interests. Both have economic power. Both can influence government decision-making and the direction that an administration might take. The same is true of the representatives and interest groups. Underlying much pluralist argument is the assumption that there is always a rough balance of forces between such groups, no matter how oppositional or polar their competing perspectives.

Central for many pluralists is the separation of economic and political power in society. Directly countering Marxist perspectives, pluralism seeks to deny that political power and state control are linked to powerful economic interests. Following on from this, the state is seen as neutral, arbitrating impartially between the conflicts of classes and other social groups. It regulates without taking sides. The state is not linked to the interests of a 'ruling class', but rather it works to represent all significant social groups. This sometimes leads to what can be called a social-democratic or reformist reading of pluralism. The state in Western Europe has introduced advanced systems of social welfare; therefore the state can no longer be seen as an instrument of the capitalist class. In short, it is possible gradually to reform the state by democratic means.

Another central value within pluralism is the belief that liberal-democratic states are not structured by a dominant ideology. Rather, there is a clear diversity and plurality of ideas, which are expressed through a variety of channels. This denies any uniformity of belief. Hence, an informed public raises issues for political discussion, which is free to express its views. Politics is thus seen as a process of choice and competition between a variety of political parties and pressure groups. Opposition political parties keep governing parties in check. Regular elections guarantee accountability and allow citizens to choose the representatives and government they want. The electoral process thus ensures the protection of the rights of minorities in opposition.

So how do pluralists conceptualize the ways in which the state should be organized? There is some difficulty in answering this question. As Dunleavy and O'Leary (1987) point out, in many cases pluralists do not have a coherent theory of the state. Indeed, many pluralists are loath even to talk about such a concept, regarding it as having clear overtones of a unified and centralized organization. Instead, pluralist theorists tend to refer to the state in terms of its discrete entities such as the police, the courts, judiciary and so on.

However, some key pluralist overviews can be identified. Dunleavy and O'Leary (1987: 41–9) further outline three models of the pluralist state: the weathervane model; the neutral state model; and the broker state model. It may be useful to consider these in slightly more detail.

First, the 'weathervane' model. Some pluralists, particularly those writing in America in the 1950s, regard the state as passive, merely a weathervane of public opinion. Its direction is altered by pressure groups in society. Policy-making and its implementation involve the success of one pressure group's policies over another. State neutrality means that state organizations are most responsive to, and biased towards, the strongest and most highly organized pressure groups.

Moreover, the existing structures of the state represent the outcome of negotiation between past pressure groups. Different pressure groups have been successful in different policy areas at different times. This has structured the form and shape of the postwar liberal-democratic state. State development is thus seen as a product of democracy, the state having been responsive to its citizens' demands.

Secondly, the 'neutral state' model. This view has been developed by pluralists who have some reservations with the above, in particular the notion that the state simply mirrors civil society. Rather, they believe the state should be 'actively neutral'. Its main task should be to act as a referee. If the state is interventionist, it should be to promote fairness. For pluralists operating within this model, the state's major role is to referee competing pressure groups, and to protect those which are weakest in terms of organization. The state should therefore mediate in the 'public interest', and be responsive to electoral and pressure groups. It also has a further role, making sure that disorganized and weaker groups are not too alienated. For those who hold such views, the state's growth is best explained in terms of responses to pressure groups, whereby public officials interpret demands and pressures to steer the liberal-democratic state along the direction pointed to by key pressure groups in the public interest.

Thirdly, the 'broker state' model. Within this model public policy decisions reflect neither the interests of pressure groups nor the pursuit of public interests. Rather, the direction of public policy reflects activities and concerns within the apparatus of the state itself. State brokers may act as intermediaries but they retain their own interests. State functionaries are, therefore, more autonomous than in the weathervane model, but they are also more self-interested and self-promoting than in the neutral model. In the broker model, state officials facilitate the acceptance of policy compromises among key groups. The broker state is not a distinct organization, nor can it be seen as passive or neutral. It consists of pressure groups of common interests formed between both formal and informal groups. One consequence is that the divisions between public and private sectors disappear.

Following on from the above, pluralists adopt a particular view of the organization and bureaucratic administration of the state. Administrative elites are seen as impartial and dispassionate, passively responding to public pressures. Most readily adopt Weber's classic concept of bureaucracy, where state administrators are seen as operating without their own preferences. However, following the models outlined by Dunleavy and O'Leary, it is clear that those who adopt the 'broker state model' may well be cynical of this view. Rather, broker pluralists expect government departments to be fertile ground for elite group formation. Bureaucracies are internally divided, and administrators' behaviour is affected by the social background from which they come.

Also depending on which model is adopted, there are consequences for the workings of the state. Within the weathervane model, for example, parliament is seen as having a diminutive guiding role. At most it is little more than a 'rubber-stamping' forum for decisions made in the public arena. Policy co-ordination, if it does occur, is undirected and unintentional. The neutral state model, however, does provide for a more sophisticated and formalized co-ordinating role by the state, whereby institutionalized pluralism is expressed through a cabinet system of government. Even within this model, however, such a role is far from advanced. This broad notion of a neutral state has led to much criticism, particularly from Marxists, and it is to these ideas which we will now turn.

Marxist theory, politics and the state

The core argument of a traditional Marxist approach to the state is easily presented. It is that the interests of the ruling classes dominate the organization and functions of the state. Further, political power and the nature and form of the state itself are closely linked. The economic organization of society and the resultant class structure provide the overriding roles in determining the nature of the state and patterns of social life. The state is therefore an extension of civil society, a political apparatus structured and shaped by class relations.

The origins of this view lie with Marx and Engels themselves. In *The German Ideology* (1970: 90) they claim that the modern state is 'nothing more than the form of organization which the bourgeois are compelled to adopt, both for internal and external purposes for the mutual guarantee of their property and interests'.

In class society the state cannot be a vehicle for the communal interest. All politics is 'class politics', capitalists and workers are constantly in conflict over the distribution of scarce economic resources. The state is therefore the product of the historical struggle between classes.

So, far from taking the role of neutral judge that others suggest, the state reinforces the social order in the interests of the capitalist class. The state is best understood as an institutional superstructure resting on the economic base. Marx outlines the importance of this base-superstructure metaphor in the following passage:

> The specific economic form, in which unpaid surplus-labour is pumped out of direct producers, determines the relationship of rulers and ruled, as it grows directly out of production itself and, in turn, reacts upon it as a determining element. Upon this, however, is founded the entire formation of the economic community which grows up out of the production relations themselves, thereby simultaneously its political form. It is always the direct relationship of the owners of the conditions of production to the direct producers . . . which reveals the innermost secret, the hidden basis of the entire social structure, and with it the political form of the relation of sovereignty and dependence, in short, the corresponding specific form of the state. (*Capital*, Vol. III, 1970: 791)

To understand fully the power of the state, it must be recognized that it is fundamentally structured by the system of economic production. The dominant economic class shapes it and the state operates in the interests of the dominant class. It is only following the proletarian revolution, with the development of a classless society, that the state as it currently exists will be dissolved.

Although these central tenets of a Marxist approach can be clearly stated, one problem for those seeking to be guided by such writings is that at no time did Marx himself approach the topic of the state in anything resembling a coherent manner. Indeed, the most comprehensive statement of traditional Marxism is found in the work of Engels, 'The Origins of the Family, Private Property and the State' ([1884] 1967). From this and much of the other, albeit partial material written by Marx, however, three consistent Marxist readings of the state have emerged.

First, an instrumental model of the state. This is often seen as the most 'orthodox' model, summed up by a much quoted passage from the *Communist Manifesto*, in which the 'executive of the modern state' is seen as 'but a committee for managing the common affairs of the whole bourgeoisie'. Underlying this are the interests of bourgeoisie, who in opposition to other social classes must try to control the state to protect their interests. Capitalists have a common interest as a class. The state must act therefore in the long-term interest of capital rather than in the interests of individual capitalists.

Secondly, the reading of the state as arbiter outlined in Marx's account of the 1848 revolution in France, *The Eighteenth Brumaire of Louis Bonaparte* (1963). Crucial here is Marx's suggestion that the state apparatus may operate in a way which is autonomous from the direct control of capitalists. Marx saw this as an exceptional historical period, in which class struggle was equally balanced. State power acquired a certain degree of independence from both capitalists and the proletariat. However, even in such an untypical regime the state's autonomy from capital on economic issues was very limited.

Thirdly, it is possible to identify a functional reading of the state in the works of Marx. This view emerges through a reading of *Capital*, Volume III (1970). The state apparatus forms part of the superstructure, which is determined by the economic base, hence, state policy is set and determined by an impersonal logic. This drives government in a capitalist society to develop the economy by its own logic and maintain social stability by coercive means if necessary.

From the above it is possible to identify two clear models concerning the relationship between classes and the state. In the first model the state generally, and bureaucratic institutions in particular, may take a variety of forms of sources or power. These need not be directly linked to the interests of, or be under the direct control of, the dominant class in society, in the short term at least. The state retains a degree of power independent of this class and its institutional forms are 'relatively autonomous'.

Following the *Eighteenth Brumaire*, power is seen as accumulated in the hands of the executive at the expense of civil society and the political representatives of capitalist class, the bourgeoisie. The state is seen as a vast set of institutions, with the capacity to shape civil society and even curtail to some extent the bourgeoisie's capacity to control the state. The very scope of these bureaucratic institutions is seen as giving the state the power not only to steer social arrangements but also to constrain the interests of capital.

The second model suggests that the state itself and its bureaucracy are class instruments, which structure society in the interests of the ruling class. At its crudest, this view suggests that the state is a simple non-autonomous reflection of the economy. Bureaucratic mechanisms extend great influence on political decisions and their outcomes. It is within the context of the second position that Lenin's analysis of the state developed. This is reflected in his insistence that the eradication of capitalist relations of production must be accompanied by the destruction of the capitalist state apparatus. The state as a class instrument has to be destroyed and replaced with direct democracy of the masses.

Lenin's views on the topic are best expressed in *State and Revolution* ([1917] 1981) where he claims the state is merely a machine for the oppression of one class by another, very often by 'a special repressive force'. The ruling class maintains its grip on the state through alliances with government. The vital business of the state takes place not in representative assemblies but in state bureaucracies where alliances are established out of public view. Hence, democratic rights such as elections, freedom of assembly or the press are merely a 'shell' and actually benefit the dominant class. Such institutions appear to be open while the dominant group controls them through ownership and control of resources.

Overall, it is important to recognize two interconnected strands in traditional Marxist accounts of the state. The first concerns the state with a degree of power that is independent of class forces. The second sees the state merely as superstructure directly serving the dominant class. Contemporary Marxist writers obviously draw on these models, but have examined in more detail the relationships between the economic base, the dominant class and the shape and form of the state.

Within this, several important perspectives have emerged. Particularly significant has been the notion of the possibility of the relative autonomy of the state from its economic base. Hence, much Marxist discourse and debate regarding the state remains structured by the exchange between two Marxist writers, Nicos Poulantzas and Ralph Miliband.

The publication of Poulantzas' first book *Political Power and Social Classes* (1973) sparked off an intense debate within academic Marxism. In direct response, Miliband's work (1969) was written from a viewpoint that has been termed 'instrumentalist'. That is, it examined how the state is used as 'an instrument in the hands of the ruling class'. Poulantzas' approach, however, is often termed 'structuralist'.

Miliband's central concern was to draw the distinction between government and the state. Certainly the government is the most conspicuous facet of the state, but that does not mean it is the most important. The state is a wide concept and includes the bureaucracy, the police and judiciary, important economic institutions such as the banks, and national, regional and local representative bodies. Most importantly, the state has a level of autonomy. What enables the state to operate in the interests of the dominant class is twofold: first, its ability to represent itself as unbiased and neutral; and secondly, the ability to make concessions to the subordinate classes which actually serve to maintain the position of the dominant group.

Overarching this, however, is a further factor, that the dominant class is drawn from those with similar socio-economic backgrounds and characteristics. Importantly, this means that the dominant group possesses shared economic and social perspectives and values. Put straightforwardly, the state serves the interests of the capitalist class because it is controlled by that capitalist class. As Miliband (1969: 22) clearly states, the ruling class 'use the state as its instrument for the domination of society'.

In contrast, Poulantzas writes that the state provides the 'factor of unity' in a social formation. It essentially plays the decisive role in mediating the central contradiction of capitalism. He analyses the unifying function of the state in terms of its impact on the working class and the capitalist class. The state atomizes the working class through transforming workers into individual citizens, while representing itself as the interest of society as a whole. For the capitalist class, however, the state serves the function of guaranteeing the long-run interests of that class as a whole. The bourgeoisie cannot be considered a unified class with unambiguous interests. Rather, it is highly fractional. The only way these can be protected is through the state's relative autonomy, that is, a state structure that can transcend the interests of only one part of the class.

Poulantzas' fundamental thesis is that functions of the state are broadly determined by the structure of society rather than by the people who occupy positions of state power. He regards the background of the dominant class as all but irrelevant, arguing that the structures of the system merely reflect the degree to which the institutions of the state are embedded in society. So, for example, he writes:

> The direct participation of members of the capitalist class in the state apparatus . . . is not the important side of the matter. The relation between the bourgeois class and the state is an objective relation. This means that if the function in a determinate social formation and the interests of the dominant class coincide, it is by reason of the system itself; the direct participation of members of the ruling class in the state apparatus is not the cause but the effect . . . of this objective coincidence. (Poulantzas, 1969: 245)

The starting point of structuralist analyses is an examination of the contradictions arising from the economic base of society and how the state operates to neutralize these incongruities. The focus of any analysis should be the class structure in society, and particularly the contradictions rooted in the economy (Poulantzas, 1978: 123–41, 255–62, 275–89, 296–307). The functioning of the state, Poulantzas concludes, maintains the unity of a social formation based on class domination. The state's role as the cohesive social factor is not reducible to 'intervention' by the state at various levels, and particularly at the economic level.

Most of those adopting an instrumentalist perspective believe that the modern state operates to secure the interests of a small, enormously rich group. The government, judiciary, civil service, and the top ranks within the police and army manage the interests of the wealthy dominant class. Following this line it is possible to argue that the Thatcher era and what has followed has seen a strengthening of the position of an elite from a particular socio-economic background.

In general, 'instrumentalist' theory has been criticized as inadequate in explaining contemporary politics of the state, much of which cannot be understood simply as the outcome of control by specific capitalists. The state apparatus it is argued, is more complex than this. Structuralist theory attempts to situate how the direction of state policy formation lies beyond the socio-economic background of those involved. The economically powerful class in society may be united by property, but different political and economic interests equally divide them. So, the dominant class includes wealth that lies in agriculture, manufacturing, the City or even in e-commerce or new technologies.

At times the interests of these groupings may coincide, at others they may radically diversify and become conflictual. A key role of the state is to preserve the control of the ruling class by creating a system which promotes bourgeois values, no matter who is in power. The state therefore becomes the structure by which the long-term interests of capital are reconciled.

Importantly, this means that the state is able to present itself in neutral terms, as the effective managers of the resources of the nation. Therefore, the state can have a degree of autonomy from the economically powerful. Clearly, if this is so, it reveals a highly contradictory process in society. On the one hand, the state continues to have the support of the vast majority, by claiming to be responsible to the democratic political process. On the other hand, however, the state remains highly undemocratic, in terms of its distribution of scarce assets, economic privilege, capital and wealth.

By pointing out much of the above, and despite what is a somewhat obscure and at times inaccessible style, Poulantzas' work is of central theoretical importance within Marxism. It moves away from the notion that the state can be understood as a simple instrument in the hands of the ruling class. Poulantzas made an important advance by relocating the line of inquiry. The debate between Miliband and Poulantzas and the subsequent discussion it invoked laid the groundwork for the next wave of Marxist and neo-Marxist writings.

In Miliband's (1991) more recent analysis, for example, he maintains that hegemonic processes are central to the bourgeoisie displacing any sense of radical alternatives to the organization of contemporary society. Miliband gives the example of class struggle in the USA, a country where organized, radical, powerful opposition to dominant class values and ideas is largely absent, as an example of a successful hegemony being constructed.

Significantly, Miliband suggests the same trends are now visible in British politics. Here, Miliband argues that the underclasses are those most economically damaged by the power struggle operating throughout all levels of contemporary capitalist society. They constitute the most deprived members of the working class: 'the permanently unemployed, the disabled and those largely or entirely dependent on payments from public funds' (Milliband, 1991: 23).

This analysis by Miliband is essentially one of power and domination, the power elite and the underclass representing the respective winners and losers of class struggle and hegemonic manipulation. Miliband also argues that the process of proletarianization of the middle classes is another aspect of a long and historic struggle with capitalism, a struggle in which the working classes have been betrayed by the adoption of social democratic policies by the labour movement.

Hence, Miliband refocuses on a central issue, namely, how to restrain capital in the face of global pressure and interdependence, and turn it aside from the inevitable consequences of its own rationale and dynamic. Given the recent move to social democracy, the weakening of the labour movement, the worldwide integration of capitalism and the inadequacies of collective services, the working classes and increasingly sections of the middle classes are likely to be ever more exploited.

We shall encounter these views again later in the book, particularly regarding the breakdown of the postwar political order, the development of post-Fordism, the emergence of the New Right and globalization. Briefly, however, on the one hand, Miliband, and other writers like John Urry, have continued to argue that the modern state operates to preserve the interests of a small, extremely wealthy dominant class. In short, the political, administrative and legal elites and the executive arm of the state manage the interests of this class.

On the other hand, the works of others, such as David Coates (1989, 1994, 1995), suggest that what is of real importance is how the economically powerful class are unified by property but divided by economic and political objectives.

Corporatism, politics and the state

Others, of course, have different ideas on these issues. One such grouping are those working broadly within the parameters of corporatist ideology. The range of views, which can be fitted under the term 'corporatist', is wide. They would certainly include writers such as Schmitter (1979) and Middlemas (1979, 1986, 1990, 1991), but also in some ways less conventional 'pluralists' such as Pahl (and Winkler, 1974) and Winkler (1976, 1977a, 1977b) might also be covered by the term.

It is, however, in the work of Schmitter that we find corporatism most clearly stated as an ideal type. For him, corporatism can be understood as:

> a system of interest representation in which the constituent units are organised into a limited number of singular, compulsory, hierarchically ordered and functionally differentiated categories, recognised or licensed (if not created) by the state and granted a deliberate representational monopoly within their respective categories in exchange for observing certain controls on their selection of leaders and articulation of demands and supports. (Schmitter, 1974: 93–4)

Fundamental to corporatist thinking is the idea that the determination of interests becomes systematized along strict guidelines set by the state. So, for example, membership of representative groups, such as trade unions or business confederations, becomes compulsory. Further, organizations such as trade unions have the power to negotiate legally binding settlements which, importantly, are recognized by the state. In response, those representing corporate interests will support agreed policies. The state directs the activities of predominantly privately owned industry in partnership with the representatives of a limited number of hierarchically ordered interest groups. Power in real terms, lies mainly in the hands of the bureaucrats and professional decision-makers.

Corporatism has, however, had a wide variety of interpretations. It has, for example, been used to refer to the system in place in Italy under fascist rule. Here, Mussolini used the concept more or less as a device of direct political control. Established trade unions were 'dissolved' and instead the corporate state was based on worker and owner syndicates. Strikes were declared illegal, and prices, profits and production rates were set by the state. Local syndicates were represented at regional and national levels through 'corporations'. The leaders of these corporations were members of a 'national council', by which the economy was centrally organized, controlled and directed.

Mussollini headed Italy's highest political body. He appointed the heads of all corporations and hence directed and controlled the economy. The corporate state in Fascist Italy was thus also used as a mechanism to quash any popular dissent, through the promotion of the notion that only the elite was in a position to discuss political issues. Further, it is clear that the state overly rewarded its supporters while punishing opposition under the guise of corporate efficiency (see Griffin, 1995; Kitchen, 1976; Neocleous, 1997; Robson, 1992).

In Western Europe corporatism has developed within the context of an accommodation between the representatives of capital and labour. Thus, at its height in the United Kingdom during the 1970s, the state reflected a clear 'corporate bias' (Middlemas, 1979: 371). Indeed, Middlemas further claims that British governments had displayed a 'corporatist bias' since the end of the First World War. Much of this was directed at running the economy rather than at any wider role within the state. In it, leading corporatist bodies included the civil service, large companies and organizations, such as the Confederation of British Industries, and the Trades Union Congress, in institutionalized state agencies.

A prime example in practice was the social contract polices adopted during the governments of Labour Prime Ministers Harold Wilson and James Callaghan. This saw the manifestation of the 'tripartiate model' and the attempt to institutionalize the support of the representatives of capital and labour as partners in the economic planning and running of the state. Indeed, in the period of the social contract between 1974 and 1977, a concordat was formed between the trade unions and the Labour government. Together they negotiated a series of non-statutory agreements on wage increases. In return, the Labour administration promoted a package of social and employment legislation and promoted the role of the trade unions, alongside the representatives of business, in determining the county's macro-economic policy.

The development of this corporate solution must be understood in the context of Britain's long-term economic decline. Throughout the twentieth century the relative weakness in the United Kingdom's domestic economy was increasingly brought into sharp relief by the growth of the USA, Germany and Japan as international trading nations. The strength of Britain's trading position had been based on its control over an overseas empire, its markets and the City of London's position as a centre of world funding, international business and foreign investment. However, one long-term consequence of this focus was a lack of investment in home industry and low growth rates in the economy of the United Kingdom. In turn, political policies throughout the last century favoured the City of London and the financial sector at the expense of manufacturing. The culmination of the above political and economic factors was an inability to compete abroad and a steady loss of markets. In response, the political parties developed a series of fluctuating policies to try to halt this decline.

Hence, corporatism may be understood as one option to achieve the halt of long-term economic decline. Winkler (1976) argues, therefore, that by the mid-1970s, the United Kingdom had taken on a more corporatist hue as a result of a slowing down of the process of capitalist accumulation. Changes in the economy involving industrial concentration, increasing international competition and declining profits all moved the state towards the adoption of corporatism.

Elsewhere, Pahl and Winkler (1974) further suggest that the corporate politics of the 1970s developed a power structure based on four major objectives. First, the elimination of fluctuations in the economy. Secondly, organization around the central principle of collaboration, placing the nation's interests before those of any individual, firm or trade union. Thirdly, that strategies should aim for controlled economic objectives and, therefore, fourthly, that there is some implicit element of discipline over those who seek to engage in different objectives.

In broad terms corporatism is most concerned with effectiveness. The role of the state is to set unambiguous national goals and to provide the framework for the necessary allocation of resources. The emergence of corporatism in practice was the result of changes in capitalism brought about largely by failed economic performance (see Cawson, 1982, 1986; Williamson, 1989).

As a result, in the United Kingdom of the mid-1970s both capital and organized labour highlighted different features and demanded different forms of economic intervention and the integration of labour into a tripartite system. It remains difficult to see, beyond perhaps some short-term income policy, how the interests of this group can be represented. Such a strategy had important consequences. As Coates explains:

Corporatism as a strategy for running the country actually *weakens* the state. It leaves politicians and civil servants dependent upon the ability of the *networks* they have built, and the private *hierarchies* which feed into them, to deliver their constituents on time, regularly and in good shape. The very building of a network precludes the possibility of major structural reform, if that reform involves a systematic diminution in the power of one of the participants to the agreement. (D. Coates, 1995: 154, original emphasis)

We shall continue to explore the roles of the state much more fully in later chapters. Before that we will, however, consider another core theoretical approach and critique of traditional social and political thought, that of feminism. In particular, feminists challenge what they regard as the tendency of much of mainstream social and political thought to universalize those political experiences associated with men.

Feminist theory, politics and the state

From within a feminist perspective, politics is seen as an activity definitely not restricted to the domain of public decision-making. Indeed, central to feminist arguments is the critique of other narrow definitions and understandings of politics as something operating in the public domain. By arguing that the 'personal is political' many feminists seek to challenge and undermine traditional divisions in society between the public and the private. Such demarcations are largely seen as conventions, which only serve to conceal relations of power between men and women. In fact it may well be that those areas marked as private actually represent the most political of all sections of social life. As Lovenduski and Randall explain:

> Intimate and familial relationships may be shown to have a political dimension: for example, how you dress your little girl, or whether you let a man open a door for you, are decisions that have a political component. Since the end of the 1960s feminist campaigns have helped to politicise and bring on to the public agenda a succession of issues formerly associated with private or personal life: abortion and reproductive rights, women's health, domestic violence, incest, sexuality and language are examples of this. (1993: 5–6)

Underlying much of the feminist analysis is the concept of patriarchy. Broadly, this refers to the traditional and systematic dominance of women by men. However, there remains much discussion within feminism as to the precise meaning of the term. A useful starting point is Walby's *Theorising Patriarchy* (1990). She argues that the concept of patriarchy may be clarified by considering six interrelated structures through which gender relations are constructed and reproduced. These are paid employment, household production, culture, sexuality, violence and the state.

In Walby's view there has been a move in British society away from a predominantly private form of patriarchy to a public one, in which the state and the market play important roles. Despite there being differences among feminists in approach (see below) and, as a consequence, differences in how they define patriarchy, the concept remains central to much feminist analysis and the view of politics that emerges from it.

There is, of course, no such thing as a feminist approach to politics. Tong (1992), in an extremely useful review of contemporary feminist thought, refers to feminism as 'kaleidoscopic' in its approaches. She suggest that while the initial impression may be one of 'chaos and confusion', in reality all are concerned with 'new relationships for personal and political life' (1992: 238). Further, as Belsey and Moore (1997: 14) suggest, feminist theories and 'the patriarchal knowledges they contest, have been in constant battle over Truth'. Thus, much of contemporary feminist theory provides a key dynamic in politics. As Mary Evans (1997: 3) argues, for feminists, 'the intellectual past should not sit like a dead weight on our shoulders, but should be used – with scepticism and even irreverence – to understand the present'.

Bryson (1992) clearly identifies the most commonly held feminist views on power, politics and the state. They include the following perspectives:

- **Liberal feminists:** who believe essentially women are rational beings just like men. Hence, they are entitled to the same legal, social and political rights.
- **Marxist feminists:** who centrally believe that those rights outlined above can only benefit a few middle-class women. Most women and men remain oppressed by capitalism. The key to women's liberation is therefore the class struggle.
- **Socialist feminists:** who seek to take the 'best' of Marxist Feminism and Radical Feminism to explain how class and sex oppression act together within capitalism.
- **Radical feminists:** who claim that the above ideas ignore the central feature of male power and that because the 'personal is political' power and politics have to be redefined in our society.

All the above feminist theories are, to a greater or lesser extent, tied up with the broader notion of social change. What follows is an outline of each of these.

Liberal feminism

For those working within the tradition of liberal feminism change has to come through the recognition and adoption of the broad claim of men and women to have equal rights. These writers draw on 'classical' liberal notions of the rights of all individuals to freedom, autonomy and a distinct voice in how they are governed. Indeed, as Carter (1988: 167) explains, 'historically, liberalism is the first social theory that offered the possibility of equality to women, since it developed in opposition to theories stressing a political, social and sexual hierarchy based on tradition, "nature" and order ordained by God in the scriptures'.

This line of thought can be traced back to John Stuart Mill's *The Subjection of Women*, first published in 1869. In this work Mill suggests that women are brought up to restrict their real nature, forced into a denial of themselves, and that they could only live through their husbands and children. The situation could only be improved by letting women realize their full potential for the benefit of both themselves and society. Mill further argues that the state had to remove legal restrictions which denied women equal civil and political rights, so that women be allowed to participate fully in public life.

Some of Mill's ideas regarding the role of the state were extremely radical for Victorian times. He did not, however, suggest any essential changes concerning family structure. He felt that giving women equal rights to work, divorce and property would also increase their choice regarding marriage. If, however, women did choose marriage, then he saw a continuation of the traditional division of labour. Individuals should have equal rights but the state should not intervene to create further social equality.

Central also to the origins of liberal feminist thought is Wollstonecraft's *Vindication of the Rights of Woman* ([1792] 1975). She applied rationalist ideas to all, arguing that women were also capable of moral self-development and were held back because they were 'socialized' into the values of weakness and femininity, and degraded by having to study to please men. Later liberal feminists built on such ideas to argue that 'freedom and equality' require legal reform and legislation, economic independence and the ability to influence politics directly, initially in demands for the vote and universal franchise.

In feminism's modern form, Friedan's *The Feminine Mystique* (1963) marks an important landmark. Friedman's work considers middle-class suburban women in the USA during the 1960s. Largely restricted to the world of home and children, such women lacked inner fulfilment and thus suffered from a lack of identity and purpose in their lives. Thus, Friedan argues that such women were kept from growing to their full human capacities, experiencing a 'slow death of mind and spirit' (1963: 266) and encouraged to define themselves in overtly feminine and domestic terms.

Friedan challenges this situation, urging the development of the full potential of women, especially in the public arena. The role of the state should be to ensure that women had equal rights to opportunities in colleges and the professions so women could develop their latent abilities. For the liberal tradition, the state should remove barriers to individual achievement through creating legal equality and preventing employment discrimination. While women were visible as sex objects they were invisible in the public domain. As she puts it with the discourse of the time:

As the Negro was the invisible man, so women are invisible people in America today: women who have a share in the decisions of the mainstream of government, of politics, of the church – who don't just cook the church supper, but preach the sermon; who don't just look up the ZIP codes and address the envelopes, but make the political decisions; who don't just do the housework of industry, but make some of the executive decisions. Women, above all who say what their own lives and personalities are going to be, and no longer listen to or even permit male experts to define what 'feminine' is or isn't. (Cited in MacArthur, 1993: 388–9)

The role of the state is therefore conceptualized as that which should ensure women have equal rights and equal access to opportunities. The state should guarantee that any obstacles to the fulfilment of women's potential will be removed, and that any form of discrimination countered legally by the state. Practical strategies would, for example, include legislation to allow women to compete on an equal basis in the labour market and the provision of childcare and equality of access to higher education.

Marxist feminism

Strategies such as those outlined above have, however, come under criticism from within feminism. In particular, those adopting socialist and Marxist feminist perspectives challenge the notion that legal reform and legislation can ever adequately tackle and redress the subordinate position of women. Rather, they point to economic issues as the fundamental source of exploitation. In this sense, both socialist and Marxist feminists draw on a common theoretical root of the class structure and the inequalities that emerge from it.

Although Marx and Engels expressed some cutting criticisms of the 'bourgeois family' in the *Communist Manifesto* ([1848] 1967), they never really discussed equality for women at any length. Instead it was Engels who sought to apply Marx's framework to the topic, most notably in *The Origins of the Family, Private Property and the State* ([1884] 1967). Here he argues that the position of women cannot be seen in isolation from the overall economic structure and social system. Rather, women are oppressed in several ways, by domesticity, by legal inequalities and by capitalism. Structural inequality surrounding gender functions to the benefit of the capitalist system, not just individual men. Central too is the position of women as a 'reserve army of labour', and the concept of the 'monogamous marriage' developed to meet the requirements of the passing on of private property within the legal family.

For Engels, it is the transition to socialism that will alleviate women's exploitation. The organization of domestic tasks, where women are largely confined to the home, would be transformed, placed on a collective basis. Women, freed from household work would be able to enter the public sphere on equal terms. Such a situation could never take place under capitalism, no matter how advanced and numerous the legal reform and legalization. Some middle-class women may benefit from such legislation, but it cannot serve women as a whole or dramatically alter their position as a group. Instead, women must be liberated from the private functions of wife and mother and be allowed to become an active public worker in a socialized economy.

For many, Marxist analyses can also directly explain the position of women in society. Under capitalism, it is their class position that best accounts for many women's lowly status and oppression. Bourgeois women simply do experience the same level of oppression as proletarian women. Women's position in society is thus the result of the political, social and economic structures of capitalism. Any meaningful attempt to change women's position must recognize this context.

For this reason feminists writing within this tradition have sought to explore and analyse the position of women in the workplace and as a 'reserve army of labour'. Women, it is argued, constitute an 'ideal type' of reserve army as they can be moved into and out of the labour market with reasonable ease, as for example, during the Second World War. By and large, however, married women are easily excluded from official statistics if it suits the state, as for example in unemployment figures. Moreover, women whose husbands are working do not put a burden on the state and those women who do work are largely restricted to highly defined sections of the labour market (Beechey, 1982).

This leads us to another major discussion within Marxist feminism, that of the arena of 'domestic labour'. There have been many debates around this issue, which Bryson summarizes as follows:

> [whether] women's domestic work should be seen as some kind of pre-capitalist mode of production outside of the money economy; whether it is essential to the reproduction of labour power under capitalism and whether in fact it does produce exchange value in the strict Marxist sense (in the form of the labour power of the adult male worker, sold like any other commodity on the market, with his overalls neatly pressed and sandwiches in his pocket). (Bryson, 1992: 238)

As Bryson (1992) points out, these debates are not merely of academic concern but structure political action by women. Thus, for some Marxist feminists, the essential features of women's work under capitalism are its trivialization and seeming inconsequence. Further, women are increasingly regarded merely as consumers and providers of service industries.

Contrary to this, Benston (1969: 16) argues that women themselves actually constitute a class because they are responsible for the production of 'simple use values in those activities associated with the home and family'. Women's oppression cannot be alleviated by allowing them to enter the labour force unless there is a parallel 'socialization' of household work, cooking, cleaning, childcare, and the like. By this means, society will finally recognize how socially necessary housework is and women will finally receive the respect that they deserve.

However, if we accept another view, that women's domestic work does in fact constitute the production of 'surplus value', it becomes strategically important to Marxists as another site for struggle. One practical strategy emerging from this would be to support demands for 'wages for housework'.

Such payments should be made by the state because it is capital which profits from women's exploitation, and payments for housework will reduce accumulation by the state.

In conclusion, Marxist feminism rests on the assertion that the social relations of the modern family, with women as reproducer and consumer, and man as producer, are capitalist constructs. Only changing the nature of the capitalist system itself can alter these constructs and the position of women in society. For women to be fully liberated requires the elimination of the basis of the capitalist economy. Society cannot be changed by appeals to reason, or justice, or to liberal conscience, but only by involvement in collective class struggle.

Socialist feminism

Obviously socialist feminism also draws on, and sometimes overlaps with, many of the same core tenets of Marxist feminism outlined above. This is particularly true of the idea that women's situation cannot be understood in isolation from its socio-economic context. Many Marxist feminists, of course, draw for their inspiration on the works of Engels and Marx. These writers are also revisited by a number of key socialist feminist writers with whom Marxist feminists have much in common. Indeed, in real terms the line between Marxist and non-Marxist socialist feminism is often, to say the least, blurred. However, as Tong (1992: 173) suggests, socialist feminism is largely the result of feminists' dissatisfaction, 'with the essential gender-blind character of Marxist thought – that is, with the tendency of Marxist patriarchs to dismiss women's oppression as not nearly as important as workers' oppression'.

Some important starting points are the works of Rowbotham (1972a, 1972b, 1973) and Mitchell (1971, 1974). In theoretical terms, such feminists highlight the intermeshing of capitalism and patriarchy. Pragmatically, socialist feminists argue that the legal reforms, which liberal feminists strive for, are mere 'tokens' and cannot hope to form the basis to improve the overall position of women. Rather, housework must be socialized and collectivized, accompanied by dramatic transformations in the economic and social structure.

Mitchell (1971), for example, seeks overtly to move away from the traditional Marxist feminist position and, in particular, the idea that a woman's position is derived directly from her position to capital. Rather, she argues that women's status is also determined by their role in both production and reproduction, the socialization of children and sexuality. She thus claims that Marxist approaches incorrectly seek to reduce women's position to the economic. Mitchell expands on this (1971: 100–1) when she says, economic demands 'are still primary, but must be accompanied by coherent policies for the other three elements (reproduction, sexuality and socialization), policies which at particular junctures may take over the primary role in immediate action'.

Indeed, Mitchell further argues that the family is the main reason that the move towards 'women's liberation' was slow. The family must be understood in broad terms, as an economic, ideological and as a biosocial unit. Even if there is a move towards the socialist mode of production, this will not ensure the end of women's oppression unless there is an equivalent transition in the psychological and ideological constructions of the family.

Moreover, many socialist feminists argue that with the break-up of the postwar political consensus on the welfare, the impact of the state on women's lives was increasingly seen as 'ambiguous'. Rowbotham (1990) argues that many of the anti-state positionings of feminists were formulated in a time when welfare provision by the state was not under challenge. Many of the assumptions of the first wave of feminists can no longer be taken for granted. The major impact of feminism on the state in the 1980s and 1990s was in relation to the continued demands to democratize and decentralize the state. In particular, the provision of welfare services continue to prove to be a major battleground, reflecting something not consumed passively but the result of active participation.

Sexism is thus best understood as a function of the capitalist system. Under socialism domestic tasks would be placed on a collective basis: women would be free of housework and able to participate fully in paid work. A socialist solution therefore involves the liberation of women from the private functions of wife and mother, allowing them to participate fully in a collectivized economy. Socialist feminists argue that liberals who focus upon legal and political reform, without seeking to change the nature of the family and economic system will fail to alter women oppression.

Further, as Smart (1991) indicates, such an analysis has become increasingly valid for feminists. Following the rise of the New Right and the acceptance of much of the rhetoric of neoliberalism, especially in regarding the nuclear family as 'conventional wisdom', the relationship between women and the state became increasingly contradictory. The burden for care on women was further reinforced. Moreover, in many ways for Smart:

> the family is becoming the main welfare agency . . . certain structural changes have occurred with the growth of the number of married women in the labour market, the extension of the period of children's economic dependence, the greater longevity of grandparents and, most recently, chronic unemployment. All these factors mean that families, or more correctly mothers and daughters, need support if they are to continue to provide care and welfare for other members whilst also joining the labour market. But it is this support that recent measures are undermining. (Smart, 1991: 167)

Radical feminism

A further perspective to be considered is radical feminism. Unlike those arguments already considered, which in various ways seek to reinterpret existing ideas, the emergence of radical feminism marks a break with previous traditions of political thought. It sets about constructing an agenda and political platform which essentially redetermines women's attitudes to themselves and those images imposed upon them by men; men's hatred of women; and the theoretical explanation of causes of women's oppression. Underlying this is the belief that neither changes in the legislative or economic systems can really transform the existing social relationships between men and women. Further, the feminist 'solutions' offered above are still all within male-defined parameters, offering only equality of opportunity and competition on male-dominated terms.

The answer for radical feminists is in a 'woman-centred' analysis of politics, especially the 'problems' of reproduction and the family. Fundamental to the project is the transformation of the social categories of masculinity and femininity. It is this notion which is central to the core theoretical statements within radical feminism, such as Firestone's, *The Dialectic of Sex* (1979). Drawing on the writings of both Marx and Freud, she argues that the biological differences between men and women mark the most basic class division of all. As she explains (1979: 232): 'Nature produced the fundamental inequality – half of the human race must bear or rear children for all of them – which was later consolidated, institutionalized, in the interests of men.'

Attempts at radical social transformation have so far failed because the repression of women and children will continue as long as the family will. Nor is it possible to bring it about by way of state institutions. The state itself functions to preserve patriarchy. In this sense reforming the state is not central to radical feminist analysis. It is merely another manifestation of patriarchal power, reflecting other deeply-rooted structures of oppression. The state is a symptom of male oppression, not the disease.

That is not to say that the state does not embody the interests of men rather than women, or that feminist demands are likely to be conceded by the state. State legislation cannot change the real position of women. Indeed, the legitimization of state intervention in key areas of social policy may only serve to increase the power and dominance of the male state.

In similar vein, Millett (1977) uses the term 'patriarchal government' to describe the institution by which 'half the population which is female is controlled by that half which is male'. In doing so, Millett argues that patriarchy runs through all economic and social structures and reinforces the relations between individual men and women in personal and sexual relationships. The conclusion to be drawn is that personal relationships and personal attitudes are necessarily political in nature. Foremost, 'the personal is political' a phrase which has become one of the key rallying cries of radical feminists over the past two decades.

It is, however, the family which Millet singles out as the key institution of women's oppression, 'mediating between the individual and the social structure', the family 'effects control and conformity where political and other authorities are insufficient' (1977: 33). Patriarchy is thus reproduced through the socialization of young people into its key values, relationships and roles.

The traditional family and the marriage institution must therefore be targets for radical social change. Indeed, Millet stresses an end to traditional sexual inhibitions and sexual freedom to undermine male supremacy and segregated gender roles.

Such ideas have led to the development of several important strategies by radical feminists, notably, the development of women's autonomous self-help groups, organized around the principal of non-hierarchy. Several of these groups also emphasized separatism and/or political lesbianism. The reasoning behind this is straightforward. Only lesbians can really be feminists because only they can be entirely 'women centred'. For many radical feminists, lesbianism is much more than an expression of sexual preference. Rather, it marks an external expression of the rejection of patriarchal heterosexual sexuality, and a rejection of controlling forms of oppression, domination and power.

The resultant discussion as to whether heterosexual women could be 'real' feminists and, wider arguments about sexuality, desire, identity and politics, structured much of the debate within radical feminism, and the feminist movement as a whole, throughout the 1980s. Later radical feminist writings have seen a shift in emphasis away from the oppression of women through social organization and physical dominance and towards a discussion of male control through ascendancy in the arenas of culture, language and knowledge.

Spender (1983, 1985), for example, argues that women's knowledge and understanding of the world has been suppressed and that there exists a long and 'forgotten' lineage of feminist thought. Likewise, Coole (1994: 1) suggests that political thought in the West 'has provided grounds for excluding women from citizenship while functioning discursively to construct the feminine identities it denigrates'. We shall return to this and other closely related ideas in Chapter 2.

For radical feminists, the kind of equality suggested by an agenda of equal rights and equal opportunities remains male defined. The notion that the main aim for women is that they should be able to compete with men on their own terms, rather than fundamentally to transform masculinity and femininity is a false one. Women should not model themselves on men, but rather should develop an analysis based on co-operation and non-aggression. The problem is not legal inequalities, or capitalism, but rather reproduction and the family.

Hence, the radical feminist perspective is overtly critical not only of mainstream social and political theory, but also of other feminisms. For radical feminists, Marxist inspired and promoted social transformation would merely mark just another coup among men. Social Democratic perspectives are suspect because when it comes to the crunch, feminists cannot expect male radicals to support them.

What is needed, therefore, at least to begin with, is some form of separatism, based around women working together with women in self-help, non-hierarchical groups. The women's movement should be, and indeed must be, autonomous. For these reasons, lesbianism plays a central organizational and political role. Revolutionary change can only come about by way of a radical transformation of society, through converting the nature of the family and sexual relationships.

Conservative feminism and postfeminism

Another view has arisen in recent years, which suggests that the link between the personal and the political, as projected by the second wave of feminist writers and activists, has become a thing of the past. Further, there has been a response to contemporary feminist debates in the form of a 'backlash' from conservative writers who have expressed strong doubts about the validity of challenging traditional gender roles. From this perspective, there is an underlying belief that women have a 'distinctive role', which should be highly valued in society and should remain 'different', rather than seeking equality.

Hence, Goldberg (1977) argues that all societies, whether developing or industrialized, past or present, traditional or revolutionary, express forms of patriarchal authority based upon universal gender differences. The 'fact' that biologically men are more aggressive leads to inevitable differences in the organization of politics and society. Goldberg concludes that as physiological differences cannot be changed, women should not seek to vie directly with men, but rather should develop their own natural feminine role.

There are other contemporary critiques of feminism emanating from the political Right (see Barry, 1994; Levin et al., 1992). Kenny (1994) offers a perspective that directly challenges the proposition that women are disadvantaged relative to men by the traditional patriarchal family. For her, the 'two-income norm' is now adversely affecting the ability of couples to start a family. Likewise, Wilson (1994), writing in the same volume as Kenny, claims that gender equality cannot be achieved in all occupations because men and women have different personalities, talents and different 'natural' interests rooted in the biological differences between them.

Others have suggested that we now live in a 'postfeminist' era. While the term 'postfeminism' remains somewhat nebulous, it is growing in usage. It first manifested in popular culture through performers such as the Spice Girls and Madonna. In populist writings it is found in the works of Wolf (1993). Indeed, the term seems to have originated in popular culture in the mid-1980s with sections of the media. If it is possible to identify that which binds postfeminism together, it is a refusal to accept any definition of women as victims and to project the notion of strong women in control across many aspects of social life. Postfeminism suggests that young women are articulating a set of ideas and forms of expression by women that regard traditional feminism as irrelevant to contemporary life and social relationships.

Elsewhere, Roiphe (1994) suggests that instead of highlighting women's strengths, the contemporary feminist movement merely demonstrate their vulnerability. For Denfeld (1995), feminism has come to represent an image of female victimization. Further, contemporary feminism merely represents an extremist cabal, which sees a continued female victimization in an all-powerful patriarchal system. This, alongside open hostility to heterosexual practices, merely alienates younger generations that believe that most of the battles around feminism have already been won.

These ideas have not gone unchallenged from within feminism. At the heart of the response to postfeminism is the re-emergence of Greer with the publication of *The Whole Woman* (1999). In this work she dismisses post-feminism as a phenomenon led by the multinationals and globalized corporations. Further, she argues that postfeminism is a luxury that can only be afforded by those in the affluent West. This broad argument is supported by several writers who claim that postfeminism lacks relevance to black and lesbian women and that it marks a break with, rather than builds upon the previous generation of feminist experiences (see Jowett, 2000; Mirza, 1998; Phillips, 1991, 1993).

Such responses have led some to talk of a 'third wave' of feminist writings located within these responses. Hence, Bryson (1999a) has further argued that the concept of patriarchy still has great relevancy and remains a piercing analytical force. Certainly it should not be abandoned by the current generation of feminist writers. Elsewhere, Bryson (1999b) suggests that the reason for the apparent decline of the autonomous women's movement is the 'normalization' of many of its activities and demands into social, academic, economic and political life.

Feminism remains a broad church; this is reflected in the range of views held by feminists on politics and the role of the state. All feminist thinking challenges traditional definitions of politics in the public arena towards the politics of everyday life. Further, feminist analysis criticizes the social construction of knowledge, power relations and identity. As Weedon defines it, feminism is a politics:

> directed at changing existing power relations between men and women in society. These power relations structure all areas of life, the family, education and welfare, the worlds of work and politics, culture and leisure. They determine who does what and for whom, what we are and what we might become. (Weedon, 1987: 1)

Foucault, politics and the state

It is possible to argue, with some justification, that no man since Marx has had such an influence on thinking regarding power and society as Michael Foucault. Pivotal to this contribution is the attempt to deconstruct existing power structures. While clearly aware of it, his writings tend to downplay the role of the material and centralized power of the state. Rather, he focuses on the role of the state as a shaper and propagator of discourses. Indeed, the concept of 'discourse' is central to the whole Foucaultian project. By this he means that broad sets of ideas, meanings and possible statements about a subject that are dominant at particular times among particular sets of people.

This, of course, in part resembles the Marxist concept of ideology. Within Marxism, dominant ideas and values are traced back directly to the class whose interests they serve. For Foucault, however, there is no presumption of necessary power inequality. Those who shape the discourse are also subject to it.

Foucault rejects the Marxist theory of ideology because it presumes that there is a 'reality' from which individuals are cunningly separated by 'false consciousness'. The concept of discourse differs from that of ideology because it does not assume that there is a 'truth', which ideology conceals. Rather, a discourse sets about defining its own truth. It defines what can be said about a particular subject, what can be seen as the logic of an argument, and what are understood as the acceptable premises in such arguments.

This reading of discourse has important consequences for understanding power. Many of the arguments outlined in this chapter suggest that we can best understand power as the imposition of a dominant will upon individuals or groups. Foucault disputes this approach, arguing that there is no such thing as power, but rather 'powers'. There are a variety of ways in which an individual, group or class can impose their ascendancy over others. For Foucault, power is based on knowledge and, in particular, the ability of discourses to define 'truth'. Knowledge does not constrain. Rather, it works by defining certain goals as much more desirable than others. As Foucault argues, power:

> is not to be taken to be the phenomenon of one individual's consolidated and homogeneous domination over others, or that of one group or class over others. . . . Power must be analysed as something which circulates, or rather as something which only functions in the form of a chain. It is never localised here or there, never in anybody's hands, never appropriated as a commodity or piece of wealth. Power is employed and exercised through a net-like organisation. And not only do individuals circulate between its threads; they are always in the position of simultaneously undergoing and exercising this power. In other words, individuals are the vehicles of power, not its point of application. (Foucault, 1980: 98)

Hence, Foucault seeks to deny that power exists as a single entity and to distinguish between different forms of power, such as repressive or coercive power or creative and enabling power, between the legal power of the state and power that is based on the possession and control of knowledge. Power, in Foucault's terms, can be thought of not as repressive, but as productive. Power produces knowledge that can be seen in the currently prevailing discourse. Above all, for Foucault, knowledge represents the power to define. Hence, power and knowledge are inseparable, knowledge decrees what can be done, to whom, and by whom.

In *The History of Sexuality* (1979), for example, Foucault focuses on creative powers. That is, the power of that which is defined as the 'norm' or 'normality' and power based on 'knowledge' of new scientific discourses.

Importantly, he introduces the notion that there can be 'resistance' to the imposition of discourses. In the same way that power and knowledge may be dispersed throughout society, so too may there be alternative discourses which may be drawn upon. In the case of the homosexual, Foucault further gives the example of how medical, psychiatric, welfare and legal discourses came together, in the Victorian era, to construct the modern homosexual as a specific 'type' of person.

The scientific truth, or in Foucault's term 'knowledge', concerning sexuality was constructed by the medical profession, moral reformers and social legislators to present homosexuals as 'perverted' individuals with a 'deviant' sexuality. Through these various discourses sexual irregularity was steadily annexed to mental illness. The notion, of the 'sick' homosexual was thus the creation of these new discourses. Once homosexuals were so identified, they were labelled and excluded from 'normal' arenas of life and normal social interaction. This disciplinary power was (and is) so successful because, ultimately, it relies on self-regulation by those involved.

What of Foucault's further notion that power and resistance operate together, and that one is never present without the other? Foucault claims that resistance is formulated on the basis of alternative discourses. Those who are 'excluded', set apart because of their homosexuality, for example, have several strategies open to them. One tactic is simply to deny the legitimacy of the category. To refuse to accept that such sexual behaviour is an indication of abnormality or deviancy. However, given the strength of the 'scientific discourse' that dominates society, such a strategy may well prove fruitless.

There is another line of resistance, however. This is to accept fully the 'label' of homosexual, but refuse to accept the wider societal implications of the label. That is, to assert politically and socially the legitimacy of a wide range of sexual orientations, preferences and relationships, of which homosexuality is just one. This would include the right to contend the legitimacy of stable homosexual 'family' relationships. In so doing, the discourse of the family could be invoked as a discourse of strength, around which resistance may well be usefully articulated.

For Foucault, power does not rest with particular individuals or groups. Rather, it is present in a multiplicity of discursive struggles. Therefore, Foucault clearly rejects those who support what he calls totallizing discourses and narratives. This obviously means that his views come into direct conflict with other theoretical perspectives, such as Marxism and feminism, which try to explain power in terms of single societal dimensions.

Ultimately, however, Foucault is not prepared to give one particular worldview the stamp of 'truth'. His core belief is that power operates not from the top down, but from the bottom up. The lives of individuals are therefore structured not by the filtering down of power and ideologies from a dominant group. Rather, those widespread oppressions in society, such as class and gender, are seen as arising from local power relationships. Those who are in a position to make use of them then appropriate these relations.

Hence, with slight exceptions, there is very little talk, or even recognition, of the state in Foucault's work. This is mainly because his concern with 'the micro-physics of power', focusing on how power is exercised in modern Western societies, means the state is seen as decentralized. Various techniques of power are autonomous, each developing its own rationality and logic, and with its own internal dynamics. Such an approach involves abandoning any notion of the economic as a fundamental determinant of change, although Foucault (1979) admits that it was initially the economic take-off of the West that necessitated these new forms of regulation and control.

Power is not seen as a property or a possession, nor does it reside exclusively with any one class to be used against another, as it is traditionally understood in Marxist social analysis. Instead, 'power is everywhere'. In rejecting class unity as the main location of political resistance, Foucault directly challenges existing political understandings and particularly the organization of many of those on the political Left. Further, his conception of positive power, rather than repression as the way in which social order has been achieved, effectively shifts the site of control into the social itself.

Evaluating theories of power and the state

So how can we begin to evaluate these notions of power and the state? Although certain theorists have argued that elite rule and democratic accountability are compatible, this remains a highly problematic and contested area. While it may be possible, in certain circumstances, to determine which elite rules, the system of concentrating power within the elite group cannot itself be challenged. The greatest input that the majority can hope for is to be allowed to decide every few years which elite will rule on its behalf. This can hardly be seen as a positive or progressive role.

It is also possible to identify several key weaknesses within pluralism. The pluralist analysis rests primarily on the belief that there exists a politically literate and well-informed electorate. In broad terms, most pluralists believe that any political changes should be incremental, and that the *status quo* should dominate decision-making. Politicians, as a group, do not favour vested interests, and competing claims for scarce resources in society can and should always be reconciled within the democratic arena.

Further, all groups are seen as possessing the ability to gain access to some section of the state apparatus. In key policy areas under represented interests, or the interested of less well organized groups, can be catered for by setting up new agencies. Strong cabinet or presidential executives are the best way of guiding policy. Further, the collective actions of the state are benevolent and have a caring overview of the needs of society. However, many pluralists are hostile to centralized states and strongly believe that decentralization ensures participation and 'control' over politicians. In pragmatic terms there is strong support for local government, with distinct powers from central government.

It is also possible to identify several further criteria of the pluralist perspective. First, there is the central belief that no single group in society is able to exercise systematic control over more than one range of issues.

Secondly, the view that there is equilibrium of power between pressure groups, especially the most important consumer groups, and particularly between capital and labour. Thirdly, the view that there is a separation of economic and political power. Fourthly, and crucially, the belief that the state is essentially 'neutral' in its character. Fifthly, most would claim that an essential part of complex society is a plurality of ideas and an absence of a dominant ideology.

For pluralists, the modern democratic state rests on the belief that politics operates through certain power centres, notably government, parliament and particularly the cabinet. There are checks and balances on these against erratic or authoritarian decisions that may be taken against majority interests. These include regular elections and the guarantee of free speech. Real power is dispersed among a wide range of pressure groups. There may at different times be coalitions of interests, but these change over time and involve different groups and organizations both inside and outside parliament. The neutral positioning of the state encourages lobbying, political campaigning and compromise between competing groups. Hence, politics is inevitably limited in its effectiveness. All of the nation's needs cannot be solved, all of the competing interests cannot be met. It is therefore essential that the protection of the voters' democratic rights is placed with parliament.

Perhaps the most telling criticism of the pluralist approach is that they operate within a highly restricted concept of what power is, and how politics actually works. In the context of the United Kingdom this means an overt focus on public policy-making, legislation and the actions of government.

Further, there is an almost unquestioning acceptance of the distinctions between public and private areas of life, the latter considered to be autonomous from the economy in particular. Pluralists tend to concentrate on political participation and decision-making in the public arena. There is little room within pluralist ideas for any operation of politics beyond the observable, the operation of interest groups who do not manifest openly, or for the state to take any role beyond that of referee.

Overall, perhaps the clearest challenge to pluralists is the charge that they concentrate their focus on a limited dimension of political power, that which is readily observable and which is seen to operate in the public domain. This is what Lukes (1974) calls the 'one dimensional view' of power.

This issue is addressed directly by Marxism's core argument, that in capitalist societies power rests with a coherent capitalist class. The state therefore acts to secure the continuance of 'bourgeois' domination. Within the United Kingdom, managers and those in leading positions in the judiciary, the law and the like are all recruited from within the dominant class and gender grouping. This 'ruling class' utilizes social networks to secure access to core decision-making roles within the state and civil society. Overall, from this perspective the state is seen as an 'instrument' of capital.

Poulantzas, however, argues that the instrumental approach of Miliband ignores, or at least is insensitive to, those structural factors that condition state action. For Poulantzas, Miliband cannot account for the role of the state in continually reproducing capitalist society, even if this means its actions may conflict with the short-term interests of the capitalist class. The state thus often acts in a 'relatively autonomous' manner in order to ensure the preservation of the capitalist order. These polar positions of 'instrumentalism' and 'structuralism' have set the parameters for a continuing debate within neo-Marxism concerning the role of the state in advanced capitalist society.

The resulting post-Marxist writings have, for example, developed a central concern with the stability of the modern capitalist state. Later in the book we shall engage with the works of two such writers, Habermas and Offe. Both have emphasized how endemic economic crisis and social conflict force a reaction, that of an increasingly interventionist state, with responsibility for the containment of these conflicts.

We shall consider these views later in relation to issues surrounding the legitimation of state power in the United Kingdom. Despite the demise of Marxist orthodoxy following the 'collapse of communism' in the revolutions in Eastern Europe between 1989 and 1991, Marxism remains influential in informing much theoretical debate.

Corporatism is another theoretical position that has important things to say on the form of politics, development of the economy and levels of state intervention within the United Kingdom. As a form of political expression it stresses the manner in which large interest groups can combine informally in co-operation to regulate the economic structure and core areas of social life. The emphasis on consensus hopefully results in a more conciliatory form of politics.

In the United Kingdom by the mid-1970s, this manifested in the concept of a 'social contract', whereby 'social partners' sought to govern the running of the state. Importantly, however, there were always key groups and dynamics which found them outside the embrace of corporatist structure, even at its height. Since the early 1980s corporatism has found itself under attack, both theoretically and pragmatically, from all sides.

For liberal theorists, the structured nature of corporatism marks the decay of pluralism. For those adopting a Weberian perspective, it marks a further development in 'rational-legal' domination, and increases the power of bureaucracies. For a number of Marxists, corporatism merely represented a stage of the development of advanced capitalism, whereby basic class conflicts were disguised.

From a Marxist perspective, rather than introducing the end to class conflict, corporatism institutionally solidifies the balance of class power at a particular point in history. Both Westergaard (1977) and Panitch (1976, 1980, 1985) have provided telling criticisms along these lines. Indeed, Westergaard suggests that corporatism is a model whereby the state is seen to exist 'above' or 'outside' competing social and economic interests.

The state, however, remains capitalist and structured by the capitalist maxim of the 'maximization of profit'. Under corporatism there is no notion of changing its mode of production, or its organizing principles. Hence for Panitch (1980, 1985), corporatism marks a political strategy to suppress working-class militancy, any opposition to its exploitation and the potential of the organized labour movement. At its heart, corporatism ensures that the capitalist class still has control of the state. Any co-operation by the trades union movement largely benefits business interests rather more than it does the labour movement.

Such a perspective was far from accepted on the political Right, which saw corporatism as a sop to the organized Left. With the emergence of the New Right, the United Kingdom state ditched any notion of corporatism. 'Thatcherism' took a very different route in the search for a successful economic system, introducing market competition as the core organizational principle. As we shall see in Chapter 3, the New Right, under the leadership of Margaret Thatcher, pursued an unambiguously 'anti-corporatist' tone, re-emphasizing the confrontational nature of politics and the primacy of the market over any form of agreed economic intervention and political consensus.

Overall corporatism has had little long-term impact on the structure of the state. That said, the concept of corporatism, albeit in a limited form, has resurfaced in recent times. In particular, the promotion of a stakeholder society by New Labour has breathed some life into the notion. We will discuss this in much more detail later, but here it is suffice to flag up a possible re-emergence of corporatism on to the political agenda, promoted by writers such as Hutton (1995a, 1997) and sections of the parliamentary Labour Party and New Labour leadership.

The very mention of a reawakening of corporatist values, however, has led to a reaction from those on the political Right. Hence, Brian Mawhinney, the then Conservative Party Chairman, in discussing the notion of a stake-holder society (see Chapter 4), revived many of the Tory demons of the recent past when he claimed that the emerging trends within New Labour in the mid-1990s were in essence corporatism. He went on to say, 'the Trade Unions, the vested interest groups, the Labour-dominated local authorities . . . it's second-hand socialist policies wrapped up in Tory ribbons. . . . It is a devious way to attempt to bring in new taxes through the back door' (*Guardian*, 8 January 1996).

In reviewing feminist views on politics and the state it is clear that we encounter not one, but several key perspectives. Sometimes these arguments and political positions are overlapping, sometimes contradictory. Lovenduski and Randall (1993: 7) point to several important trends in contemporary feminist analysis. They suggest a coming together of the politics and strategies of radical and socialist feminists. It is the strategies of liberal feminists, and the attempt to integrate more women into public life, that have, however, become most influential and clearly seen in the British context.

Further, Lovenduski and Randall (1993: 353–8) suggest that the decline and deradicalization of the women's movement has been accompanied by, and 'in many ways was a consequence of, its greater involvement with state agencies and the growing presence of feminists in mainstream institutions' (1993: 15). This increasing involvement by feminists in the agencies of the state, and the increasing impact of feminist ideas in these areas, is one of the greatest 'gains' of the contemporary women's movement.

The feminist gaze thus proves to be an incisive analytical tool. Some of the more interesting material in the most recent wave of feminist writing seeks to embrace and encompass several strands of feminist thought. The works of Jagger (1983) or Young (1990), for example, often seek to integrate socialist, Marxist, radical and indeed psychoanalytical approaches within feminism. Such an approach, as Tong points out, has the potential to 'resolve the existing differences among many currents of feminism' (1992: 193).

Obviously, however, it is also important to highlight the major traditions of thought within feminism. Depending on which strand of thought is adopted, there are competing feminist views of the state. Overall, for many feminists, practical political issues and actions are as important, if not more important, as theoretical issues. Nonetheless, feminist writings have become increasingly sophisticated in their writings on power and the state.

Many feminist writings now seek to distinguish between the experiences of groups of women, such as those differentiated by class, ethnicity and race (see Anthias and Yuval-Davis, 1982; Lorde, 1992; Mama, 1995). Other feminists reject all universalizing discourses, seeking to locate their views within postmodernist thought. Most postmodern feminists seek to connect modernity with masculinity. Hence, the supposedly neutral universal truths of modernist thinking are actually deeply located in male power. Truth is not seen as external or neutral, but rather constructed through multiple determinants of experience, such as exclusion and repression (see Flax, 1990; Grosz, 1990, 1994; Spivak, 1992).

One important point highlighted in recent feminist writings is that women's experience of politics, and their comparative positions in the social structure of the United Kingdom, varies considerably. Rowbotham (1993: 1) highlights the importance of this. Rather than seeing women as a homogeneous grouping on to which a prescription for change can be applied, she argues that the emancipation of women and gender relations must be understood in relation to other aspects of women's lives. Further, nobody is simply a woman. Women are born into a particular family, class and race and at a particular time in history.

Foucault's work has been open to several political critiques. First, the notions of 'resistance to power' appear extremely unrealistic to some. Indeed, it appears at times to be built on a series of somewhat prosaic statements rather than any coherent political strategy. Secondly, there is the anarchistic thread that runs through his work. If power and resistance are 'everywhere', how are we to evaluate one form of resistance against another? For example, how are we to decide which would be progressive and which would be reactionary? The only way out is to introduce value judgements, which at the same time would seem to suggest that, to some extent at least, we are able to stand outside of power. Thirdly, Foucault at times seems to embroider and accent the role of the deviant. One way this is done is by regarding their actions as unique and difficult to clarify for their purposes of normalization (Foucault, 1977). Another is through the construction of particular individuals who are seen as standing up to and resisting power, shrugging off its effects (Foucault, 1979).

Politics and the state: some conclusions

How then should the individual hope to understand and have any meaningful input into the political process? Indeed, it must be asked whether, in contemporary society, individuals have any chance of influencing the political world around them, or altering the decision-making processes often made at national and supranational levels?

Although the state remains central to most of our lives, its place is seen as challenged by several current trends. This can be seen in what Jessop (1990) calls a 'hollowing out' of the state. This is a process whereby many of the functions once performed by the state have gradually been transferred to other institutions. It can be seen in developments such as privatization (see Chapter 3) and globalization (see Chapter 7).

Despite this, it would seem that in the United Kingdom the legitimacy of the state, certainly outside Northern Ireland, is rarely questioned on a mass level. One example of when this did happen in Britain, however, was with the mass protests surrounding the Poll Tax in the early 1990s (Tonge, 1994). Another recent example was seen in the widespread and co-ordinated protests against the level of taxation on petrol and other fuels organized throughout 2000? Although such events are rare, it does not follow that uncritical attitudes towards the United Kingdom state and its actions are the norm.

Even in time of 'war' this is often the case. It is clear that many Britons opposed the sending the task force to the Falklands/Malvinas in 1981, even though a majority may have supported it. At the time of the Gulf War, while there was considerable populist support for 'Desert Storm', there was also a solid core of opposition, and a reasonably coherent 'anti-war' movement. During 2001, tens of thousands of individuals took to the streets in organized protests in opposition to the bombing of Afghanistan. Yet such voices of discord were able to gain little prominence in the political arena of the time. Many opposition groups still often claim exclusion from the political agenda.

From what has been said already, it should be apparent just how 'contested' notions of power and debates concerning the roles of the state remain. This chapter has outlined some of the conventional building blocks that are often drawn upon to try to answer these questions. As we shall see, there are those who believe that ideologically single theories cannot account for the plurality of identities that exist in the modern world.

Further, we shall also encounter arguments that the ideological positions we have reviewed have largely been made irrelevant by a new postmodern frames of reference, or that the politics and power relationships within individual nation-states have been rendered immaterial by the forces of globalization.

The theories outlined above cannot, however, be ignored. Much of the rest of the book will introduce material which either seeks to build upon, or at times fundamentally challenges the models already discussed. The ideas in Chapter 1 remain core reference points for orienting individuals to the political world and for providing explanations in relation to the market economy, conflicts over national and political identities, and the contemporary politics of social inclusion and exclusion. To begin with, let us consider in more detail the nature of the state and the dynamics of power as it continues to develop within the United Kingdom.

DISCUSSION QUESTIONS

- How should we best understand the concept of the state?
- Discuss the view that only Marxists have produced a coherent analysis of the contemporary state.
- How useful are pluralist theories in explaining the relationships between power and the state in contemporary societies?
- What chance do people have of influencing the political world?

2

Legitimacy and Power in the United Kingdom

<table>
<tr><td>Key concepts and issues</td><td>Key theorists and writers</td></tr>
<tr><td>

- The end of political consensus
- Legitimacy and the state
- Fordism and post-Fordism
- Nationalism and the state
- Nationalisms within the United Kingdom
- Race, ethnicity and politics

</td><td>

- Benidict Anderson
- Andrew Gamble
- Ernest Gellner
- Antonio Gramsci
- Jürgen Habermas
- Stuart Hall
- Eric Hobsbawn
- Bob Jessop
- Tom Nairn
- Claus Offe

</td></tr>
</table>

In the historical shift to the modern world, political identity, institutionally secured order and legitimacy came to revolve around nationhood, statehood and citizenship . . . pragmatically, a modern polity came to be a state within whose boundaries a nation of citizens lived, hence nation-statehood. (Preston, 1997: 10–11)

The starting point for much of this chapter is the debate surrounding the construction of, and later challenges to, a 'postwar consensus' of politics. It will then explore some central issues surrounding nationalisms and national identities within the contemporary United Kingdom and how these contribute or inhibit the continued legitimacy of the 'British' state.

Following the end of the Second World War it is widely accepted that there existed a common political agenda, determined around the major ideas of Beveridge and Keynes and which commanded the dynamics and policy-making decisions of the United Kingdom. Such a programme was seen to dictate for around 30 years after the war and to form the basis for a social democratic state, which found commitment from across the party political spectrum.

The origins of this social democracy rest within the socialist reformism tradition and in particular with the idea that social problems and inequalities can be alleviated by direct state intervention. The classic focus for such intervention and redistribution has been the welfare state. Social democracy is also directly associated with progressive taxation, increased access to housing, education, social services and other mechanisms for removing social problems affecting the poor.

The basic assumptions underpinning this have been highlighted by Donnison (1982: 20–2, cited in Lowe, 1993). These were that the growth of the economy and the population would continue. Although inequalities in incomes would persist, their harsher effects could be gradually softened by a social wage, and despite conflicts about important issues the peoples of 'middle England' would eventually support equalizing social policies and programmes.

From the middle of the 1970s, however, there began to appear the notion of political crisis and the expression of a widespread feeling that the policies of consensus were failing to fulfil even its most basic goals. In part, this was precipitated by a prolonged recession in the world economy and increasingly open challenges to state authority. It was exhibited in a sharp polarization between political parties, culminating in the demolition of the existing political consensus following the 1979 general election, which marked a decisive political break with much of what had gone before.

There was, for example, a clear shift away from the concept of a welfare state which provided a 'safety net' for all, towards a system whose emphasis was on market forces. This was seen by the New Right as an attempt to address its concept of the crisis created in the previous decade. There are, however, several other crucial aspects to understanding the concept of 'crisis'. First, it is important to recognize the significance of uneven economic development throughout the capitalist world and within the United Kingdom. This will be a focus for Chapters 6 and 7. Secondly, it is important to consider the significance of nationalist movements, which were taking on increasing significance in the late 1970s. Another issue which brings into sharp relief the political crisis of the United Kingdom state is the situation in Northern Ireland, a discussion of which will provide the focus for Chapter 5. In this chapter, however, we shall concentrate on the formation, and later decline, of the political consensus after 1945. This will form the base line for discussions of contemporary politics.

Post-Second World War consensus

But what was the postwar political consensus? Gamble (1985) argues that its formation can be seen at three levels. First, the formation of the coalition government followed by the election of a majority Labour government marked the evaporation of the political pattern of the 1920s and 1930s. In particular, the postwar period saw the emergence of a new two-party electoral system with very stable support for both groupings.

Secondly, there were major policy shifts, involving reconstruction pro-grammes and the legitimation of an extended role for the state. In particular, the Beveridge Report provided a blueprint for an advanced welfare state and Keynesian economics, with the commitment to full employment, provided a major dynamic to policy formation.

Thirdly, the consensus involved an important shift of power between capital and labour. Labour gave a new role and increased importance to the trade unions, involving them directly in economic policy-making.

Perhaps even more importantly, the Conservative Party showed more willingness to administer than to dismantle the welfare state. This ensured that the new policy direction was consolidated in the 1950s. In the decades that followed, Conservative administrations demonstrated no great desire to undo the social reforms introduced by Labour. Both parties came to regard such policies as 'acceptable'. Coates (1995) agrees with the identifi-cation of the core values of social democracy: a commitment to full employ-ment, rising living standards, international competitiveness and generous provision of welfare, underpinned by economic theories based on the works of Keynes.

This postwar political consensus also extended to foreign policy. Both ideologically and pragmatically, the United Kingdom was in a continued alliance with the USA. This was clearly reflected in the United Kingdom's commitment to acceptance by the North Atlantic Treaty Organization (NATO) of the USA as leader of the new political and economic order of the West. The United Kingdom fell in line in the 'Cold War' against communism.

There was, of course, a cost to all of this. Coates (1995: 141) suggests that the price of USA help was immersion into the Western anti-communist military, economic and ideological system. Keynesianism and Cold War ideology went hand in hand. At the heart of the accommodation between the political Right and Left in Britain was agreement around the role of NATO and the benefits of collective welfare. It is crucial to assess the strength of consensus. The United Kingdom elections of 1964 and 1966 revealed no real disagreements over policy between Conservatives and Labour. The only real choice offered to voters was to choose between which political grouping was best able to modernize British society.

By the mid-1960s the nature of the consensus had begun to change, to take on a more corporatist shape. Most noticeably there was a reintroduction of a series of incomes policies, some voluntary, but most involving legislation. Between the early 1960s and the late 1970s there was a clear attempt to bring together leading representatives of the trade unions and business to agree policy on prices, productivity and strategic investment. Although, even at its height, the British road to corporatism was not far travelled, the government did support large programmes of investment, often guided by an agreed policy with the unions and industrial leaders. There was also often to be seen an agreement to pursue common goals, largely in the face of foreign economic competition.

There are counter-perspectives to this, challenging the strength and solidity of the consensus. Indeed, several writers, such as Jenkins (1987) and

Evans and Taylor (1996), have cautioned against a too facile or too obvious view of the existence of the postwar agreement, while Pimlott (1989) has proved most sceptical, describing the idea of consensus as a 'mirage' and an 'illusion'. For most commentators, however, there is some agreement that such a consensus existed. If this is so, then there is an important question to be answered, namely, why was there a break-up of the political and economic consensus that stamped the mould of the United Kingdom in the postwar period?

How did the consensus break up?

There are several features to be considered in trying to answer this. For example, it has been argued that there were important changes in the direction of the major political parties themselves. Throughout the decades following the Second World War it is alleged that decline in inequality and class had eroded ideological differences which were seen as something of the past. This was given sociological expression by Bell (1962), who talked of the 'end of ideology' (see Chapter 6). His ideas became almost the conventional wisdom of the day, academically, politically and certainly at the 'common-sense' level. In party terms this found expression through the development of 'Butskellism' (made up from the names of Butler and Gaitskell, leading figures in the Conservative and Labour parties), which demonstrated the level of ideological consensus at the time regarding politics.

In the early 1960s, however, increasingly polar views within the political arena were beginning to be expressed. This is sometimes referred to as the rise of ideology, with both a 'New Right' and a 'New Left' gaining control of respective parties. Hence, it is argued that the consensus was destroyed by resultant growth in adversary politics driven by these new ideologies. The failure of modernization, which had provided a key element to consensus, was central to this process. This caused deep disillusion in the electorate and the existing political policies were increasingly discredited by high unemployment (in relative terms) and poor economic performance.

Elsewhere Leys (1983) suggests that the crisis of the late 1960s and 1970s can be identified as a coming together of both economic failure and political inadequacy. However, what made the crisis so significant was that it began in a period of unparalleled prosperity for most of the rest of the industrialized world. The position of the United Kingdom state has to be understood in terms of continued relative economic decline.

By the middle of the 1970s Leys suggests that the failure of the two main political parties to halt economic decline reflected in falling electoral support. Leys outlines the consequences as follows:

> The social-democratic values to which even the Conservatives had subscribed during the 1950s were losing some of their authority. The parties themselves,

faced with the intractable problem of economic decline, became increasingly polarised. Political currents previously considered 'extreme' – the market-oriented doctrines of the 'New Right' and the more radical socialist policies of the 'Labour left' – gained ground in the parties outside parliament, and in the case of the Conservatives, captured control inside the parliamentary party as well in 1975. (Leys, 1983: 65)

It is possible to engage with a further set of arguments that go beyond the British state and point to major shifts regarding Britain's position in the world economic system. Such sentiments find resonance with Gamble (1981: 4–5) when he argues that the problems of the contemporary United Kingdom state are best understood in terms of 'one hundred years of decline'. Over that period, Britain has passed through three main periods of degradation. The first phase was between 1880 and the outbreak of the First World War, when Britain first suffered major competition from industrial rivals. A second phase, between the two world wars, saw Britain attempting to, but failing, to build itself as a world power. Crucial too, however, was that Britain managed to avoid the worst excesses of the economic slump of the 1930s. In the third phase after 1945, Britain was forced to withdraw from the Empire and failed to expand as quickly as other capitalist societies during the postwar boom. The period also saw Britain subordinated to the United States, financially, militarily and ideologically.

Britain's continued decline has seen its overall position change from one of world leadership to that of dependency. Its accumulation and profits remained linked to the world capitalist economy, but it was able to exert less and less influence over its direction. Britain's position was becoming increasingly weak. For many years, however, the buoyancy of the capitalist economy disguised the broader trends of decline. With the economic downturn of the 1970s, the camouflage was removed as a new phase was ushered in, starkly revealing to many the full extent of Britain's economic and political decline (see English and Kenny, 2000; Tomlinson, 2001).

From several very different perspectives, social democracy was seen to be failing to deliver economic prosperity or to preserve public authority. By the late 1970s, a section of the Conservative Party did not seek to disguise its rejection of consensus. Margaret Thatcher emerged as the leader of this New Right faction. The subsequent political developments were complex and will be considered in detail in the next chapter.

In broad terms, however, the emergence of the New Right marked a clear rejection of the primacy of the ideas of John Maynard Keynes, as the motivation behind economic policy, and their replacement by the works of Adam Smith. These new neoliberals argued that only if inflation was overcome could unemployment be brought down. Pragmatically, it manifested in a strong attack on public expenditure and the commitment to the removal of all 'obstacles' to free market.

This increasing disillusionment with the path of reform and its financial cost gave rise to the election of the Thatcher government of 1979. Keynesian ideology gave way to monetarism, marked by the shift from fixed to floating exchange rates, which, it was claimed, was increasingly discredited. The end of consensus resulted in a dramatic slowing down in public sector spending. Fiscal crisis and 'the politics of the budget' increasingly became central to the political agenda. Recession and subsequent unemployment meant the role of government intervention and the form it should take came to centre stage.

Those on the New Right actively promoted their *laissez-faire* views that the state should intervene as little as possible in the running of society and the economy. The problem of unemployment could best be understood not in terms of deficiencies in demand, but rather in terms of gross inadequacies in the supply side of the economy.

The impact of the New Right on the existing arrangements of social democracy was therefore no more clearly seen than in the changing relationship between the state and the labour movement. From within the perspective of the New Right the 'real' cause of high levels of unemployment was inflation. In turn, this lay in excessive demands by labour and the inadequacies of supply. The remedy to the ills of the United Kingdom economy was to release the forces of competition. As a result, any notion of a corporatist approach was rapidly dispatched.

The structured assault by the New Right on the labour movement that followed was far from coincidental. Overtly, the New Right challenge to the trade unions and collective bargaining was on the grounds of 'national efficiency'. Such an understanding is extremely superficial. Rather, this renegotiation of power away from representatives and organizations of collectivism was a crucial strategy in a wider offensive on the existing postwar consensus. Within a short time of its election in 1979 the Conservative government had broken the institutionalized bargaining between the state, big business and trade unions. Gone too was any notional commitment to the co-operative management of economy.

Instead, the first Thatcher administration began to challenge some of the essentials of the universal welfare state and the ideological cornerstones of social democracy. In its place it sought actively to promote the 'freedom' of the individual and the primacy of the market in the areas of both the economy and welfare. As Gamble (1994a) explains, those promoting the views of the New Right believed that the social democratic state had gradually undermined institutions such as the family, which was seen as essential to the maintenance of social order.

As we shall see, the years of Thatcherism dramatically changed much of the understanding of what politics involved and how the state and society should be organized. The neoliberalism of the New Right offered one clear set of explanations and cures for the perceived problems of United Kingdom society.

We will deal with this perspective in detail in Chapter 3. Such views, however, were not the only understandings on offer at the time. Indeed, the political and social organization of much of the West was coming under severe criticism from across the political spectrum.

Contradictions of the state

Much of capitalist society was, by the 1970s, experiencing rapidly rising inflation and unemployment. The response of wage restraint in an attempt to control inflation saw the destruction of widespread political support for the social democratic consensus. As a result, in 1979, the United Kingdom elected a government that no longer expressed support for social democracy and who put forward its own programme to halt the economic decline. The dominant emphasis by many social commentators during the 1950s and 1960s, which had been on social integration, stability and consensus, had evaporated. By the late 1970s writers were talking about social disintegration, instability and disharmony. As always, there were differing explanations. One grouping, as we shall see, developed theories of the 'overloaded state', based on an ever rising set of social expectations.

Importantly, however, other writers were putting forward alternative explanations to the crisis within the capitalist bloc, centring on the legitimacy of the capitalist state itself. The dominant ideological perspective on the liberal-democratic state is that it ensures legitimacy through the promotion of individual liberty and sensitivity and responsiveness to public opinion.

For many Marxists and neo-Marxists, however, this representation of liberal democracy is mere counterfeit. The core values of such democracy are little more than a superficial disguising of the workings of the 'ruling class'. Miliband (1969, 1970), whose views we have already encountered, talks of liberal democracy as a 'capitalist democracy'. He makes clear that it serves the interests of private property, the long-term goals of capital and is grounded in an imbalance of political power. From within the Marxist perspective, the state gains legitimacy not from rational consent, but rather by ideological manipulation.

Indeed, the role of ideology is central in understanding the traditional Marxist approach to the state. Marxism highlights a definition of ideology, which is seen to be inappropriate to the 'real' and 'objective' situation of those involved. A poor peasant worker, who is deeply religious and, for example, also believes that in working hard and accepting a lowly place in society, she will be rewarded in heaven, is suffering from false consciousness. Religion here is an ideology in that it keeps her in her place and supports the existing structure and, hence, the dominant groups in her society. It disguises the 'truth'. In so far as the comforts of religion are false comforts, she is alienated from true sources of personal satisfaction.

Ideology serves to mask the contradiction in society between the exploitative economic relationships that it involves and the need for some kind of minimum consent from those who are disadvantaged. While there may be external trappings of democracy, such as a free press and autonomous and competing pressure groups, these cannot camouflage society's domination by 'bourgeois ideology'.

In this sense ideology works to conceal the essential contradictions of capitalist society in the interests of the ruling class. This group has the ability to structure intellectual as well as material production. As Marx and Engels themselves argue:

> The ideas of the ruling class are in every epoch the ruling ideas, i.e., the class which is the ruling material force of society is at the same time its ruling intellectual force. The class which has the means of production at its disposal has control at the same time over the means of mental production, so that thereby, generally speaking, the ideas of those who lack the means of mental production are subject to it. The ruling ideas are nothing more than the ideal expression of the dominant material relationships, the dominant relationships grasped as ideas; hence of the relationships which make the one class the ruling one, therefore the ideas of its dominance. (Marx and Engels, 1970: 61)

Hence, once a class has become dominant it will present its own interests as being the common interests of the whole of society. Within capitalism the ruling class dominate educational, cultural and intellectual life. It will further represent its own ideas as rational, universal and the only ones with validity. As we have seen, Althusser (1971, 1977), for example, highlights the role of ideology and the ability of the bourgeoisie to ensure its core values are accepted by means of the 'ideological state apparatuses', such as the formal education system and the Church. He also, of course, stresses the role of 'repressive state apparatus' such as the police and the military.

All of this is not to say that the views of the ruling class do not go unchallenged, or that there are not counter-positions. Here, Gramsci's (1971: 1929–35) argument that the bourgeoisie continues its position of dominance by making concessions to subordinate groups such as the working class remains central. Such capitulation, however, is never great enough to undermine the position of the dominant group. The ruling class maintains a position of dominance not simply through unequal economic and political power, but through its repressive potential, and hegemonic processes. It is through the primacy of ideas promoting beliefs benefiting the ruling class that its dominance is ensured. All the major institutions of capitalist society were marked by the domination of bourgeois ideas in every aspect of life.

The major function of the values of the dominant political culture is social control. It produces clear beliefs and patterns of behaviour, such as obedience to the state and acquiescence in the arena of politics. In other words, what we have is a hegemonic dominant value system. While the machinery of the state enables, if necessary, the ruling group to dominate society through coercion, its more important and common role is that of intellectual and moral leaderships. This gives the ruling class its 'success' not through coercion but through consent, achieved by the manipulation of civil society and its major interlocking institutions such as the Church, education and the media.

Succeeding from this there are direct consequences for the dynamics of politics. The hegemonic position of the ruling class can only be rivalled by the construction of a counter-hegemony. The bourgeois hegemony can only be challenged by proletarian hegemony, through cultural revolution to establish socialist principles and value systems in place of capitalist ones. Gramsci's work on the state was particularly influential in the direction taken by Eurocommunism in the 1980s. It produced an analysis blending Marxism and liberalism and which at times came to resemble social reformism and social democracy more than Marxism.

Moran (1989: 44–7) points out that Marxist analyses, which accept much of the above, can make sense of that which is ignored by other models of the state. As such, these perspectives bring to the centre of the political agenda the nature of the legitimacy of the state. Several commentators in the contemporary period have focused on the major reasons why the legitimacy of the state may be called directly into question.

One such writer is Habermas (1988, 1989), especially when he refers to a 'legitimation crisis' in the period of late capitalism. This manifests from at least three 'crisis tendencies' that are outside the control of liberal democracies: the economic, the administrative and the motivational. These arise from the necessity for the capitalist state to meet what are often conflicting and contradictory demands, for example, support for capitalist accumulation and eliciting popular support for the 'neutral democratic state'.

At the core of Habermas's argument runs the following. As the state increasingly intervenes in more areas of life, it is seen as having ever increasing responsibility for them. This stimulates core demands: for higher benefits; for fuller participation; for democratic rights. The state cannot possibly meet all these demands. Or at least it cannot meet such demands without threatening the essential nature of capitalist production and profit.

What then happens is that the state is forced to strip away its veneer of neutrality and overtly acknowledge its support for the dominant class. By bringing this into the open, the state faces a process of declining legitimacy as it seeks to maintain its core values. It is this that is seen as central and a fundamental threat to the stability of advanced capitalist society. The weakening legitimacy of the capitalist state surrounds several important contradictions. Deeply ingrained in capitalist society are the central bourgeois values of formal 'participation' and 'democracy' of the masses. However, formal democracy has to be prevented from becoming 'real' democracy. Habermas argues that to do this the major tactic of the capitalist state is that the public realm should be depoliticized.

The tensions between, on the one hand, the demands of the capitalist economy and, on the other hand, a fully democratic political system means that the liberal-democratic state is inherently unstable. The democratic emphasis forces a government response to populist demands, often in response to highly organized pressure groups. As a result, public spending and the responsibilities of the state in economic and social life spiral increasingly upwards. Increased public spending creates a fiscal crisis, high taxation rates and high inflation, all of which creates disincentive to capitalist enterprise.

Consequently, Habermas believes that this legitimation crisis will be the final blow to the capitalist system. To identify the final nail in the coffin, however, we need to turn to another of Habermas's categories, that of motivation crisis. Legitimation crisis must rest on a motivation crisis, the discrepancy between the needs declared by the state and the motivation supplied by socio-cultural system.

Habermas further suggests that capitalism is based on a particular value system that is eroded by its very success. Traditional values such as the Protestant work ethic and vocational ambition are replaced by bourgeois values of possessive individualism, which threaten to destabilize the state further. In an argument that parallels that of the New Right, he believes that an advanced welfare system has eroded the work ethic. Such developments threaten a motivation crisis and in its wake a legitimation crisis as the capitalist state is faced with actively resisting democratic demands or risking economic desolation. In turn, Habermas has been criticized on several issues. The most serious of these, perhaps, suggests that his ideas are at times internally inconsistent and that he does not use empirical evidence to support his arguments.

In broad terms, however, the approach finds resonance in works of both O'Connor (1973, 1987) and Gough (1979). Gough's writings on welfare developed in the context of what he perceived as the uneasy truce between the major conflicting interests of capital and labour. For Gough, capitalism seeks to accumulate profit and ensure a healthy workforce with necessary skills, while labour is always seeking to improve the social and economic position of the working class. Overriding this, the state always seeks to maintain political stability. Thus, when faced with organized and collective protest, the state is likely to concede some ground by way of wages, welfare benefits and the like, to ensure its own legitimacy is maintained.

Elsewhere, O'Connor (1973, 1987) takes a similar line but focuses directly on the functions of public policy in advanced capitalist society. The capitalist state, he argues, 'must try to fulfil two basic and often mutually contradictory functions – accumulation and legitimation' (1973: 6). Above all, the state must ensure the long-term efficiency and profitability of capitalist industry and, at the same time, it must promote social harmony in order to legitimize the capitalist system. Such goals, however, are in essence contradictory. Increases in spending on ensuring social harmony means that funds are constantly diverted away from the profitable areas of the economy. Yet, all public expenditure has these two functions to fulfil.

O'Connor further divides public spending into three other categories. First, 'social investment', which, for example, can take the form of government aid to industry. Secondly, 'social consumption', which, for example, includes expenditure on education, health and housing provision. This lowers the reproductive cost of labour, thus raising profitability. Thirdly, 'social expenses', for example spending on social security, policing and social work, all of which promote social harmony.

These state functions for O'Connor are essentially contradictory. They create a fiscal crisis of the capitalist state because of the increasing difficulties involved in raising the revenue required to meet the cost of expanded public services. At the same time, however, the state cannot afford to ignore these demands because this would have direct consequences for the levels of profitability and social harmony within the state should such social expenses not be met. The work of O'Connor has also raised criticism. That the categories used were too abstract. That he dramatically under-estimates the real benefits derived to the working class from the provision of public services within the advanced welfare state, and that he under-estimates the contribution economic growth can make to political stability rather than instability.

For Offe (1982), the contradiction is that while capitalism cannot co-exist within the welfare state, neither can it exist outside the welfare state. Further, Offe (1984) argues that the state cannot be seen as 'merely capitalist', as in the work of Poulantzas. Nor can it be regarded as 'a state within capitalist society', as in the writings of Miliband. Rather, the most fundamental facet of the state is that it is bound up in the contradictions of capitalism itself. Hence, the capitalist state is always faced with contradictory roles and tasks. The most important of these are the contradictions that arise for the state between sustaining private accumulation and presenting itself as a 'neutral arbiter'.

Offe is also concerned with the 'crisis' of modern capitalism. He locates this in the breakdown of the postwar welfare consensus. He argues that the private capitalist economy is not self-correcting, as classical political economy claims. Rather, the private capitalist economy is subject to several inherent crises. The interventionist welfare state developed as both a way of ordering capitalism and as a way of legitimating it by being regarded as the source of impartial administration and reform.

The state thus becomes intertwined with the contradictions of capitalism itself. Hence, the state is dependent (for its revenue) on a successful capitalist economy but is unable to intervene too directly. The origins of the welfare state rest in the contradictions between democracy and capitalism. The conflicts between the states need to sustain its legitimacy and the best conditions for private accumulation.

The state's legitimacy and power comes, in part, from the belief of the population that the state acts impartially in the political process. To help sustain mass support the state must expend large revenues to finance welfare programmes. For Offe, the welfare state emerged to 'reconcile' the demands of citizens for a more secure standard of living and the requirements of capitalist economy, within which accumulation is the primary momentum. Because democracy and private accumulation are irreconcilable, the major function for the welfare state becomes that of crisis management. The state in capitalist society is caught between conflicting demands. Offe emphasizes the fundamental nature of the welfare state in actively seeking to reconcile contradictions. This reconciliation, however, is not stable. The welfare state is central to the process of continued negotiation of contradictions within capitalism.

The demands surrounding the legitimacy of the state and the needs to sustain private accumulation can pull in opposite directions. Since state power derives in part from the legitimacy achieved through the political process, the state cannot be 'seen' to be anything other than neutral. To sustain aggregate support it requires substantial revenue to finance welfare, etc. However, this state revenue derives largely from the taxes on profit and wages. Therefore the state is obliged to assist in the process of capitalist accumulation and act in a biased and partisan manner to assist the processes of capitalist accumulation.

The work of Offe marks a break with traditional Marxist assumptions, and his ideas have influenced many later 'post-Marxist' or 'neo-Marxist' analyses of state. Central here is Jessop's (1982) argument that all general theories of the state must be abandoned. Even Marx and Engels were not single minded on the relationship between economic class power and state power. The notion of 'base-superstructure', whereby changes in the economic base are paralleled by developments in the political superstructure, is only a guiding structural principle. For Jessop, capitalist forms of production do not ensure that the state form is essentially capitalist; each nation-state has its own form and direction.

Importantly, Jessop sees no valid ground for assuming that the state is essentially class unified rather than fragmented. Rather, for Jessop (1982: 10), its unity must be constituted as 'different forms of the state and state intervention are required by different modes of production and that the nature of state power is determined by the changing needs of the economy and/or by the changing balance of class forces at the economic level'.

While the above writers are not a coherent school, all can be seen as engaged in discussing what may be termed a 'legitimation crisis theory of state' (Held, 1984).

The 'overloaded' state

At the same time several writers were developing a different view of the difficulties of contemporary politics (see Brittan, 1975, 1977; King, 1976; Nordhaus, 1975). Taking pluralism as their starting point, those who characterized the overloaded state saw power as shared between a diverse number of competing groups. Hence, the outcomes of political contest are determined by the democratic processes adjudicated by government.

Increasingly in the postwar period, Keynesian economics had generated mass affluence and prosperity, which had resulted in ever-rising expectations and demands on the state. These took the shape of increasing wage claims, welfare provision and the expanding educational system. Further, aspirations and expectations were increased by a 'decline in deference' and decreasing respect for authority.

This in turn brought about a whole series of consequences. Private initiative was undermined, the egalitarian ideology gained in prominence and only served to promise much more than the state could ever deliver. Within this context, however, organized groups such as business or consumer organizations and trade unions continued to make further demands on governments on behalf of those they represent.

In response to this, and in an attempt to secure votes, politicians often continued to promise more than they could deliver, even though they responded to a set of demands which cannot all be fully met. Continued competition between political parties leads to ever more unrealistic sets of promises to the electorate and attempts by the government to appease them, for fear of losing future votes.

This rejoinder becomes increasingly bureaucratic and fails to meet the demands upon it. Increasingly the state cannot provide effective leadership and is faced with excessive public spending as one of its few retorts. The state becomes overloaded through a 'vicious circle' which can only be broken, if at all, by decisive political leadership, which is less responsive to democratic demands.

The state 'in crisis'

Despite a common starting point, that of analysing a transforming society facing political dilemmas, theorists of 'legitimation crisis' and of 'overload' envisaged very different political consequences. For legitimation crisis theorists the crisis offered the potential for progressive change. Although the works of Offe, Habermas, O'Connor and Gough presented sophisticated models for the understanding of political change, they did not necessarily influence the political agenda directly. Rather, it was those operating within the parameters of political overload who claimed that the state was becoming too bureaucratic and governments policies were based too strongly on appeasement of the labour movement and who most directly engaged the broader population.

It was this perspective, which paved the way for much of the populist discourse of the late 1970s, that was harnessed by the New Right. In turn this was given increased prominence by Thatcher's consistent airing the view that British society was becoming ungovernable. Although this became deeply located in the populist consciousness, this is not to say that it presented itself as a convincing political ideology. Indeed, much of the dynamic of the overload thesis seemed designed merely to justify and bring about those political changes which were to welcome in Thatcherism. We shall engage with this in much more detail in Chapter 3.

A more recent notion of crisis surrounds the transition of economic organization of contemporary Western societies. Since the early 1970s, this marks what Harvey (1989: 189) calls a 'sea change in the surface appearance of capitalism'. The changes which have taken place, and the break-up of the stable economic and social relations referred to above, have motivated a further set of discussions surrounding the transition from 'Fordism' to 'post-Fordism'.

Fordism, post-Fordism and the state

The definition of Fordism is still contested, but it is certainly possible to outline its major contours. To begin with, it involves the use of techniques of mass assembly-line production, structured by a logic of rationalization and the 'scientific management' promoted by Taylorism. The system relies on huge capital investment in, for example, large-scale plant, factories and machinery. Such plant is utilized by an inflexible production process and organized through rigid and hierarchical management structures. One result is a standardized product, matched by the growth of mass consumption. It was this method of organizing production that strongly influenced the agenda of capitalist production.

These social institutions of mass production, collectively referred to as Fordism, began to emerge in the USA early in the twentieth century, and were at the centre of a decades long process of social struggle and labour politics. This extended into the immediate post-Second World War era, but it was Cold War ideology that played a crucial role in the political stabilization of Fordist institutions in the USA.

This provided the common ground on which de-radicalized industrial labour unions could be incorporated as junior partners in a coalition of globally-oriented social forces. These worked together to rebuild the 'free world' along liberal-capitalist lines, and to resist the encroachment of the presumed 'red menace' of communism, internationally and at home. Institutionalized Fordism, in turn, enabled the USA to contribute almost half of world industrial production in the immediate postwar years, and thus provided the economic dynamism to spark reconstruction of the major capitalist countries after the Second World War. It also provided support for the emergence of both the consumer society and the military-industrial complex in the postwar USA.

It is Henry Ford who is usually credited with constructing the modern model of mass production which bears his name. The term dates from the development of the first moving assembly lines, put into operation at the car plant in Michigan around 1914. One consequence was the displacement of older, predominantly craft-based production, where skilled labourers, following the completion of an apprentiship, exercised substantial control and high levels of autonomy at work. Fordist production entailed an intensified industrial division of labour and the increased mechanization and co-ordination of large-scale manufacturing processes to achieve a steady flow of production. It also meant a shift towards the use of less skilled labour performing tasks minutely specified by management with greatly heightened control over the pace and intensity of work.

Fordism thus represented a historical break, through the rationalization and mechanization of material and assembly (see Hounshell, 1984; Walker, 1989). At the core of this Fordist reorganization of production was the construction of new relations of power in the workplace. The promise of massive increases in productivity led to the widespread imitation and adaptation of Ford's basic model of production, first throughout the industrial core of the economy of the USA, and then in other industrial capitalist countries.

Underlying Fordism is the use of semi-skilled labour paid to perform repetitive and routine productive tasks. In return, wages are tied directly to productivity. Wages rise in line with productivity, increasing the market for mass-produced consumer goods and further capital investment. Fordism also depends on a particular model for the organization and workings of the state.

The state is a regulator between capital and labour, seeking to limit the self-interest of both. The state also has a crucial role in operating a Keynesian model of fine tuning the economy to ensure, as far as possible, full employment and low inflation.

From Fordism to post-Fordism

As capital became more multinational in form, it became more and more difficult for nation-states to regulate their economies through traditional Keynesian methods. It was possible, of course, that capitalism could have sought to remain within the broad parameters of established Fordist production. This, however, proved extremely difficult. Partly, this was because of the nature of Fordism itself, resting on the intensive accumulation of capital and long-term investment necessary to perpetuate the system. Above these, the market for consumer goods became saturated, thus dramatically reducing the ability to fuel growth.

How then did capitalism alter its form? For some, the introduction of new technologies, job reskilling and an increased centralization of managerial control marked a restructuring of Fordism in an attempt to solve some of its crisis. Indeed, for some, what is being experienced is a fundamental restructuring of both economic and social relations.

This has led several writers to claim that the capitalist response to the crisis is best seen in terms of a move to what is known as post-Fordism. This refers to the end of the old manufacturing economies and a move to a different kind of economic order. Thus, there is a break with Fordism by introducing more flexible systems of production of both commodities and capitalist profit. Central to this are the increasingly 'high-tech' nature of production and the new economic possibilities of microchip technology, computers and robotics. If the heart of Fordism was the control of consumption, then the heart of post-Fordism is the control of production to conform with ever-changing demands of consumption.

Such a post-Fordist system is thus based on what Harvey (1989) names 'flexible accumulation' and what Hall and Jacques (1989) refer to as 'flexible specialization'. These writers identify a new era that has flexibility as its identifying hallmark, overcoming the inflexibility of an economy organized around Fordist lines. The era dominated by a skilled male manual working class, and based on the mass production of standardized products, is gone. The workplace is transformed largely by electronics-based technology and, in turn, the marketplace is dominated by international financial markets and multinational companies.

For Jessop (1989, 1990, 1992), the transition from Fordism to post-Fordism is central in the understanding of the crisis that has unfolded over the last 30 years in the British political economy. He argues that a critical role of the state is organizing appropriate political and economic conditions for the successful accumulation of capital. Thus Jessop et al. (1988) suggests that Thatcherism, rather than simply reacting to economic crisis, took a proactive role in transforming British economy and society via radical form and the assertion of ideological programme. This was achieved by the state building its own 'power base', a coalition of different social groups, including the skilled working class, those in the City of London and the moral Right.

Certainly, the move towards flexibility, in terms of the production of specialized goods and services, and the setting of the agenda concerning consumer choice coincided with the rise of the New Right and the active promotion of economic individualism. As the crisis of Fordism became more apparent, there was a growing response from the state in terms of the running of the economy. Hence, the Conservative administration elected in 1979 set about restructuring labour practices and challenging the labour movement as part of a wider programme of a post-Fordist restructuring of the economy, based on increased unemployment and reduced government spending.

Ideological strategies of the state

Underlying much of the discussion in this chapter has been the roles of ideology. If, as has been argued, ideology is best understood as a perspective on knowledge and signification, we need to ask about the ways these are deployed in the service of political power. In other words, we are forced to ask again the fundamental question 'how does politics work?'

One view of ideology is as 'distorted communication', a notion largely associated with Habermas (1987a, 1987b, 1987c), who argues that we can envisage an 'ideal speech' situation in which communication is perfect. For Habermas, this rests on four validity claims, that: what is communicated is mutually intelligible; the propositional content is true; each contributor has the right to act as he or she does; each speaks or acts sincerely. In the end Habermas is still concerned with distinguishing socially determined ideology from universally valid knowledge. We are still faced with the problem that there is a social basis to all knowledge and that 'truth' may still be deployed ideologically.

We can also encounter the view of ideology as knowledge employed in the interest of the ruling group. Although they all subscribe to slightly different versions, Giddens (1979) and Thompson (1984, 1990, 1993) both follow this line of argument. Eagleton's *Ideology* (1991), while certainly not written from the perspective of orthodox social science, provides an important reference point. He details several major strategies regarding how ideology works.

First, 'unification ideologies' strive to establish a monolithic internal unity that hides contradictions and conflicts. The ultimate successful ideology would be one that goes completely unrecognized. As Eagleton puts it, the final alienation would be not to know that we were alienated.

Secondly, 'action-orientation ideologies'. These are not just speculative theoretical systems; they actively shape desires and wants. They work not just at the level of Giddens's discursive consciousness, but also at the level of practical consciousness. Ideologies are 'lived' experiences, not just thoughts and abstractions.

Thirdly, 'legitimation', which is one of the ways in which ideology works to establish a group or sectional interest as broadly acceptable to society as a whole. Eagleton distinguishes between the 'normative' acceptance by those who have a commitment to legitimated norms and values and those who have a 'pragmatic' acceptance, 'in which subaltern groups endorse the right of their rulers to govern because they can see no realistic alternative' (Eagleton, 1991: 52).

Fourthly, 'universalization', is one of the most common and powerful ideological strategies, in which 'Values and interests which are in fact specific to a certain time and place are projected as the values of all humanity' (Eagleton, 1991: 56). Thus, for example, in the politics of gender it is often held to be true that in all known societies men are the aggressive hunters and women are the nurturing homemakers. This is not actually true as a glance at the anthropological record will soon show you, but it is widespread common-sense among those who would confine women to the home and motherhood. This is closely connected to the next strategy.

Fifthly, 'naturalization'. If a group can have beliefs that operate in its interests accepted as natural, self-evident and commonsensical, it puts itself in a very powerful position. As long as the 'divine right of kings' was widespread commonsense, the traditional European monarchs, certainly prior to the 1790s, could remain confident that they would continue in power.

Giddens (1979: 195) summarizes this position well when he argues that the 'interests of dominant groups are bound up with the status quo. Forms of signification which "naturalise" the existing state of affairs, inhibiting recognition of the mutable, historical character of human society, thus act to sustain such interests'.

This idea is closely related to the concept of 'reification', which refers to the process by which the products of human social action come to be seen as natural, external realities that govern human behaviour. One clear example of the strength of ideology in action is found in expressions of national identity. It is to this that we shall now turn.

Defining nationalism

It is all too tragically obvious that nationalism is far from archaic relevance. Rather than, as it was claimed for many years, an antiquated ideal, it is clearly of growing importance in industrialized societies and beyond. Several of the most momentous events of recent times in Europe, for example, the political violence following the break-up of Soviet bloc, the reunification of Germany, and the bloody occurrences in former Yugoslavia, have all demonstrated the contemporary fervour of nationalism.

Such events have given weight to the claim of McGarry and O'Leary (1995: 13) that nationalism is 'the most potent modern principle of political legitimacy'. We do not, however, have to travel to the heart of Europe to find political and social turmoil surrounding nationalism and national identity. Within the United Kingdom the relevance of nationalism to contemporary social and political identity is also paramount. This is particularly true in the context of constitutional political devolution within the United Kingdom, through the Scottish Parliament and Welsh Assembly. Both of these represent areas with long histories of distinct national identities. While the same cannot be said for Northern Ireland, here too there remains the possibility of a long-term devolved administration being in place, following agreements around the peace process.

So how should we understand nationalism? To answer this is a much more difficult task than it may at first appear. At its basic level, the nationalist perspective on the world is simply demonstrated by the high political priority on the integrity of the 'nation' against internal separatist and external pressures. All these are aspects of an ideology that sees the nation as the primary historical, social and political unit. Indeed, a central tenet of nationalism is that the political state of the nation should coincide with the group of distinctive people and culture.

Many nationalists invoke or at least seek to invoke notions surrounding the historic unity of a people. This is most often done through a discourse of shared values and origins. Nationalism seeks to create a strong sense of mutual belonging which is seen to rest on particular constructions of the past and common ancestors. Some of nationalism's most fundamental power rests in the strength to convey such ideas in terms of commonsense values, often so much so that it appears to require little or no definition or explanation. Hence, despite its crucial political importance, defining nationalism remains no easy matter. Indeed, Hobsbawm (1992) points out that because of the conflicting definitions of nation the study of nationalism must assume no a priori definition of what it is that constitutes a nation. Nevertheless, he does offer a tentative definition of the term 'nationalism', arguing that it is less difficult to discover what nationalists believe the nation to be.

Giddens (1985) also regards nationalism primarily as a psychological phenomenon which involves the affiliation of individuals to 'a set of symbols and beliefs emphasising commonality amongst members of a political order'. This has to be distinguished from a nation which is a 'collectivity existing within a demarcated territory, which is subject to a unitary administration, reflexively monitored both by internal state apparatuses and those of other states' (1985: 116). The nation-state, which exists in a complex of other nation-states, 'is a set of institutional form of governance maintaining an administrative monopoly over a territory with demarcated boundaries (borders), its rule being sanctioned by law and direct control of the means of internal and external violence' (1985: 12).

Others, such as Gellner, stress the primacy of material conditions in shaping political thought and social change. Hence, nationalism becomes a theory of political legitimacy, 'which requires [that] ethnic boundaries should not cut across political ones, and, in particular, that ethnic boundaries within a given state . . . should not separate power-holders from the rest' (1983: 12). He also poses what he calls the 'false theories of nationalism'. One example is that it is natural, self-evident and self-generating and that its absence must be due to forceful repression. Another is that it is due to the 'wrong address' theory, favoured by many Marxists. The spirit of the awakening message was intended for classes, but by a postal error was delivered to nations. Yet another false theory is that nationalism is the re-emergence of the atavistic forces of 'blood and territory'. Hence Gellner (1983: 55) concludes that, 'it is nationalism which endangers nations, and not the other way round'.

National consciousness can be actively promoted, and nations created, by a state strongly promoting centralization and uniformity. Here, Anderson (1983) provides a key reference point for contemporary studies of national-ism. There are necessary preconditions, partly material and partly psycho-logical, for the emergence of nationalism. The principal material condition for the development of nationalism was 'print-capitalism', which spread the ideology and integrated the masses in political participation. Print-capitalism thus consolidated the diverse spoken languages in early modern Europe and concentrated them into a smaller number, which were widely distributed through books and pamphlets. This formed the baseline for 'national con-sciousness' by connecting the readers with one another through common texts.

Anderson (1983) also importantly points out that while members of even the smallest nation can never know all their fellow nationals, in the minds of each member lives a distinct image of their community. A nation is therefore an imagined political community and imagined as both inherently limited and sovereign. The nationalist community is, in Anderson's celebrated and much-used phrase, an 'imagined community'. For Anderson, communities are imagined because they have to be, and the form the imaginings take give the political societies not only an order and structure they would otherwise not have, but an order without which they would not even exist.

Nationalism as a political movement

Nationalisms, of course, are not just theoretical and psychological constructs, but represent themselves as social and political movements. For Alter (1989: 22), national consciousness can be actively promoted, and nations created, by a state whose general modes are centralization, uniformity and efficiency. The process of nation-building can then proceed within a framework that is identical to the state's frontiers. In other experiences, the process of nation-building set in before nation-states came about. It transcends existing bound-aries and often leads to the formation of new states. Shared language and culture often underlay the process, the ultimate goal of which is the cohesion of a cultural nation within a single state.

There are then important ideological features to consider. As McLennan (1995: 134) points out, as popular movement, nationalism must aspire to do several things. First, to project a set of 'shared ideas' among a particular social group. Secondly, to form a relatively 'coherent system' of political and social belief. Thirdly, to develop a distinctive picture of 'power relations'.

Nationalism as an ideal type is reducible to several core propositions. Most nationalists, for example, believe that the world can be understood as naturally divided into nations. Each nation has its own unique character, resulting from its history and culture, and in many cases its language; each nation should be independent, running its own affairs; and that the first loyalty of the individual is to the nation-state. These basic beliefs have helped form the idea that each nation should construct itself into an autonomous state. This obviously is a doctrine of great potency. Moreover, only a short time ago nationalism was seen as a spent political force in the modern world. It is important, therefore, to highlight some of the different forms nationalism can take.

It is, for example, possible to find nationalism blending with conservative perspectives, as in the United Kingdom when politicians seek national regeneration by invoking the memory of heroic leaders or deeds, for example, through Winston Churchill or events at Dunkirk in the Second World War. It can be seen in the 'celebration' of such events, most recently seen in the controversies surrounding the 50th anniversary of the D-Day invasion of Normandy by Allied forces. This form of nationalism may manifest around calls for 'renewal' and 'regeneration' within an old-established state. This often involves direct appeals to national pride. Some, for example, would claim this construction was a key part of the first Thatcher administration with its calls to the economic and moral revitalization of the nation.

We can also recognize nationalisms in the 'liberation struggles' against an empire or colonial power. Usually, the primary goal here is the creation of a new state independent of the existing controlling power. Nationalism can also be seen as the basis for ethnic and group separatism in existing multinational states. Indeed, some of the most recent developments in nationalism have been based in old-established loyalties and demands for greater autonomy within established multinational states. These could include Bretons in the French state, the Basques in Spain, and indeed the Welsh and Scots within the United Kingdom state.

Hence, from the revival of Scottish nationalism, on the one hand, to the escalation of ethnic conflict in, and demise of, the USSR, on the other, there is little sign of nationalism losing its special power to mobilize and motivate political and social movements. Indeed, as Anderson (1983) suggests, nation-ness is the most universally legitimate value in the political life of our time.

We are therefore forced to return to the central nationalist tenet that the boundaries of the political state should coincide directly with a distinctive culture and social grouping. In attempting to develop this into a popular movement, nationalism aspires to do several important things: first, to project a set of shared ideas among a particular social group; secondly, to form a coherent system of political and social belief; and thirdly, to invoke a distinctive picture of power relations and legitimacy of the state.

The strength of much nationalist discourse is encapsulated in the above. Let us now consider the different ideological bases of nationalism within the United Kingdom. The politics and ideology of Northern Ireland's politics will be considered separately in Chapter 5.

Nationalisms in the 'United' Kingdom

Traditionally, the 'British' have been regarded as having an unified political culture, within which class has been the major dividing line. However, political nationalism has constantly re-emerged as a core issue within the United Kingdom's politics. This has manifested in the growing articulation of political separatism in both Scotland and Wales, and in a return to sectarian division and militant nationalism in Northern Ireland.

The notion of 'being British', or there being a homogeneous British national identity, is extremely problematic. Not least, issues concerning social differences located in race, ethnicity and other minority identities increasingly undermine any concept of a unified identity. The United Kingdom contains at least five national identities and groupings, the English, Scottish, Welsh, and in Northern Ireland, the largely Protestant unionist majority, who identify themselves as 'British', and the mainly Catholic Nationalist minority, who claim their primary political identity as 'Irish'. The notion of a British nation-state is ever more nebulous and for some, an increasingly meaningless concept.

The differing civil societies within the British state have produced a set of 'dual nationalities'. At times, many would identify as British, at other times, returning to a Welsh, Northern Irish, Scottish or English identity. To highlight this, Nairn (2000) has entitled the United Kingdom as 'Ukania', to stress the ambiguity with the supposed unified British nation-state and the continued divisive potential of nationalism within the United Kingdom.

Nairn has also suggested 'the nations of the old composite state are likely to end by throwing it off; and afterwards, they will evolve into differing selves – the identities for so long occluded by the superimposition of Britishness' (Nairn, 2000: 93). The United Kingdom certainly was never really unified in institutional terms, even less so in terms of popular consciousness or populist cultural and political identity. There are also major differences, for example, in the history of the economic development of three peripheries, around Central Scotland and South Wales along with the North East of Ireland around Belfast. The United Kingdom of Great Britain and Northern Ireland is increasingly falling short of any idea of the monogamous and homogeneous nation.

Next we shall contemplate carefully the thesis that the failure to meet the ideal of the nation-state is leading to the demise of the United Kingdom. In particular, we shall consider the cases of Scottish, Welsh and English nationalism. The issues surrounding Northern Ireland will be dealt with separately in Chapter 5.

The existence and persistence of nationalisms within the United Kingdom has been explained in a variety of ways. Nairn (1997) suggests that the development of nationalism was as a direct response to uneven development. In general, it is possible to identify two major forms of nationalism in the United Kingdom. First, that type of nationalism associated with underdevelopment, such as that found in Wales, in nineteenth-century Irish nationalism and in contemporary Irish nationalism. Secondly, there is a form of nationalism associated with economic over-development by a political core, such as Ulster unionism.

The perspective of Hechter (1975) also locates nationalism's progress in uneven development. His central thesis is located in the notion of 'internal colonialism', whereby the centralizing colonial powers are at best insensitive to, and at worst actively exploit, cultural differences. This provokes a back-lash, a political reaction against this exploitation from the peripheral nations.

Hence, it was with the 'modernization' of the UK economy that conflicts between national and sub-national politics were intensified in the late 1960s and early 1970s. There were particular reasons for nationalist upsurge. In Wales, for example, there was a 'last chance' feeling about the decline of the language, while in Scotland there was a general loss of confidence concerning its position in the British state and, in particular, debates about the ownership of North Sea Oil revenue. There were also more generalized concerns about the prominent role of popular culture originating from the USA. Moreover, regional economies were being increasingly penetrated by multinational and transglobal economies.

Welsh nationalism

The development of Welsh nationalism needs to be set, however briefly, in a broader historical context. In the nineteenth century the character of Welsh national identity was largely shaped by non-conformist chapel services in Welsh, the production of Welsh language newspapers and political struggles against English landlords. The use of the language declined dramatically, but Welsh identity continued to be expressed through strong identification with Welsh social institutions such as *eisteddfods* and Rugby Union. Hence, the focus on extending cultural expression and the influence of the Welsh language has remained central to politics of Welsh nationalism.

Linguistic decline and an awareness of external economic influences brought about a rise in support for the nationalist movement. The Welsh nationalist party, Plaid Cymru, was formed in 1925. Support for the party, however, was largely restricted to the rural west, where use of the language was uppermost. In the predominantly working-class south of Wales, most people found political expression through the labour movement. Broad support settled at around 10 per cent and when devolution proposals were put to a referendum in 1979 they were decisively rejected, with only around 20 per cent in support.

Throughout the 1980s electoral support ebbed away for Welsh nation-alism, and it increasingly became limited to identifiable social groupings. Its activist core remained that section of 'middle-class professionals' who stressed the cultural before the material, and those who lived in geographical areas where the language remained strong. While the decline may have been note-worthy, nationalism was far from a dead issue. In Wales, while the idea of a people with a separate sense of identity has never found political expression in the formation of a state (as in Scotland), it certainly has a deep root in culture.

Indeed, in terms of achieving some of its long-term goals, Plaid Cymru has been very successful, through the wider use of the Welsh language as a medium in schools and the establishment of a Welsh language television channel.

Scottish nationalism

The situation in Scotland was different. Scotland was a state in medieval and early modern times (James I of England 1603–25 being James VI of Scotland). Scottish society retained a level of civic independence (for example, in its own educational and legal systems) and distinctive sense of history, which developed into a characteristic identity. Scotland also developed its own separatist political organization in the shape of the Scottish National Party (SNP), which was founded in 1933.

The SNP made some of its earliest advances in rural Gaelic Scotland and some of its initial activists advocated the re-creation of a 'traditional Scotland'. This, however, became less and less central to the SNP, the major concern of which has been to gain control over Scotland's resources for the Scottish people. Unlike most nationalist movements, including those in Wales and Ireland, the contemporary SNP has displayed a decided lack of interest in restoring a 'traditional' culture or a national tongue.

The fortunes of the SNP have varied considerably over the past 70 or so years. The decades of the 1950s and 1960s were reasonably barren, but the SNP won its first seat in a general election in 1970. By the October 1974 general election, it secured 11 seats, harnessing 30 per cent of the vote. In a referendum in March 1979, a majority of 51.6 per cent voted for the formation of a new Scottish Assembly. The turnout, however, was low at 32.5 per cent and some way below the 40 per cent necessary to bring about any constitutional change. With the failure to achieve devolution, the SNP vote declined to around 10 per cent of the popular vote, but rose again in the late 1980s.

Since then, there has been a dramatic increase in the endorsement for Scottish nationalism. The SNP has increased working-class support and produced programmes that are recognisibly Left of centre. The SNP have been able to mobilize urban support around concerns regarding Scotland's economic problems, the consequences of de-industrialization and the consequences of Westminster administrations' opposition to collectivism and welfarism. Much of the dynamic came from resistance to the Poll Tax in Scotland (see McCrone, 1992; Sheridan and McCombes, 2000). Part of the opposition involved the highlighting of what was distinctive about Scotland's social and civic institutions and the organization of a coherent campaign to preserve these.

The contemporary SNP has cross-class appeal and draws support from across all socio-economic groups in Scotland. At one level this is a hindrance to expanding electoral support (Denver, 1997). At another level, there is some reason for the SNP to be optimistic. There clearly is a wider pool of support on which the SNP might draw. This wider expression of Scottishness was given clear assertion in the 1997 referendum when 74 per cent supported a

Scottish parliament and 63 per cent indicated that they wished it to have tax raising powers.

As Mohan (1999) points out, however, to be fully understood these arguments need to be placed in the broader context of British nationalism. In particular, the reassertion of nationalism cannot be understood simply in terms of discontent from within the regions. It must also be understood as a reflection of the severe contradictions within a centralized state and the lack of correspondence between state and nation (McCrone, 1992). The key to understanding nationalisms in the United Kingdom lies therefore as much at the centre as at the periphery.

English nationalism

At the core of understanding constructions of nationalisms within the United Kingdom remains the overlap between the concepts of 'Britishness' and 'Englishness'. Not that the notion of Englishness is a highly developed one. As Paxman (1999) points out, for many years the imperial English rarely questioned identity and tended to use Englishness and Britishness as interchangeable expressions of identity.

Part of that contradiction remains that the United Kingdom, for many, still involves an overarching ideological identity of Englishness. While territorially England represents only around half of the United Kingdom's land mass, demographically, militarily, economically and politically the English still dominate the United Kingdom.

Indeed, more often than not, England and Britain are seen as one entity. This can clearly be seen in the way much history is written, whereby English history and British history are seen as synonymous. The English national myth surrounds 'freedom', partly because the conquest and assimilation of the other 'nations' into what was to become the United Kingdom took place so early in the state's history. Hence, often at a populist level, the English habit is subconsciously to include them without consideration for difference of culture or politics.

Much of the strength of ideology of British nationalism, for example, comes from the existence and performance of the symbolic rituals of state. Occasions such as the State Opening of Parliament or the Queen's Birthday celebrations symbolize the historic unity and greatness of the 'Kingdom'. All of this tends to emphasize the Englishness of British nationalism. The construction of such boundaries and the notion of Britishness involved seek to erase differences between the English, Welsh and the Scots (Hickman, 1998). The symbols and rituals of nationalism tend to be packaged to be, at the same time, both inclusive and exclusive. British national identity does not preclude other forms of identity, but rather it seeks to subsume other identities.

This notion of Britishness also involves constructing what it was not to be British. The images and icons of what constitutes the nation also involve the social construction of the 'Other', those set aside from the nation. It was in this context, for example, that the development of ideas, such as those about the 'wild Irish' that became deeply ingrained in popular culture, must be understood (see Curtis, 1997; Pickering, 2001: 142–6).

Such processes do not guarantee success or social harmony. Indeed, as Hechter (1975) has argued, modernization and increased contact between ethnic groups within a state does not necessarily bring ethnic unity but is just as likely to bring ethnic conflict. For him, Scottish, Welsh and Irish nationalism are the result of 'internal colonialism' by the English core.

Within Hechter's model of internal colonialism there are several requirements. First, where cultural division already exists between core and periphery, the division of labour is seen as one in which 'best jobs' are dominated by core. Secondly, when residents in a culturally distinctive periphery perceive this division, national identity becomes more salient. So, for example, a large proportion of people north of the border readily identity themselves as Scots, highly conscious of differences with English.

Nowadays the Celtic fringes of the United Kingdom are increasingly devolved and separate administrations have become a political reality. Nonetheless, the construction of Englishness as Britishness and Britishness as Englishness remains strong in the core areas. Two faces of Englishness were clearly revealed in the pages of the British press on Monday, 24 June 1996. The first surrounded the fortunes of the England team in the 'Euro 96' soccer competition. The second, the place occupied by the United Kingdom in Europe, following the strategy evolved by the British government to win the 'beef war', after restrictions placed on the export of British beef in the light of the BSE outbreak.

It is worth considering some of this in a little more detail. Much reflects the core of political English nationalism throughout the 1990s, where the issue of Europe and opposition to the European union (EU) and later monetary Union and the introduction of the Euro (€) have been central. The split in political Conservatism in the run-up to the 1997 general election was apparent for all to see, as was the antagonism between the Eurosceptic and European integrationist factions of the party (see Chapter 3). These divisions remained tangible throughout the 2001 election campaign. The face of English nationalism can, however, also manifest in a much more populist form.

Football and English nationalism

Many supporters of its national soccer team find one expression of nationalism in the populist assertion of Englishness. There were some overt examples of this when, in 1996, the European Football Championship was hosted by England. During the tournament the England team beat Spain, in a penalty shoot-out, to reach the semi-final stage. The previous week had seen an increasingly xenophobic and jingoistic media campaign against England's opponents. The popular press had, for example, encouraged England to 'give the Spanish El' and the Netherlands 'edam good thrashing'.

Such demands were, however, to prove but a tame prelude. The victory over Spain meant a tie against Germany. This precipitated an overt response from the tabloid press. So, the *Daily Mirror* (24 June 1996), drawing directly on representations of the Second World War and the representation of that period in boys' comics, led with the headline: 'ACHTUNG! SURRENDER For you Fritz, ze Euro 96 Championship is over'. This was pasted against photographs of two of England's 'heroes' from the previous rounds, Paul Gascoigne and Stuart Pearce, both of whom were pictured wearing army helmets. Alongside this, a full-page statement by the editor, parodying Chamberlain's famous statement before the outbreak of the Second World War, made clear that the *Daily Mirror* had declared 'football war on Germany'. This war included such 'victories' as 'invading Berlin' – sending a reporter to pose for a series of publicity shots. Or, as the paper put it, they 'penetrated the Fatherland. To shake the nerves of the so-called indomitable Jerries. We have come fully armed with a special St. George flag and thousands of leaflets bearing the warning: "Achtung! Surrender! Remember 1966!"'

Other tabloids followed similar lines. The *Daily Star* (24 June 1996) led with the headline 'Herr We Go Bring on the Krauts'. The edition carried 11 'jokes' to add to those 'taking the field against Terry Venables' brave boys'. These included:

> WHAT'S the quickest way to lose 16 stone of ugly fat?
> *Give a German the wrong directions to Wembley*
>
> WHY are Germans rubbish at golf?
> *You can't keep them out of the bunkers*

The *Daily Star* gave further reasons why England must win, including:

> Herr Kohl is the fattest and ugliest political leader in Europe.
> They don't eat our beef.
> They pinch all the sunbeds on holiday.
> They earn a lot more than us.

Stridently British nationalism, now predominantly based both geographically and ideologically in England, has for many years been seeking to dominate social and political relations within the United Kingdom, to disrupt relations with the rest of Europe and to provoke further nationalist reaction. It has also sought to continue to define the 'Other' in terms of citizenship within the United Kingdom. This reaction is central when we consider the multicultural dimensions of British society and social structure. Many discourses of Britishness continue to exclude immigrants or non-white British citizens from their core.

Race, ethnic politics and the state

The discourse of race within the United Kingdom needs to be set in the context of the rise and fall of the Empire in the nineteenth and twentieth centuries. The construction of such a discourse is complex. It has not helped that the discourses surrounding nationality, national identity and citizenship have developed in the absence of any written constitution to establish its criteria. While it was not until 1981 that the formal category of 'British citizen' existed, it was always informally constructed within an interchange of notions of nationality and national identity. This meant that who was entitled to British nationality and citizenship, and the perceived rights and duties that accompanied it, have all been flexible entities.

There are two major aspects to this construction of Britishness, one cultural and social, the other empirical and legal. It is possible, for example, to trace a whole series of legislation from the 'Aliens' Act' of 1905 to the 'Immigration Act' of 1988. All of these redefined what it was to be a British citizen. However, as these immigration laws construct constituencies of 'belonging', they are also cultural processes, whereby representations of national belonging are reproduced. The construction involves who is, or can be, British and who defines the terms of Britishness.

Gilroy (1992) ably demonstrates how symbols of 'race' are actively mobilized in conservative rhetoric about national decline. Such notions are often presented alongside ideas about the dilution of a homogeneous national stock. This has manifested in two recent sets of arguments and debates. The first concerns the debates surrounding immigration and asylum claims to the United Kingdom. The second concerns the continuing social and physical marginalization of sections of the United Kingdom's ethnic communities.

There is now a commonly expressed populist view that the United Kingdom is too easily accessible for all those seeking to move there. Further, it is claimed that only a tiny proportion of refugees and asylum seekers are 'genuine' and the United Kingdom takes in more than its fair share of such people. While it is undeniable that asylum applications to the United Kingdom have increased significantly over the past few years, this trend reflects global factors rather than United Kingdom support provision for asylum seekers. Relative to their population, many other European countries take far more asylum seekers than do the United Kingdom. Indeed, Britain is ranked at only 8 out of 13 (1.21 per thousand population), behind such counties as Luxembourg, Belgium, the Netherlands, Austria, Ireland, Sweden and Denmark.

Such statistics have not held in check a glut of negative images of asylum seekers within local and national media coverage. Such portrayal not only creates a difficult and dangerous climate for asylum seekers; we believe it also damages race relations more generally in the United Kingdom (Campaign Against Racism and Fascism, 2000: 8–13).

Elsewhere, crucial evidence is emerging that sections of the United Kingdom's ethnic groups are increasingly socially, politically and physically marginalized. As research (*The Observer*, 28 July 1996) indicates, white Britons are now less likely to have non-white, ethnic group neighbours than before and that racial segregation had increased by 2.8 per cent over the past decade. Further, the 1995 Rowntree Inquiry reported that in 1990 only 18 per cent of the 'white' population were in the poorest 20 per cent of the population, against more than a third of the 'non-white' population. The report also revealed 'alarming' disparities between different ethnic groups. Between 1988 and 1990, 21 per cent of those aged 16 to 24 had no qualifications. This figure, however, rose to 48 per cent for Pakistanis and 54 per cent for Bangladeshis. Over this period, 8 per cent of white men were unemployed, but the figure rose to 14 per cent for all ethnic minorities, and 22 per cent for Pakistanis. The disparities were even greater for women. While 66 per cent of white women were in work, only 48 per cent of ethnic women were in employment. Indeed, for Pakistani women this figure fell as low as 16 per cent (*The Independent*, 10 February 1995).

One manifestation of the increasing marginalization of sections of the United Kingdom's ethic community was seen in the riots that took place throughout the summer of 2001 in northern English towns such as Oldham, Burnley and Bradford. All saw violent confrontations between young Asians and the police, culminating in clashes in Bradford throughout the 7–9 July in which 200 police officers were injured. As Kessler suggests:

> Pakistani and Bangladeshi youth in these and other towns feel – just as Britain's Afro-caribbean communities felt in Toxteth, Handsworth and Brixton in 1981 – that the law can no longer protect them, that violence is their clearest voice. That there is anger and overwhelming frustration is undeniable, no matter how many TV pundits would like to suggest that the trouble is just high spirits. (Kessler, 2001: 17)

As Kundnani (2001) points out, the riots signalled the rage of deprived young Pakistanis and Bangladeshis of the second and third generations, who had lived with rising rates of unemployment and high levels of social and physical segregation. The segregation of these communities, the roots of which lay in racism, came to be perceived as 'self-segregation' and the attempt by Asians to create their own exclusive areas because they did not want to mix with white people. Mutual distrust flourished and was reproduced through a series of self-fulfilling prophecies.

Some of these tensions in day-to-day living have manifested in politics elsewhere. There is some evidence to suggest that since the inquiry into the killing of the young black man, Stephen Lawrence, there has been a political backlash, particularly from marginalized white working-class people. One result has been an increase in support for neo-fascist and extreme Right parties in some of those areas, such as North-west England, which have experienced some of the greatest racial tensions. In the 2001 general election, for example, the British National Party (BNP) improved its vote to an average of 3.9 per cent of the poll in the seats that it contested. In two Oldham seats it polled 16.4 per cent and 11.2 per cent of the votes cast (*Searchlight*, July 2001: 4–5).

The categories of race and nation have been used in different ways and at different times to construct what it means to be English and/or British. Central here has been the marking out of groups as excluded, as the 'Other'. Historically, this has been applied, among others, to Jews, the Irish, and later those whose origins can be found in the wave of immigration from the New Commonwealth after the Second World War. Most recently, this has been seen in the construction of 'bogus' and 'legitimate' asylum seekers.

As the Runnymede Trust Report (2000) highlights, many customary images of Britain are England-centred, indeed Southern England-centred, and leave many millions of people out of the picture. Further, as Parekh suggests (*The Daily Telegraph*, 18 October 2000), although this particular view of Britishness is changing, it is still the case that when people think of Britain they instinctively think of white people, and believe that Britain belongs to them.

For many within the ethnic communities this remains central to why black and Asian people are subjected to discrimination. As Hall (*The Observer*, 15 October 2000) suggests, British society can be roughly divided into three groups. Some think that Britain's multicultural character gives it vibrancy and cultural energy. Others may tolerate 'multicultural drift' but are not committed to it. Another grouping, however, is passionately hostile to the idea and feels threatened and culturally undermined by it.

Conclusions

The construction of the legitimacy of the 'British' state remains central to the understanding of politics and the notion of citizenship and nationhood within the United Kingdom. Even the relatively few examples above should illustrate some of the complexities and problems of considering nationalisms. It is certainly difficult to identify a single quality that all nationalisms have in common. That does not mean, however, that there are no relationships between the various uses of the term, even when they are applied to very diverse national groups. It also helps to temper any desire to find a general theory of nationalism.

Perhaps what is most significant about the idea of nationalism is not that it points to a historical and political reality, but is in the strength of its conceptualization. It is an attempt to give meaningful explanation to social and political life and to impose a meaning on otherwise disparate and often unconnected events. The state in this sense is not only a territorial and political entity, but also an 'imagined community'.

Hence, the nation needs to be understood not just in terms of its geographical and political boundaries, but also in terms of its social boundaries. We must also understand the nation as socially constructed. This involves assumed cultural values and attributes, and presumed normative behaviour. Integral to the construction of Englishness/Britishness is the identification of a series of 'Others'. Importantly, the Runnymede Trust has called for a 're-imagining' of contemporary multicultural Britain, which should take account of patterns of cultural pluralism, patterns of postwar migration, end of Empire, devolution, globalization and closer integration with Europe.

Some argue that the range of cultural diversity in the United Kingdom today irretrievably undermines any notion of a single British identity. More and more people seek to express identity through multiple and hybrid cultural forms. There are serious questions to be asked as to whether Britishness has a future, or if ideas of Britishness can accommodate these differences? Some of these issues will be discussed later in the book, particularly in the context of the development of 'new politics' and globalization. Much of the globalization process is driven by the ideology of neoliberalism, which emphasizes individualism and is antagonistic to state intervention. In the next chapter we shall consider the influence of neoliberalism on the politics and society of the United Kingdom.

DISCUSSION QUESTIONS

- What evidence is there to support the view that nationalism is the most universally legitimate value in contemporary political life?
- How powerful a social and political force is nationalism within the United Kingdom?
- Examine the proposition that the British political system, once regarded as the paradigmatic stable democracy, is in severe and deep crisis.
- How are contemporary discourses surrounding nationality, national identity and citizenship constructed in the United Kingdom?
- What evidence is there that ethnic minorities are actively engaged in the political life of the United Kingdom?

Section II

Society and the State

3

(Re)defining Politics: Neoliberalism and the State

Key concepts and issues	Key theorists and writers
• Neoliberalism and neoconservatism	• Milton Friedman
• New Right ideology	• Andrew Gamble
• The New Right in politics	• Stuart Hall and Martin Jacques
• Thatcherism	• Fredrick Hayek
• The legacy of Thatcherism	• Bob Jessop
• The New Right and morality politics	• Roger Scruton

Neo-liberals argue that inequality is both inevitable and desirable. Attempts to offset inequality through state interference will inevitably lead to the erosion of human freedom, preventing individuals making choices about how to spend their income. The inevitability of human diversity within civil society will ensure that the state acts on only a partial, and therefore distorted, understanding of individuals' needs. (Faulks, 1999: 74)

The neoliberal agenda of the New Right, which manifested itself in the leadership of Margaret Thatcher, directly dominated both party and ideological dimensions of United Kingdom politics during the 1980s. Its legacy was still profoundly felt throughout the rest of the 1990s and remains a potent political ideology and reference point into the new millennium.

At this chapter's core, therefore, is an outline of the major neoconservative and neoliberal perspectives. It will also trace in some detail the political emergence, and later decline, of Thatcherism. Equally importantly, however, the chapter will further discuss the main consequences of the period of New Right dominance, not just for party politics, but for United Kingdom society more generally. Finally, it will discuss the legacy of Thatcherism and its effects on contemporary politics.

Indeed, a core set of questions to be considered in the remainder of the book surrounds how much Thatcherism altered United Kingdom society, and to what extent political formations since have changed as a reaction to the parameters set by neoliberalism as interpreted by the New Right. In broad terms, Thatcherism will not only be considered as a response to decline and as a set of economic, social and moral propositions, but also as a starting point for understanding the emergence of New Labour and the subsequent direction of many of its policies (see Chapter 7).

In one sense the New Right, which emerged in the late 1970s and then dominated politics in the United Kingdom throughout the 1980s, was not really new at all. Certainly, many of its ideas and propositions had been in circulation for a long time, without attracting any widespread consideration or support. Friedrich von Hayek, for example, had argued from the 1930s for the primacy of a free market and the minimal state. More recently, writers such as Milton Friedman and James Buchannan had, from at least the early 1960s, and while remaining tangential to mainstream politics, consistently advocated New Right theories.

In another sense, however, the New Right was dramatically different and its emergence marked, if not a rupture, then certainly a new dynamic in United Kingdom politics. The widespread political, social and economic crises of the late 1960s precipitated a dramatic readjustment in United Kingdom politics. One result was that the domestic postwar consensus broke down.

It was within this context that the New Right emerged to dominate the political agenda in the United Kingdom. Its rise was centrally connected to its opposition to a social-democratic consensus and the collectivist values within the politics of the United Kingdom. However, despite a core opposition to the values of social democracy, the New Right was always a coalition of diverse political forces. This is partly illustrated by the fact that despite the depth of the literature available, there is no agreed term to characterize the New Right within British politics in the 1980s. Different commentators have applied a variety of labels, such as the 'radical right', 'authoritarian right', 'neoliberalism', 'anti-collectivism' or 'neoconservatism'.

It is, of course, possible, and indeed important, to differentiate between various components and factions within the New Right. Here in Chapter 3, we shall focus on the influence of the authoritarian Right and neoliberalism on New Right politics since 1979. While recognizing the wider social forces, which may be brought together under the banner of the New Right, it was Margaret Thatcher who proved to be the concentrate for much of the dynamic behind its direction within the United Kingdom. Therefore, throughout the rest of this book, we shall also refer to a more limited phenomenon, of Thatcherism. Certainly neoliberalism, the New Right and Thatcherism are not synonymous terms. To begin with, therefore, some key elements that make up New Right ideology need to be identified.

Neoliberalism

Much of the dynamic within neoliberalism has its origins in a particular reading of classical political economy. Indeed, some would argue that the origins of modern liberal democracy may be found in the American Revolution of 1776 and the French Revolution of 1789. In the contemporary period, however, neoliberals place stress on the free market, minimal state intervention and the primacy of personal choice.

Green (1987) identifies four basic 'schools' of thought within neoliberalism. These are the 'Austrian School', represented most clearly by the works of Hayek. In perhaps his most famous work, *The Road to Serfdom* (1944), he explains how state intervention based on collectivism will bring about a totalitarian society.

Elsewhere, the 'Chicago School' is clearly represented in the works of Milton Friedman and best known for the promotion of 'monetarism'. This theory, adopted as it was by the Conservative administration in the early part of the 1980s, argues that the money supply should only expand in line with production. If it expands any more quickly there will be only one result – inflation. There is also great emphasis on the market as the primary provider of goods, and they remain hostile to almost any type of state intervention.

The thinking from the 'Virginia School of Public Choice' takes a slightly different tack. Here, neo-classical economics is used to explain the behaviour of politicians and bureaucrats. All individuals are deemed to be 'rational utility maximizers'. The result of this is that state services are put in place to serve the interests of the providers, not their clients. The real problem is that this leads to state 'overload' (in the form that we have encountered it). The perceived answer is again to return to 'the market'.

Finally, 'Anarcho-Capitalists', which is by far the most diverse (and perhaps the least well known) of the above groupings. Writers such as Nozick and David Friedman, who place emphasis on 'unrestrained freedom', represent this perspective. Indeed, for some authors, such as Friedman, the argument is for an absence of any state structures in society whatsoever.

Neoconservatism

Several of those on the New Right drew on a different source for their inspiration. Here again we are not talking of a coherent 'school' of thought, but rather a fairly diverse grouping. That is not to say, however, that there are not key themes that may be identified. There is a common emphasis by such neoconservatives on authority, traditions, law and order and morality. The 'cause' of many contemporary social problems is seen as the increasing permissiveness in society. In particular, the 1960s are seen as the turning point in the moral decline, and break-down in authority, of contemporary society. Hence, they tend to emphasize the roles and responsibilities of the individual before the collective. This has been clearly seen in policy towards the 'family', of which more in later chapters of the book.

There is, however, no necessary alignment between neoconservatives and neoliberals. Indeed, over issues such as individual freedom and the role of the market there may well be open conflict. The social and political forces that brought the two together manifested itself in the late 1970s, as Thatcherism. It was a particular set of social and political dynamics, rather than the individual, which marked the merger of such complex political forces and expresses it in a populist form.

As we shall see, many would argue that the manifestation of the New Right administration and its ideological positioning has structured much of the terrain of the United Kingdom's polity ever since. It is therefore necessary to consider a little more fully just what Thatcherism was.

Thatcherism: a new beginning?

Thatcherism, recognizing a crisis in Conservatism's traditional support, set about creating a new social and political coalition. Hence, the general election of 3 May 1979 saw the New Right exploit some of the widespread popular feelings surrounding disillusionment with the crisis of the state. Such views were clearly represented by the Conservative Party at the time when it projected itself as being able to cure all the ills of the country and to reverse Britain's long-term economic decline. The 1979 Conservative Party Manifesto claimed Britain was 'faced with its most serious problems since the Second World War'.

In response, the Convervatives set out five major tasks to be undertaken. First, to restore the health of economic and social life by controlling inflation and striking a fair balance between rights and duties of the trades union movement. Secondly, to restore incentives whereby success would be rewarded, and jobs created in an expanding economy. Thirdly, to uphold parliament and rule of law. Fourthly, to support family life by helping people to become home owners, raising standards of children's education and concentrating welfare services on effective support of the old, the sick and those in real need; and fifthly, to strengthen Britain's defences and protect interests in an increasingly threatening world.

In one way the emergence of Thatcherism can be seen as a direct response to demands which are necessarily made on the state in order to implement the above principles. Here, the theory of 'overload' mentioned in the previous chapter is important, and it is one to which we shall return. In particular, on the part of the New Right, there was a recognition, not always made overt, that government could no longer 'solve' all the fundamental economic, social and political problems of society. Almost immediately this involved a downgrading of expectations. The responsibilities of the state were reduced in the popular consciousness, and at the same time the notion of individual responsibility was upgraded.

There exists a vast literature on Thatcherism. This includes a variety of critical analytical perspectives (see Hall, 1988; Hall and Jacques, 1983, 1989; Jessop et al., 1988; Wilson, 1992), ideas about Thatcherism as a response to the restructuring of international capital (see Overbeek, 1990) and detailed discussions of Thatcher's leadership 'style' (see Riddell, 1983; Young, 1993; Young and Sloman, 1986).

Other literature reviews the changing face of United Kingdom politics and society during the 'Thatcher years' (see Edgell and Duke, 1991; Kavanagh, 1987). Some provide detailed considerations of the effects on various aspects of United Kingdom society, such as the economy, civil liberties, Northern Ireland and welfare (see Ewing and Gearty, 1990; Gaffikin and Morrissey, 1990; Johnson, 1991; Loney, 1986). Yet more is based on major criticisms offered by political opponents (see Ali and Livingstone, 1984; Hirst, 1989) and the legacy of the Thatcher era (Riddell, 1989, 1991).

One thing which is clear when we consider all the above writings is that the Conservative government of 1979 sought to mark out a distinct break with much of what had gone before. The New Right 'vision', with Margaret Thatcher and Keith Joseph in the vanguard, emerged from a distinctive recognition of the relative weakness of support for the policy parameters which had been set in place. In particular, they sought to challenge any existing commitments by the state based on the ideologies of Keynes, Beveridge and the Fabians. As Kavanagh (1987: 6–7) explains: 'One can disagree about the exact date – the defeat of the Heath government in 1974, Healey's budget in 1975 which abandoned full employment, the IMF rescue in 1976 or the Winter of discontent in 1979. [but] The consensus had few credible defenders by 1979.'

So, for example, the vision manifested in direct conflict and often confrontation with the existing institutionalized arrangements of bargaining, between the state, big business and trade unions, and with the notion of a universal and state-provided welfare system. All of these were effectively challenged and, at least in part, undermined. In its place came the endorsement of individualistic perspectives and market forces as the major methods in governing and determining the economy and the provision of welfare.

The origins of Thatcherism

If the emergence of the New Right is to be located in the breakdown of postwar consensus (as discussed in previous chapter), it is important to try to understand this in terms of the wider phenomenon of disillusionment with the state. Thatcherism in part drew on academic arguments and those writers such as Scruton (1990) and Paul Johnson (1980), who stressed a 'failure of values'. Johnson, for example, argues that there were inherent weaknesses in the postwar United Kingdom settlement. The 'Beveridge–Keynes' state provided a public monopoly in welfare which was 'justified' as working on behalf of the poor. However, this in fact undermined political democracy by making promises that could not be met. Overall, it worked against a clear understanding of real social needs and future economic possibilities.

So why did the New Right become dominant? After all, as the above indicates, free market views had been in currency since at least the 1950s, although admittedly these had been tangential to mainstream Conservative

Party ideology. However, within party political Conservatism much of the internal momentum for change came from the two election defeats in 1974. The then leader, Edward Heath, had actually begun to adopt some New Right policies around 1970 but was quickly forced to abandon them. The New Right tendency within political Conservatism, initially spearheaded by Keith Joseph, its chief ideologue, and then by Margaret Thatcher, who was elected leader of the Conservative Party on 11 February 1975, began to gather momentum.

Thatcher, despite what has been claimed, offered no dramatic change in political attitudes or direction at the time. Indeed, Loney (1986: 44) describes her rise to power and the subsequent shift to the Right as largely 'fortuitous', based more on disillusionment with Heath's leadership than any widespread conversion to a new ideology. Slowly, however, a distinctive set of social policies began to emerge from within, promoting New Right virtues and largely based on economic restraints on public expenditure. Much of the policy remained shadowy but there was a clear commitment to reducing overall public expenditure, except in specific areas such as defence and law and order.

In terms of populist support, rather than the acceptance of any dramatic ideological shift to the Right, the real prelude to the political rise of Thatcherism, may well have been the events of late 1978 and the so-called 'winter of discontent'. This saw a massive number of days lost through industrial disputes largely surrounding wage limits in the public sector. It brought to a head increasing criticism regarding the provision of state services as being out of touch with ordinary people.

One result was that welfare came back to the core of the political debate, this time not in terms of 'need', but rather of the increasing cost of welfare provision. Hence, by the mid-1970s, after a quarter of a century of steady growth and near-full employment, it was clear that the consensus that had existed around welfare was fast disappearing. It was at this point that the neoliberalism of sections of the New Right came to the fore. By the late 1970s there came an overt challenge to the postwar consensus and calls for extreme constraint on the welfare resources provided by the state.

In fiscal policy they argued that the nature of the contemporary state had produced an 'overload' (see previous chapter). Further, it was claimed that most of the major social problems of the late 1970s were merely the latest dire examples of a century of national decline. It was the New Right which best recognized this populist concern and constructed a meaningful political discourse within which only they could be called upon to halt the degeneration and repair the damage. To do so they called for a government that was much less interventionist and that restored greater individual choice and personal responsibility.

Thatcherism's political philosophy

The above, however, does not fully explain the subsequent direction taken by the neoliberals headed, in party political terms, by Margaret Thatcher. How exactly was Thatcherism different and how did some of the New Right ideological positions outlined above come to influence the Thatcher administration so strongly?

New Right ideology always had wider political dimensions, far beyond its narrow economic focus on public expenditure. This sometimes caused some confusion in the analysis. Partly, this is because, as Kavanagh (1987) suggests, the terms 'Thatcherism', 'monetarism' and the 'New Right' are often incorrectly used interchangeably. He further explains the vital differences:

> A monetarist believes that excessive increases in the supply of money (that is, above the increase in production in the economy) cause inflation, a case of too much money chasing too few goods. Too often in today's political rhetoric, however, the term refers not to an approach but to a right-wing Conservative, who questions Keynesian policies. But there are varieties of monetarism and monetarism is analytically quite separate from, and has no necessary links with, a market economy, high unemployment, lower public spending, balanced budgets, and so on. Similarly the term 'New Right' is too often used to lump together various social and economic doctrines and policies and political personalities. It is important, however, to separate those libertarians who favour a reduction in the role of the state in both social and economic areas from those who are concerned with the restoration of the authority of the state and hostile to many aspects of 'permissiveness'. (Kavanagh, 1987: 10)

At this point it may be useful to outline some of the central political tenets of traditional Conservative thought, if only to highlight where Thatcherism departed from it, how far and in what ways. Central to inherent Conservative thought is the belief that the core purpose of politics is to provide a mechanism for social harmony. Underlying this is the belief that human nature is imperfect, and therefore that inequality is innate and inevitable in society. Society is held together by strong leadership and discipline and rests on the foundations of organically evolved social institutions such as the Church and the family and shared customs and traditions. Both politically and socially, it is continuity that is more important than change. It is the rule of law that provides the basis of all freedom. Hence, the government should exist merely to provide checks and balances and manage political change only when it can no longer be resisted.

However, Thatcherism quickly placed itself outside this tradition of Conservative thought and action. There was still a strong emphasis on such issues as freedom, property and the nation, but this was to be achieved by a new conviction, and the resolution and strength to bring about radical social and political change.

So let us consider the ideological basis of Thatcherism, the thinking which underpinned the policies and strategies of the Thatcher leadership. Ideologically, Thatcherism stressed neoliberalism, freedom of the individual, voluntary rather than state action in welfare provision and the notion that inequality and unequal rewards are necessary to society.

First, Thatcher upheld the virtues of 'the market', by way of its commitment to the neoliberal view that the market was the best mechanism for producing and distributing resources in society. Such views draw heavily on classical liberalism and the belief that competitive markets, with minimal involvement by the state, is the best means to ensure economic growth. In the contemporary New Right vision, the market is seen as more efficient, responsive to peoples' needs and productive than any other state system could possibly be.

Secondly, there was an emphasis on individualism. Again, this draws directly on ideas within liberalism, where the individual is seen as self-reliant and responsible for his or her own actions. It is therefore seen as a mistake to involve the state in economic affairs, or any other aspect of people's lives, as this would result in the state taking away individual responsibility. This is particularly clear in the area of welfare where provision such as social work and benefits are seen to create a 'dependency culture'. The postwar welfare state has damaged the individual ethos, which had to be restored by the 'rolling back of the state'.

Many on the New Right drew ideologically on works of Hayek and his 'truth of individualism'. This represented the freedom to buy, sell and accumulate, and marked the crucial foundations upon which many other 'liberties' in society rest. It is what Hayek (1944, 1949, 1960) terms the drift towards 'collectivism' which represents the greatest threat to individual freedom and hence the foundations of society. Thus, while socialists have promised the 'road to freedom', it in fact represented serfdom.

Thirdly, a key ideological feature was the commitment to 'strong government' and 'authority'. In spite of the claims outlined above, promoting the market and individualism, underlying these was an equally intense ideological commitment to strong government. Hence, Jessop et al. (1988) refer to this aspect of Thatcherism as 'social authorianism'. It manifested itself in several ways: overt campaigns for more 'law and order'; the tightening of security services and controls of information; a patriotic, nationalist and sometimes jingoistic approach to foreign policy and defence. It is useful to consider these main features of Thatcherism in more detail.

The free market

While it would be entirely wrong to suggest that Thatcherism was solely about economics, it is nonetheless true that its economic position constituted a large part of what the New Right was about. In broad terms this meant commitment to a limited government or a non-interventionist state, and the goal of economic liberty or unregulated capitalism. Such economic thinking amounted to a fundamental rejection of Keynesian economic management practices. The only alternative was the free market. Arguments for the free market assumed a number of formats, including that it:

- represents a just mechanism for rewarding talents and abilities;
- nurtures self-reliance; and
- benefits everyone in society, through the 'trickle-down' effect.

Thatcher, in particular, objected to what she termed the nanny-state and the dependency culture, which had enveloped society and people's attitudes. Many of us had become welfare junkies who had abdicated responsibility for our own lives, relying excessively on the state to cushion our existence. The wealth-creators, it was argued, would carry the poor in their wake. Sometimes referred to as the trickle-down effect, this argument holds that eventually everyone's standard of living would rise. Naturally, some would benefit more than others, but that is simply a reflection of their superior talents and abilities.

Hence, fundamental to Thatcherism was an ideological commitment to *laissez-faire* economic policies. This was displayed in several crucial ways, notably through the promotion of private enterprise and in a commitment to reduce 'public expenditure' (which was rarely matched in reality) because it was seen as necessitating high taxation. Moreover, the results of public provision were seen as wasteful, inefficient, misdirected and often abused by those who did not merit or deserve it.

This ideological commitment manifested in a series of policy directions. These included 'monetarism', designed to curb inflation by controlling the money supply and a drive towards 'private enterprise', whereby public services and utilities were largely jettisoned in favour of massive privatization programmes. The free market, it was claimed, was the premium mechanism for rewarding individual talents and nurturing self-reliance. Thatcherism further objected to the creation of the dependency culture. To remove this scourge from British society the circumstances must be created whereby those capable should be allowed to create wealth. Some would clearly benefit from this more than others but, due to the trickle-down effect, everyone's standard of living would eventually rise.

These values manifested in different ways. The initial response of the neoliberals to the economic situation took the direction of a strict control of the money supply. This was seen as a direct mechanism to control inflation. As such, the policies drew directly on the works of Milton Friedman (1962, 1980), who claims a direct and causal link between money supply, the amount of bank notes and credit available in economy and inflation. The rate of inflation is seen as being determined by the rate of growth of the money supply. So, one can control inflation by controlling monetary growth. If governments borrow, or simply 'print money', this will not increase production but merely push up prices. This in turn will generate the demand for more wages, resulting in higher inflation. It is high inflation that provides the greatest threat to the stability of contemporary society.

Governments must actively counter this tendency. In particular, they must show the labour and trades union movement that if wage claims are not matched by increases in production, then the result will be unemployment. This 'fear' of unemployment, what New Right called 'economic realism', should be used to keep wage demands and inflation low. Unemployment cannot be artificially kept below its 'real' rate without accelerating inflation.

A second fundamental tenet of New Right ideology was the belief that market forces work for the benefit of everyone. Reading this through the works of Hayek and Friedman, the New Right argued that pursuing selfish economic interests by some could benefit all. Competition among supplies ensures profit is not too high. If it is efficient, business will prosper, there will be employment and wealth for all and consumers will benefit through the wide variety of goods made available.

In the wider economy some enterprising groups succeed and some fail. This ideology was to be transferred *en masse* to create new social relations in a social structure based on inequality. Some on the New Right almost regarded this as desirable. Material deprivation was seen as making individuals more economically dynamic and people more willing to work to their full potential.

What in the opinion of the New Right had stopped this was the ever increasing and monopolistic state intervention. It is this that destroyed individual freedom and undermined individual efficiency. Paramount here in the mind of the Thatcher government was the role of the trades union movement. There were several constantly repeated 'images' of trade unions: that they were controlled by political extremists; used coercive methods; and extracted wage rises far beyond those 'justified' by production. Overall it was the labour movement and the trade unions which stopped the true movement of market forces and individuals reaching true potential.

For these reasons one of the first tasks the Thatcher administration undertook was confrontation with the labour movement through set-piece industrial clashes, especially the Miners' Strike of 1984 and 1985, and through the implementation of restrictive legislation. Both reflected one core belief of the New Right, that of anti-collectivism. Further, those on the New Right also believed that there was a 'natural' rate for unemployment. Any notion that governments could intervene to achieve full employment was at best misguided, at worst harmful to society.

From the perspective of those involved in the New Right, the decade beginning in 1979 marked a rapid and positive metamorphosis in the fortunes of the United Kingdom. This involved greatly reduced rates of inflation, greatly increased levels of industrial input and 'productivity'. Alongside this was an advanced programme of privatization, including 'British Aerospace', 'British Telecom' and 'British Gas'. During the same period, public borrowing was reduced, and there were substantial reductions in income tax. Moreover, there had been dramatic changes in the public attitude towards widespread support for the values of self-reliance and the virtues of the 'enterprise culture'.

Individualism and social authoritarianism

One of the things that might be engraved on Thatcher's epitaph is her now infamous remark that there is no such thing as society. Of course, this is plainly nonsense, but there is a latent argument here from the political Right that needs to be addressed. One interpretation of what Thatcher really meant was that society is nothing other than a loose collection of self-interested individuals who come together with no other purpose than to protect their persons and their property rights and to pursue private rather than public ends. The major functions of the state are thus defined, in the same way as did Adam Smith, as those of non-intervention.

Much of the New Right expressed great alarm over the perceived breakdown of law and order and the moral malaise, which it claimed was infecting society. They frowned upon moral relativism, increasing secularization and the decline of traditional values. The resolution to the problem was to re-establish respect for authority and law and to restore social discipline within society, hence, the frequent accusations that they were peddling an outdated Victorian morality. However one interprets that, it seems undeniable that the New Right believed that freedom requires order in society. That while, on the one hand, it was libertarian, it was decidedly authoritarian on the other. It is in this sense that the minimal state is also a strong state.

It is clear, therefore, that the New Right did not speak with one voice. For some, social and economic issues were secondary to constructing a new social morality. Edgar (1983), for example, argues that in the wake of the Falklands War the social authoritarians in the New Right were able to rise to prominence at the expense of those promoting economic liberty. One result was that this section of the New Right could see no contradiction between getting the state out of the boardroom and into the bedroom.

Many sought not only to define 'morality', but also to police and regulate it. Scruton (1986), one of the key thinkers of the authoritarian Right, for example, argues that social policy should be formulated by the state in order to promote the 'normal heterosexual family'. Alongside this can be seen other coherent social movements around the notion of a 'moral crusade'. One of the clearest examples of this can be seen in the case of the New Right's positioning regarding sexuality and sexual politics. Hence, with Section 28 of the 1988 Local Government Act, the Conservative Party made clear what forms of sexual relationships they saw as legitimate and what forms they did not. Clearly, in interventions into sex education, the Convervatives made it clear that 'individual freedom' and 'free market' had distinct limits. This period also saw the increased enforcement of legal sanctions in defence of 'fundamental moral values'. Indeed, throughout the time of Thatcher's governments, pressure groups concerned with 'the family' and 'morality' increasingly came to centre stage.

It is important, therefore, to investigate more fully the relationships between Thatcherism, sexual morality and those organizations based on a moral crusade, to identify how Thatcherism also shifted the moral agenda, and claimed it as a political one. There were two key sets of issues upon which the authoritarian Right focused, in order to shift the moral agenda: first, the regulation of human reproduction, as manifested in issues surrounding contraception, abortion, AIDS, and so on; and secondly, in the changing representations of sexuality, which can be clearly seen in shifting definitions regarding, for example, obscenity, and the redefinition of formal sexual education.

Such issues were brought together, at least in the mind of the authoritarian Right, in a much wider debate concerning the moral decline of the country, for which much of the blame is laid squarely at the feet of the 'permissive society' of the 1960s and 1970s. For many within the authoritarian Right the solution to many of today's social problems still rests in a remoralization of society. The remedy, which often manifests itself in calls for a restoration of 'Victorian Values', is seen as a return to the certainty of a former golden age.

The starting point for much of this is the construction of a mythical family, located somewhere around the mid-1950s. Within this supposed time of marital peace and harmony we can readily view striking images of a white middle-class married couple, mummy and daddy playing with their two children, one boy and one girl, in a snug middle-class living room. This, of course, is a scene that was no more stereotypical in 1956 (the year this author was born) than it is now. Within the Conservative mind, however, the perceived ethics of personal liberation, equal rights, and especially the rise of the women's movement of the 1960s, have all caused the downfall of the so-called golden age.

Durham (1991) makes many such issues explicit. He suggests that for the political Right the crisis of 'modern Britain' is seen as revolving around increasing divorce rates, one-parent families, the legalization of abortion, homosexuality, pornography, young people out of control, children committing ever more serious crimes, and the like. From within this perspective the United Kingdom is facing imminent social collapse.

We will encounter these perspectives at several other points in this book. For now it may be useful to move beyond these ideological aspects of Thatcherism to consider some of the major effects that Thatcherism had on the nature of politics and society in the United Kingdom.

What did Thatcherism change?

So far we have largely considered the ideological basis for the growth of neoliberalism and the authoritarian Right, as it developed through Thatcherism within the Conservative Party. However, it is also important to consider how this set of ideas materialized 'in practice'. Here we shall consider several key areas: economic policy; the welfare state; the construction of 'freedom'; law and order; and Europe.

Likewise, the core institutions of the state were challenged and to some extent restructured. The New Right no longer sought to guarantee full employment, or to negotiate income policies, or to have a consultative role for the trade unions. They closed or downgraded corporatist institutions and actively promoted the reintroduction of 'market forces' to as much of public sector as possible.

This was seen in many ways: local authorities were expected to tender for services; the concept of universal grants dissolved; and in general the public sector was increasingly expected to 'model' itself on, and take direction

from, large private capitalist organization. There was also an overall attempt
to replace and redraw boundaries of the state to leave large areas of economic
and social life 'free' from intervention.

Also, however, throughout the Thatcher period, the central state was
strengthened. Indeed, to use Gamble's (1994a) term, Thatcherism twinned the
'free market' with the 'strong state'. Hence, for example, the abolition of the
Metropolitan and the Greater London Councils must be set against the
creation of 'national curriculum' in schools and the dramatically increased
police powers and a strengthened 'secret state'.

Ewing and Gearty (1990) ably demonstrate the tendency of Thatcherism
towards the strong state, which created a crisis surrounding civil liberties in the
United Kingdom under Thatcher. These ranged from a vast extension of police
powers and wide-ranging restrictions on public protest to unprecedented
restrictive legislation on the freedom of expression for gays and openly
discriminatory legislation surrounding nationality, immigration and citizenship. Further, Thornton (1989) argues that the Thatcher administration had a
dramatic effect on freedom in the United Kingdom. He provides another
overview of the Thatcher 'era', arguing that civil liberties were not just eroded,
but rather that they were deliberately attacked and undermined. The scale of
the assault was breathtaking, from censorship of the media to the invasion of
privacy, from increased police powers to injustice and unfairness, from a
denial of basic rights to institutionalized intolerance and discrimination.

The provision of the state welfare proved another central target for New
Right policy. This will be considered in detail in Chapter 4. However, within
the broad terms of this chapter it is worth noting that the objections were
three-fold. The provision of welfare by the state was seen as too expensive,
costing too large a stake of public expenditure; it was also regarded as having
weakened the moral resources of the United Kingdom. Importantly, it was
argued that the welfare state had creating a dependency culture. Finally, it
was suggested that the provision of welfare was based on state monopolies,
which were regarded both as inefficient and as removing any meaningful
levels of choice to the individual.

The notion of 'law and order' was also extremely high on the agenda of
the newly elected Conservative government in 1979. Before the election
Thatcher had identified the fall of a golden age, reflected in rising crime rates,
increased lawlessness and lack of respect for authority. The 'causes' of these,
like much else, were laid squarely at the door of the 'permissiveness' of the
previous generation and the 'weakness' of past administrations, both Labour
and Conservative, in tackling the issue. Hence, the issue of law and order was,
from the 1979 election onwards, treated as a special case, and given a
privileged position in budgetary terms within the new administration. As
Savage puts it:

> There is no denying that the pre-election commitments on law and order
> were translated into action from the earliest days of the 1979 Thatcher
> government. Both in terms of the provision of resources and in terms of

legislative reform, the government was quick to move on what they saw as an issue of priority for the new administration. (Savage, 1990: 90)

All of this provides evidence to support Gamble's (1985) argument that the attempt by the New Right to dismantle the postwar consensus made it more, rather than less, interventionist.

The legacy of Thatcherism

Given the above, it is now part of conventional wisdom that the Thatcher years altered UK society forever. However, in terms of analysis, it is important to try to distinguish between what Thatcherism claimed to do and what it actually achieved. It is important to try to highlight the gap between the 'rhetoric' and 'reality' of Thatcherism. Did Thatcher succeed in 'the great moving Right show'? One of the central organizing principles of Thatcher, for example, was the desired claim 'to roll back the state'. Yet as Clarke and Langan (1993: 54) point out, throughout the 1980s 'the government proceeded in a relatively cautious fashion in the welfare sphere'. Indeed, Le Grand (1998) argues that one of the most striking features of the first eight years of Thatcher's government was how little it affected the welfare state. It was only extremely late in the Thatcher administration, after 1988, that there was any systematic attempt to introduce 'the market' into health, education and social services.

It should be equally clear, however, that Thatcherism did dramatically shift the ideological parameters of politics in the United Kingdom. If, for example, we stay with the notion of the rolling back of the welfare state, Mishra (1990) distinguishes a number of different stages in the 'offensive'. There was the general ideological attack on welfare, largely propagandist and populist in character. This did not necessarily manifest itself in policy changes or legislation. However, what it did result in was the creation of an anti-welfare climate of opinion.

Certainly there is a clearly identifiable legacy of Thatcherism. One important feature of the pre-Thatcherite state, as we have seen for example, was its commitment to a 'corporate bias'. With the development of Thatcherism, the co-operative management of the economy was rapidly removed as an organizing principle. Put plainly, the ascendancy of the New Right saw the overt challenge to social democracy and the attempt to recast the United Kingdom along the lines of neoliberalism and free market economics.

What were the foundations of the postwar state that the New Right sought to restructure? The broad parameters of 'social democracy' have been discussed in Chapter 2, but the core understandings of it are neatly summarized by Coates (1995: 160) as follows:

- that we lived in a Cold War world, divided between a free society and an evil empire;

- that as part of the free bit, we possessed a post-capitalist mixed economy capable of being managed by the state for socially-desirable ends;
- that it was the state's job to guarantee full employment, rising living standards and basic welfare provision; and
- individual citizens had a right to all three of those.

Gamble suggests that Thatcherism was an ambitious, often contradictory, attempt to create conditions for a new hegemony. Further:

> The Thatcherites were more adept at staking out new ground and repudiating the old consensus than at making sacrifices or seeking the compromises necessary to build a new one. If there was one idea running through the whole project as it unfolded it was that to win hegemony Conservatives no longer needed to make the kind of concessions to the demands of the labour movement that they once believed necessary. (Gamble, 1994a: 208)

So, for example, there was, on the one hand, an overt commitment to anti-statism and the deconstruction of the social democratic project. On the other hand, however, this was replaced by a politically aligned state apparatus. Central to the New Right, neoliberal ideology was individual liberty, yet throughout its administration there was a constant constriction on the policies and groups supporting civil liberties.

Likewise, the dominant rhetoric of economic prosperity has to be set against the actuality of economic hardship and the devastation of whole occupational communities. There was a clear break between the theory and practice of Thatcherism. As Christopher Johnson points out:

> The paradox was that Mrs Thatcher came to office promising to get the Government off the people's backs, yet used her complete command of the apparatus of power to intervene in the economy as much as any of her predecessors had, only in different ways. Her interventionist temperament was at odds with her philosophical liberalism. (Johnson, 1991: 253)

Yet for the Thatcher administration there was little contradiction between such factors. As Coates puts it:

> There was no tension – in Thatcherite liberalism – between the criteria guiding public and private funding. Thatcherite Conservatism wanted the same criteria (of profitability, commercial viability, self-reliance) to operate across the public and private sectors. This 'rolling back the state' was but a mechanism for enabling society to be run as the government wanted it to be run. If the 'market' rules as co-ordinator of economic/social resources now, it does so because the government willed it. This 'rolling back of the state' was in that sense a political choice, not an imperative. (Coates, 1995: 158)

Alongside the above, the New Right expressed alarm surrounding what it perceived as the breakdown of law and order and the spread of a moral malaise throughout society. It dismissed those who promoted cultural and moral relativism, and in their place gave primacy to traditional values. One of the ways to solve such problems was to restore the declining respect for authority and discipline in society. Hence, for the New Right freedom also required order in society. Thatcher's style of British nationalism also had important consequences. This sense of identity rested on notions of a strong defence, including the retention of a nuclear arsenal and 'permission' to base US cruise missiles, a willingness to confront Argentina over the Falklands, a confrontational style in Europe and a vigorous assault on the forces of Irish republicanism.

Sexuality, morality and the New Right

Many of the views of the New Right regarding morality remain deeply engrained in the popular consciousness. At a fringe meeting of the Conservative Party Annual Conference of 1993, for example, Michael Howard voiced support for the programme operating in New Jersey, USA, where extra benefits are denied to a second child (and any subsequent child) born to mothers dependent on social security. Indeed, at one point shortly before the 1997 general election, lone-parent families seemed to be targeted by sections of the Conservative Party as being responsible for most of the contemporary evils in society.

Hite suggests that this was merely representative of a political force that had been building up for some time. As one Conservative MP she cites puts it: 'if women have sex, they will have to learn that there may be consequences'. Hite further seeks to place such views in an international context, when she argues that:

> The use of catch-phrases 'preservation of family values' and 'return to traditional values' became a hallmark of the Reagan–Bush years in the United States during the 1980s, and now is the hallmark of reactionary groups in the United Kingdom. In the States now, these phrases are no longer mainstream, they represent the radical right of the recently defeated Republican Party. (Hite, 1993: 5)

Further, as Hite points out, the idea that there was a golden age of family life in the 1950s or earlier smacks of a type of Western fundamentalism which wants to put women back into the kitchen (Hite, 1993: 5).

Such Conservative views tap a deep vein in British public consciousness. Open any newspaper on any day and the chances are that you will see signs of a new moral panic. One of the most common stories is that the family is in crisis. A typical example of this occurred at the end of January 1996 and surrounded the 'marriage' of a 13-year-old English girl to an 18-year-old

Turkish man. Moral indignation, throughout the press, was rife and largely blamed the social services. The traditional concern from the Right is focused on what happens when traditional family structures break down and there is a reduction in parental control.

It is possible to outline the main projection of such an argument as follows. A steady rise in single parents, the ever-increasing liberalization of the legal system, the influences of feminism and the lack of discipline brought about by 'trendy' teaching methods, have all resulted in ever-rising crime rates and the virtual collapse of society. Such reasoning has great appeal. It attacks a vulnerable group in society and seems to be able to unite political Left and Right. Central to this is the social construction of the contemporary family, particularly in its nuclear form. However, as Greer (1971) observes, the nuclear family is possibly the shortest-lived familial system that has ever developed, emerging as it did within the class relations brought about by the onset of industrialized capitalism.

The contemporary family is also deeply structured by class. The concept of childhood is relatively recent (Postman, 1983) and children have often been sent away to work, while parents in wealthy families would have their children wet-nursed and looked after by nannies. Even now boarding school remains a popular choice for the better off and there is no outcry about the abrogation of responsibility and lack of parental care.

One key source for constructing a wider definition of the 'family' surrounds sexuality. The lesbian and gay experience illustrates that many homosexual couples with children are not as restricted as heterosexual couples into fulfilling gender roles and can draw more on external support. It is important to stress the centrality of friendship networks to gay and lesbian families. Many lesbians and gay men rely far less on their family of origin than they do on the strong mechanisms of social and emotional support that have developed with friends and constructed community. Writings on contemporary gender politics highlight the ways in which people are fixed into prescribed gender roles. It is still this which is central in defining politics and morality.

Analysing Thatcherism

The legacy of Thatcherism remains deeply implanted in the social and political fabric of the United Kingdom. It can be found throughout its economic and political structures, views on social authority and in the profound social and geographical divisions that remain manifest today. Equally important are the continued ideological parameters which have been set, and the ways in which many people explain and understand their social and political world. It is crucial, therefore, to try to understand this aspect of the politics of Thatcherism in more detail.

Even at the time of development Thatcherism did not go unchallenged from within the political Right. Thus, Green (1993) makes some cutting criticisms of the economic rationalism of the Thatcher years. For him, while the Thatcherite emphasis on the virtues of self-sufficiency was necessary to halt

Britain's economic decline, there were missing ingredients. These involved the civic virtues of solidarity, service of others, duty and self-sacrifice. This reinforces some of Green's other views (1990, 1996), particularly when he argues that the welfare problem is not primarily a financial but rather a moral one.

Another important starting point in understanding Thatcherism is the work of Stuart Hall. Drawing directly on Gramsci's notion of hegemony, which we have already encountered, as the construction of social authority throughout all levels of society, Hall concentrates on the ideological dimension of Thatcherism. For Hall, Thatcherism is best understood as an attempt to discredit the previous hegemony, namely, social consensus and social democracy, and the apparent inability of either the Labour or Conservative parties to manage the state effectively.

From this perspective, Thatcherism succeeded in shifting the political terrain dramatically to the Right. It sought to organize several diverse interests and groupings around the central themes of anti-statism, anti-collectivism and anti-socialism. This manifested itself in the ideological, political and legislative assault on the postwar settlement and the values of collectivism, redistribution and corporatism.

Another identifying feature of Thatcherism was the ability to project the ideology successfully at a populist level. What Hall (1984) terms 'authoritarian populism', prospered mainly due to the perceived failures of social democracy. Indeed, Thatcherism fed off a wide range of 'discourses' constructed to challenge the central beliefs of the benefits of the established social democracy. These included, for example, law and order, the nature of the family, the future of welfare and education. What Thatcherism constantly sought to do (and in its own terms successfully did) was to explain all society ills in terms of the 'evils' of collectivism and socialism. It was this focused attack on social democracy that dramatically redrew political boundaries. Thatcherism thus created a new ideological space, giving expression to the mass experience and to the political questioning of the benefits of social democracy as commonsense.

All of this suggests, however, that Thatcherism may be regarded as an extremely coherent movement. This has been questioned by many. Overbeek summarizes the major problems with Hall's analysis as follows:

> [first,] it tends to blame (the leadership of) social democracy for the rise of Thatcherism (which goes much further than saying that social democracy was unable to formulate a creditable socialist response to the crisis); secondly, it tends to analyse Thatcherism exclusively in political and ideological terms (as an -ism), and to ignore the identification of class forces whose interests are represented in the new project; and, finally, it tends to view Thatcherism as primarily reactionary and destructive. (Overbeek, 1990: 177)

One important criticism of Hall's analysis is that it projects Thatcherism as seeking to return Britain to the past. This was an easy impression to get of course with a constant refrain in the rhetoric being talk of a 'golden age of Victorian values'. Yet clearly Thatcherism also sought to project a distinct image of the future with new forms of capital accumulation beyond those of Fordism.

Further, as writers such as Atkins (1986), and Overbeek (1990) point out, the Thatcherite project of de-industrialization makes most sense when considered in the context of the globalized economy (see Chapter 7). Capitalist production, the search for profit and the location of capital are directly linked. The physical relocation of capital in the 1980s was partly a result of the failure of Fordism and the move away from mass manufacturing and skilled, unionized production plants, towards firms using reasonably unskilled, low-wage workers, mainly engaged in component assembly (Murray, 1989). Such considerations have led to the development of some of the most notable criticisms of Hall in the works of Jessop et al. (1988, 1990). For Jessop, Thatcherism is also a hegemonic project within the post-Fordist era. However, Jessop argues that Hall concentrates too much on ideological features of Thatcherism. Rather, it is important to recognize that there were clearly identifiable capitalist interests locked into Thatcher's project. The New Right's support of the introduction of post-Fordism into the United Kingdom was a distinct attempt to change the existing socio-economic structure and social relations.

Hence, for Jessop, Thatcherism is best understood in more materialist terms than Hall. It can be regarded as a differentiated accumulation strategy, a reassertion of the major financial logic of British society. However, Thatcherism recognized that this could not be sustained on a rational basis. Therefore, another key strategy was to destroy central parts of old economic structure, particularly the United Kingdom's traditional industrial base. This cleared the way for the establishment of new forms of accumulation based on integration into the world market and new enterprise by way of deregulation, privatization, denationalization and tax cuts. Jessop further questions whether Thatcherism succeeded in creating new consensus. Much support for Thatcher may have been calculative, in people buying council homes, for example, rather than an acceptance of its broader ideological position. Nonetheless, it set in motion an acceptance of a more individualistic set of cultural and political values.

Gamble also regards Thatcherism as an attempt to organize a new hegemony in British politics. For him, this has four key components: electoral hegemony; ideological hegemony; state hegemony; and economic hegemony. In this sense, hegemony cannot be seen simply in ideological terms, but rather 'it involves the successful interweaving of economic and political as well as ideological leadership' (Gamble, 1994a: 207).

From Thatcher to Blair and beyond

Although the road of social and political change mapped out by Thatcher was long travelled without realizing its hegemonic project, and while Thatcher herself has long since met her political demise, that is not to say that neo-liberalism has not had long-lasting effects on society. As we have seen, Thatcherism went far beyond Margaret Thatcher, who clearly remained central to setting the political and policy programme throughout her administration. However, even after her downfall, the 'Thatcherite' agenda continued to define many of the parameters of social and political debate in the United Kingdom.

This is a point to which we shall return at several times during the remainder of the book. Briefly, however, Thatcher's replacement as Prime Minister by John Major saw, after a very short time, the re-emergence of a Thatcherite agenda, particularly in its populist messages. In part this was an attempt to unite political divisions within the Conservative Party. However, despite an overt attempt to distance himself, John Major demonstrated no significant break with much of the strategy outlined above. As Hall explains, at the time John Major:

> reaches for the popular themes of crime, law and order, family breakdown, and social disintegration. He reaches for Thatcherite common sense, or rather his version of it: 'Back to Basics'. He attempts to combine the impossible – respectability and enterprise. (Hall, 1993: 3)

From the early 1960s, there has been a series of protracted bids to reinvent a new Conservativism. The struggle for the mantle of party political Conservatism is still very much a live one. This is manifested as a whole series of contradictions and confrontations, for example, in the run up to, and the period following, the general election of 2001. Those who uphold a free market approach, those who believe in libertarian and individualist trends, alongside those who stress either authoritarian or communitarian directions, are all seeking to take contemporary Conservatism and the Conservative Party in very different directions.

Overt tensions have arisen, for example, between internationalizing the economy of a medium-sized, Western industrialized power and traditional English nationalism (see also Chapter 2). Deep fissures have opened up over attitudes to the European Union, where a core of English nationalists and defenders of 'traditional values', the family and social order form the basis of continued Euroscepticism. They reflect the concerns of many on the political Right over the 'loss of sovereignty' and what they see as the negative cost of EU membership. As Thatcher herself expressed it during the 2001 general election campaign:

> All my life, our problems, our wars have come from mainland Europe. All my life the upholding of liberty has come from the English-speaking peoples of the world. The thought that we might be absorbed into Europe is to me utterly repugnant, and I'll fight against it as long as I have breath to do so. (*Daily Mail*, 22 May 2001)

Despite the contemporary fragmentation of parliamentary Conservatism, the ideas of the New Right have been central in redefining politics in the United Kingdom. The political agenda set by Thatcherism, and opposition to it, continues to define the parameters of much of the wider social and political debate. It is possible to suggest that reaction to the New Right's brand of nationalism and centralism set in place the foundations for the growth of nationalisms in Wales and even more so Scotland (see previous chapter).

Further, the dynamics of New Labour, Blairism and 'third way' politics can only really be understood against the backdrop of the New Right. The term New Labour remains contested but it began to be used by Labour Party modernizers after Blair had been elected as leader in 1994 to define the direction in which they sought to take the party. Blair and his senior colleagues have used the term consistently ever since (Heath et al., 2001). We shall discuss the politics of New Labour much more fully in later chapters. One immediate question, however, is how far New Labour policies have broken with the traditional themes of social democracy. On this theme Novak (1998) has gone so far as to claim that New Labour's recent electoral success was really a victory for Margaret Thatcher's ideas. How far this claim can be sustained will provide some of the subject matter for the remainder of this book.

Conclusions

Since the early 1980s, the political and economic doctrine of the New Right has re-established itself in a more assertive form, called neoliberalism. Indeed, neoliberalism, driven by the USA, has established itself as the dominant political discourse and form of economic organization across much of the globe. It has been reinforced by the fall of the Soviet bloc, the US- and UK-led military coalition during the Gulf War and the intervention in Kosovo in 1999. Unrestrained neoliberalism has also provided the context for the dramatic liberalization of the economy and its enforcement by multinational corporations, which determine the structure of world politics following neoliberal principles. Globalization promotes and legitimates neoliberal ideology. Part of this process of globalization involves the fragmentation of national and local interests. The thrust of neoliberalism and the resulting claim that all areas of social and political life should be subordinate to the interests of the free market and guided by the multinationals has met with increasing resistance. We shall deal with this in more detail in Chapters 6 and 7.

First, however, we will consider another highly politicized area, that of social welfare provision. Here too we find complex debates concerning the role of the state. The contemporary structure of welfare provision is also intertwined with globalization and the strength of neoliberal ideology, promoting as it does the superiority of the private provision of services over the public. The spread of contemporary neoliberal values through globalization emphasizes the individual above the social and sets the context within which debates about welfare are structured. Globalization structures responses to social problems and the development of distinct welfare policies, emphasizing the role of the market and the limitation of public spending. As such, it is only the latest in a series of ideologically determined political influences on social welfare and policy. Let us begin, therefore, by considering the structuring and restructuring of welfare provision in the United Kingdom.

DISCUSSION QUESTIONS

- Critically evaluate the views of the New Right in politics.
- Outline and account for the long-term effects of Thatcherism on British politics and society?
- Did the emergence of New Labour mark a break or continuity with the main tenets of Thatcherism?

4

The Politics of Welfare and the Welfare State

Key concepts and issues	Key theorists and writers
• Development of the welfare state • Ideologies of welfare • Reconstructing contemporary welfare • Stakeholding, citizenship and communitarianism	• John Clarke • Amitai Etzioni • Vic George and Paul Wilding • Will Hutton • Charles Murray

> The postwar welfare state comprises a configuration of powers, controls, opportunities, rights, inclusions, exclusions and memberships. Its foundation held out the promise of abolishing the iniquitous, dispassionate and grossly impoverishing operations of an unfettered market capitalism by democratising and humanising the social conditions under which national prosperity was organised and its growth directed. Yet the promise had a hollow ring that echoed down the decades since its declaration. Only some inequalities and impoverishments were attacked by Beveridge's proposals and subsequent British welfare policy. (O'Brien and Penna, 1998: 184)

This chapter follows directly from what has gone before, but has a precise focus in considering the politics of welfare and welfare policies. Underlying this is an attempt to highlight the impact of some of the recent political changes outlined in previous chapters on the restructuring of the welfare state. It is not an attempt to provide a pocket history of the welfare state, or trace detailed social policy. Rather, it seeks primarily to examine the opposing definitions and theoretical interpretations of welfare and how these are made manifest in differing political visions of the role of the state in welfare provision.

That said, the chapter seeks to locate such discussions in the 'realities' of contemporary welfare provision. As we have already begun to see, the period since 1979 has seen a radical shift not just in policy, but also in rapidly changed attitudes towards the state's role as a central provider of welfare services. Indeed, following recent economic, social and political changes, many would now question whether it is, in any meaningful way, possible to talk of a welfare state in the United Kingdom today. Certainly, welfare provision has been and is likely to remain a pivotal item on the political agenda. As Clarke and Cochrane put it:

> The welfare state – or more accurately, the state's role in providing welfare – has been one of the central political issues through the 1980s and 1990s. It has featured in the legislative programmes of successive Conservative governments under the leadership of Margaret Thatcher and John Major, through which all the major institutional arrangements for social welfare have been reconstructed.

Further, they say:

> Welfare has also been a consistent thread of political debate and conflict – with arguments raging about its cost, its social consequences, the best way to organise its provision, its implications for the 'economic health' of Britain, the balance between public and private and so on. (Clarke and Cochrane, 1994: 5)

Foundations of the welfare state

But what exactly is it that has been so much altered? The easiest starting point to understand the foundation of the British welfare state is the 1942 Beveridge Report. This is commonly regarded as the 'blueprint' for the modern welfare state. In broad terms, at this time, the United Kingdom faced social problems which were common to all Western nations in the aftermath of the Second World War. Practically, this involved a controlled economic reconstruction. There were other important considerations, however, not least of which was the need for the state to control the populist radical politics that was emerging. The major ideological problem facing the British capitalist state was how to develop a free market economy with minimum interference, and to ensure as high a degree as possible of social harmony.

A further consideration, and one that should not be understated, was the role played by the United Kingdom in the emerging 'new world order'. David Coates (1995), for example, argues that the postwar world was structured by the dominance of the USA over the 'West' and its division from the 'East'. A weak British economy was dominated by the fiscal and military power of the USA. America began to establish a hegemonic position, within which the British government had to choose between supporting a foreign policy that was either pro-Soviet or pro-USA.

It was against this backdrop that the foundations of the modern welfare state in the United Kingdom were laid, and within which its initial development took place. Overtly it manifested itself in the Labour victory at the 1945 general election and the attempt to implement a 'national revival' based on the ideas of John Maynard Keynes and William Beveridge. The activation of a commitment to social justice and egalitarianism saw the promotion of welfare, which was made overt in a whole series of legislation implemented between 1944 and 1948.

This resulted in a much-expanded role for the state in areas such as health, education, housing and social security. Underpinning this, was Beveridge's commitment to overcome what were termed the 'five giants of social evil': want, disease, ignorance, squalor and idleness. Pragmatically, this resulted in the development and expansion of several different 'welfare departments', and tiers of government by which it could be managed.

The development of state welfare

It was these economic and political parameters that directed the development of the British state and the political consensus which emerged over the welfare state. The core economic foundation for this were the belief in, and a commitment to, the notion that a managed economy could deliver near full employment. Importantly, however, despite a commitment to the principle of universal provision, the state was never seen as the only agency supplying welfare services. Underlying the welfare state was the understanding of continuing provision of welfare by the family and by the private sector. As Clarke and Langan explain:

> In addition to its direct role in the provision of health care and education, the state was required to support the institutions of the market and the family, filling gaps where the market and family failed, but with no intent to replace them as the main source of support to individuals. In their different ways the programmes of public housing, income maintenance, services to neglected children and so on, assumed the needs would be met primarily through (male) waged work and the services which the wage can buy, and through services provided within the family by wives/mothers. Even in the income maintenance programmes, the predominant mode of providing for benefits was to be social insurance, which presumed a pattern of sustained employment in order to accrue a contribution record. (Clarke and Langan, 1993: 23)

Even if we take this on board, in other central areas such as education and health, the state was certainly seen as the key provider.

Expansion of state welfare

The 30 years following the end of the Second World War saw the provision of state welfare expand in a coherent and structured manner. The state took a pole position and began to expand in central areas of welfare provision, particularly health and education. However, even in these areas there were always alternatives offered by the private sector – private health provision, private provision of care, and private health insurance schemes remained intact. That said, between 1950 and 1975, the percentage of the GNP allocated to public expenditure rose steadily (Clark and Langan 1993: 32–4).

Clearly, the structure of the welfare state was determined by ideological direction and by decisions regarding its cost. The demands made on the welfare state by those 'in need' also, in part, moulded its shape. There are several important factors here: the increasing demands from an ageing population, the 'rediscovery of poverty' and the steady rise in state benefits paid by the state between 1950 and the mid-1970s. Alongside this has to be set the increasing organization and articulation of those in need. Hence, the 1960s onwards saw the development of a 'welfare rights movement', including professional bodies, charitable bodies and pressure groups of those expressing need.

For some, the period after 1945 and up to 1979 marked the zenith in British politics. Conservative, Liberal and Labour parties all accepted common tenets surrounding the Beveridgeian 'welfare state' and the Keynesian 'managed economy' as the basic building blocks of a 'modern' society. Government and its social services, accountable to this consensus, were therefore the natural engines of progress. Although economic crisis, political accidents and sheer ineptitude would often compel governments temporarily to abandon these aims, in the long term they would seek to return to these core values and programmes of increased industrial investment, low unemployment, increased equality of opportunity, and some notion of redistribution.

The result was not a monolithic politic. There were, for example, strongly felt differences regarding the implementation of nationalization, comprehensive schooling, pensions, the precise charges made for welfare services and the like. Nonetheless, as we have seen in Chapter 2 the degree of party political consensus surrounding the legitimate role for the state in providing welfare was remarkable.

Contesting the welfare state

As previous chapters have also highlighted, these guiding principles remained relatively undiminished until the mid-1970s. However, by that time, it had become increasingly apparent that the very fundamentals of welfare provision were being questioned (see Chapter 2). Any consensus that existed on the nature of the existing welfare state and its continuing development along agreed lines was beginning to be challenged from a variety of political perspectives and ideological positions.

This contestation came from a variety of sources, some of which have been reviewed in Chapter 1. Throughout its existence, many socialists have pointed to the failure of welfare to redistribute societies goods effectively. They also highlighted the continued level of economic and material inequality that has existed since the end of the Second World War. It is important to remember that in the 1970s the political Left was highly critical of the state's provision of welfare. This analysis suggested that welfareism was largely 'functional' to capitalism. Collective social consumption benefited capital through ensuring a healthy, reasonably well-educated and largely deferential workforce. Throughout the 1970s, Marxists continued to stress the welfare state as a tool for reproducing and preserving capitalism, rather than as a mechanism for social change.

Further, many feminists highlighted the gendered nature of the provision of welfare and its continued, but clandestine, reliance on women in the role of informal 'carers'. Others pointed out that sections of the welfare state, especially public sector services, drew heavily on black people, whose position in the labour market meant that their wages remained 'cheap' compared to the private sector. In this sense both female and ethnic labour subsidized the cost of welfare provision in the United Kingdom.

The late 1970s, however, saw the emergence of a more resonant challenge, whose origins lay in a re-thinking and re-articulation by the political Right. The logic of much of the analysis of the Left at the time was that the welfare state would endure in a more or less consistent and uncontested way. No matter how far Right the administration moved, the consensus around welfare would remain undiminished. However, the re-expression of the old liberal values, with the work of Hayek at the vanguard, and its political manifestation as Thatcherism, essentially refuted this.

As the needs of capitalism changed, the New Right found itself in a position to challenge the parameters of existing social democracy. Among much else, it sought to contest the assumptions of the recent past, articulating the failure of Keynesian demand management to sustain economic growth or to control inflation or sustain mass employment rates. Essentially those on the New Right disputed the need for established welfare services, and the provision of welfare directly by the state.

Many suggested that postwar prosperity had seen off Beveridge's giants. They condemned and dismissed policy-makers and academics for inflating notions of need (Dennis, 1997). They also damned politicians for acceding to populist pressures to increase welfare benefits. Above all, they saw this as a disincentive to competitive participation in the labour market. In place of a broad collective approach to welfare, the New Right stressed self-reliance, and the inability of the state to provide effectively for its individual citizens through comprehensive welfare. George and Wilding summarize the broad approach of the New Right to the welfare state as follows:

> The New Right believe, quite simply, that creating this kind of purposeful collective enterprise is impossible. The argument has three related parts – firstly, to seek to create a comprehensive welfare state ignores the nature of spontaneous order; secondly, it assumes that such rational planning is possible and finally it assumes the possibility of a common purpose in society. (George and Wilding, 1994: 21)

At the heart of the New Right critique of welfare politics, according to George and Wilding, is the belief in a spontaneous order, drawing deeply on traditional Conservative thought. Here, we encounter the notion that social institutions and social order arise out of human action, rather than human design. Not only that, but also this natural emancipation is far superior to any possible human construct. As long-term and mass unemployment became a reality and linked to wider social problems of family break-down and crime, the New Right critique expanded to include others (see Dennis, 1992; Murray, 1990, 1994a). They became defined as that grouping dependent on welfare benefits, the so-called 'underclass'. They were seen as the result of a long-term dependency culture, fostered by over generous levels of welfare provision (see Chapter 6).

Reconstructing welfare

There are two crucial aspects of the impact and legacy of the New Right on the British welfare state. First, there is the ideological debate surrounding the politics of welfare. Secondly, there is the actual realization and manifestation of this ideology in policy. There is, of course, no complete or neat fit between the two. The ideology of the New Right and neoconservatives is extremely complex, as Chapter 3 has shown.

Any ideas about welfare are often mediated by others arguments, for example, in competing notions of what constitutes a normative family or through issues of traditional morality. Throughout the 1980s there was, therefore, no simple dynamic such as 'rolling back the state', which directed Conservative Party policy and the major changes implemented by Conservative administrations. Rather, this period has to be seen as being directed by a much more manifold and fluid process.

The initial New Right criticisms of welfare focused on its excessive cost. First, its essential claim was that rising demands through increased benefits and spiralling services brought about by demographic changes was making the state provision of welfare economically unenviable. Such criticisms remained central throughout much of the 1980s and 1990s.

Secondly, the New Right argued that the welfare state was inefficient and hopelessly flawed in comparison with the market as a mechanism for providing welfare. The state is characterized as an unwieldy bureaucracy, whereas the market is seen as flexible and responsive to individual needs. In response to the state monopoly of welfare provision, the New Right sought to introduce 'the market' based on competition between different providers of welfare. This, it was claimed, would be more 'customer-centred' and based on choice. In the words of Marsland (1994: 14), the welfare state is 'outmoded, ineffective and destructive'.

Thirdly, the New Right expressed grave concern regarding the culture of welfare. It consistently argued that the British welfare state produced undesirable social consequences, particularly in the creation of a dependency culture undermining the work ethic and providing a disincentive for people to become involved in the labour market. As Loney argues:

> Benefit levels have been attacked for being too generous and destroying work incentives. Poverty researchers are denounced for exaggerating the numbers of those in poverty and deflecting attention away from the needs of the 'real' poor . . . poverty is seen as the creation of the naive if well meaning reformer, who through a plethora of income support programmes and an army of social workers destroys the incentive for self-sufficiency and creates a multitude of welfare recipients reared on a diet of dependency. (Loney, 1987: 10)

People, rather than taking responsibility for their own affairs, have looked to the state to provide for their needs. A recent example of this attitude can be seen in the hostility expressed towards 'single mothers'. Fundamentally, those on the right of the Conservative Party have consistently claimed that the existing level of state benefit encourages lone parenthood by protecting women from the consequences of their behaviour. According to George and Wilding (1976), the New Right (anti-collectivists) sought to implement several underlying values to address this. In place of the consensus they put stress on:

- liberty of the individual, especially in relation to economic activity;
- voluntary rather than state action in the provision of welfare; and
- inequality, in that, unequal rewards were seen as necessary to reward success and provide for wealth creation.

The New Right offered general ideological criticisms of the welfare state. Its major critique was that the welfare state was inefficient, ineffective and simply cost too much. Hence, a fundamental target has been the circumscription of spending. This has manifested itself at several levels – in tight annual budgets and reduced targets for public spending. More frequent reviews of public spending also showed a strong commitment to contain the cost of welfare provision. The reconstruction of welfare in the 1980s and 1990s revolved around cost containment, the changing mixed economy of welfare and the creation of 'quasi-markets', and the growing notion of a 'tough' welfare state. All of these drew directly on the parameters set in place by the Thatcher administration.

Wilding (1992) seeks to identify and categorize the legacy of Thatcher further. This includes the powerful ideological and pragmatic challenge it offered to collectivism, the promotion of markets and private provision, and the 'cuts' in public provision. It also involved an emphasis on effective and efficient forms of 'new managerialism'. Thatcher's legacy also included greater social divisions throughout the United Kingdom, the discrediting and downgrading of local government and the introduction of a mixed economy of welfare provision. Further, the endowment resulted in a redefinition of citizens' rights and the discrediting of the social-democratic concept of universal citizenship. Moreover, the emphasis on the regulatory state had a direct impact on the Labour Party, which was increasingly forced to adopt Thatcherite policies.

So while, perhaps some reports of the death of Britain's welfare state have been exaggerated, the broad parameters and overall goals of the system have changed dramatically since its formation. New Labour has overtly set about the task of 'modernizing' welfare provision. Part of this appears to draw directly on the agenda and experiences of the USA, and the introduction of terms such as 'welfare to work'. Many are increasingly suspicious of what they see as a continuation of a long, slow retreat from the central components of the welfare state as it was once envisaged through Beveridge.

Contemporary ideologies of welfare

While much of the ideological debate regarding welfare has been dominated by argument over the extent to which New Right and neoliberal values have remained dominant, there are, of course, counter-perspectives. George and Wilding (1994) have updated their previous model to outline six major ideological schools of thought regarding the welfare state: the New Right, the middle way, democratic socialism, Marxism, feminism and greenism. Many of these reflect the material on the nature of the state that we encountered in Chapter 1. It is useful briefly to outline those perspectives other than those of the New Right:

- **The middle way**: the core belief of this grouping is in a 'controlled' free market as the best way to organize the economy. In other words, capitalism needs to be managed. Examples of believers and practitioners of the middle way would have been Macmillan and Butler, and Beveridge and Keynes.
- **Democratic socialism**: here the welfare state is seen as a staging-post in the transition from *laissez-faire* capitalism to socialism. This transformation is to be a gradual one through the democratic process and parliament. Hence, primacy is given to the development of progressive social policy as the mechanism for bringing about a more just society.
- **Marxism**: for most Marxists the welfare state 'distorts' the real functions of state welfare, presenting as it does the 'caring face' of capitalism. The welfare state is neither wholly malevolent nor wholly benevolent, but a form of capitalism. However, in any capitalist society, conflict and exploitation are inevitable. The welfare state is a mechanism for incorporating the demands of the working class. Hence many Marxists prefer to use the term 'welfare capitalism'.
- **Feminism**: George and Wilding claim that there are four essential starting points for this perspective. First, the activities of the British welfare state have focused on women. Secondly, if this is to be understood, a form of analysis must be used that focuses on women in essentially male drawn parameters. Thirdly, the focus must make the analysis of women central.

Fourthly, and underpinning the whole of feminist analysis, is the belief that women's position must be understood as systematic subordination with deep structural roots.

- **Greenism:** as a distinct ideology, Greenism is a recent product and is reflected in two main factions – 'weak' and 'strong' Greens. Weak Greens largely accept the structure of contemporary society, but emphasize that economic growth and consumption must be 'environmentally friendly'. Strong Greens, however, see little difference between capitalism and socialism, as both are committed to industrialism. There have been attempts to combine Green ideology with feminist, social-democratic and Marxist perspectives, all of which see different root causes for the emphasis on industrialism. Because of the nature of Greenism, there is no coherent perspective on welfare. There are, however, criticisms of social policy which cannot accommodate general principles of egalitarianism, community and individual self-reliance, public participation and 'respect' for the environment.

Other perspectives are emerging, such as the vision of the social-democratic welfare state set out in the proposals outlined by the Labour Party's 'Commission on Social Justice' (1994). While it has been called a 'Beveridge Plan for the next century', in essence it demonstrates a coming together of the 'middle way' and 'democratic-socialist' perspectives. Most recently, this has been referred to as the third way in politics. We shall consider this further in Chapter 7.

In the report, three main rival strategies are outlined. First, the 'investors', who combine an ethical commitment to equality of opportunity, a vision of the 'good society', and an understanding of how contemporary capitalism works, and how it can be changed. They claim to be the heirs of the reforming tradition, but to have learnt lessons from the 'social market', as in Scandinavia, 'active states', such as Japan, and the 'entrepreneurial capitalism' of the United States.

Secondly, the 'deregulators', who are the 'neoliberal free-marketeers of the New Right'. It is this grouping that has dominated thinking on politics and welfare in Britain and the USA for the past two decades. Their 'vision', it is claimed, is one in which entrepreneurs are unencumbered by state intervention, state regulations, employment laws or social responsibilities. The motor of 'competitiveness' and the drive towards production costs that are ever cheaper will drive the economy.

Finally we encounter the 'levellers', which the report characterizes as being mainly concerned with the distribution of wealth, independent of the economy. The levellers share many of the basic goals of the investors, but differ on the proper tactics involved in achieving these. The levellers' strategy is for social justice based on redistribution and an advanced benefit system, rather than a policy of increased opportunities.

In the report, primacy is given to the investors; hence it outlines six fundamental principles for the United Kingdom's economic development, which follows this perspective. These are that:

- Markets should be the servant and not the master of the public interest.
- Innovation wins markets; 'value added' creates wealth.
- Labour is the key resource; long-term unemployment is a costly waste.
- The key to a good standard of living is to be found in high real wages and high employment; high productivity and high mobility should go together.
- The economy is not a self-regulating system; economic policy has social effects, and social inequality rapidly produces high economic costs.
- Under-investment, not under consumption, is our central problem; investment in skills, research, childcare and community development is the precondition for future property. (The Observer, 23 October 1994)

These six fundamental economic principles are to be matched by six principles of welfare strategy, namely:

- Freedom from poverty is the basis of social justice and the quickest route out of poverty is a good job at a fair wage.
- We must help the economy grow as well as distribute wealth more fairly; central to good social policy is an effective economic policy.
- Insecurity comes from risk, security from the ability to manage change; in the new welfare state services are as central as cash to helping people negotiate social and economic change.
- Strong families are vital social institutions. The unpaid work of parents and other carers must be supported, as much by the workplace as by the welfare state.
- Social policy exists to promote autonomy and choice for individuals and families.
- The modern welfare state must be tailored to the changing shape of people's lives. (*The Observer*, 23 October 1994)

The patriarchal welfare state

Just how far the modern welfare state is able or willing to change shape is, however, a matter of no little debate. The welfare state that has developed in the United Kingdom is both capitalist and patriarchal in character, intertwined and mutually reinforcing (Hay, 1996: 12–14). In particular, the welfare state, as it has realized, rests fully on the construction of a distinct public/private divide.

The archetypal contributor to the welfare state was perceived as the adult male worker (Harris, 1977) and the unpaid caring role taken on by women (Ginsburg, 1992). Indeed, as Pateman (1989) suggests, 'the importance of women in the welfare state and the importance of the welfare state for women' is disproportionate. She demonstrates how welfare agencies are a major source of paid employment for women, but there remains a rigid segregation of tasks and salaries along gender lines. Further, women are largely excluded from executive and policy-making roles within the welfare state.

One of the foundations of the welfare state was that the interests of the male worker were synonymous with the interests of society. Certainly, at least up until the beginning of the 1970s, the welfare state directly ratified the dominant sexual division of labour in society, excluding women from the world of work and confining them to the domestic sphere. Further, the whole of social policy rested on the notion of the married male breadwinner earning a family wage sufficient to meet the needs of other family members. Central to this construction was the idea of a wife working unpaid at home, caring full time for children and other family members.

Throughout the 1980s and 1990s the political debate regarding access and entitlement to welfare provision intensified. The results are particularly pertinent to some sections of the community, for example, the long-term unemployed, migrant groups and more recently asylum seekers. One other key group is single mothers, who are almost unique among groups blamed for social degeneracy by being scapegoats as both its cause and effect.

A new consensus of welfare?

We have already encountered the notion of post-Fordism in Chapter 2. Some writers have sought to set the significant changes in welfare provision within the context of the shift from Fordism to post-Fordism (Burrows and Loader, 1994). The discussions regarding the nature of Fordism and post-Fordism and the consequences for the nature of welfare provision are complex, as is the controversy regarding the nature of welfare 'restructuring' (see Clarke, 1993; Cochrane, 1992; Jessop, 1990, 1992; Stoker, 1991). At its broadest level, however, Fordism represents a set of social relations based on mass production, mass consumption and mass public provision of welfare. Post-Fordism, however, can best be understood in terms of flexible production, segmented consumption patterns and a restructured welfare state.

The debate over the future welfare state has therefore to be placed in the context of the wider discussions regarding the direction of politics in the United Kingdom. Take, for example, the following extract from a keynote speech made by Tony Blair, in Singapore, where he outlined a future vision for the United Kingdom. This included widespread reforms of the welfare state, highlighted as follows:

> Our Welfare State . . . is one of our proudest creations. But it suffers today from two important weaknesses: it does not alleviate poverty effectively; and it does not properly assist the growth of independence, the move from benefit to work. Too many people go on to benefit to stay there. The result is that it neither meets sufficiently its founding principle; nor is it cost effective. . . . [T]he system will only flourish in its aims of promoting security and opportunity across the life-cycle if it holds the commitment of the whole population, rich and poor. This requires that everyone has a stake.
>
> The alternative is a residual system just for the poor. After the Second World War, the route to this sort of commitment was seen simply as universal

cash benefits, most obviously child benefit and pensions. But today's demands and changed lifestyles require a more active conception of welfare based on services as well as cash, childcare as well as child benefit, training as well as unemployment benefit. (*The Guardian*, 12 January 1996)

The controversy concerning the future of the welfare state continues to intensify. One of central issues for Hutton (1995a, 1997, 1999) surrounds what he calls the democratization of welfare. He argues that at the heart of the welfare state must lie a conception of a just society, involving the guarantee of a reasonable level of income for the disadvantaged and the expression of belonging and social citizenship. To achieve this there is the political require-ment that those in the top income brackets must accept the notion of pro-gressive taxation. Hence, the system must ensure that the middle classes, which are disproportionately heavy contributors, get enough out of the system. This return is both direct, in terms of provision, and indirect, in terms of social cohesion.

This requires well-designed and high-quality welfare services. The acceptance of such a settlement also assumes, however, a broader public morality, which insists that universal participation is the only moral basis upon which the welfare system and society as a whole can be constructed. But it was this very ethic that was erroded by the New Right requirement that the welfare system conform not to notions of citizenship and democracy, but to the dictates of the market. People were urged to opt out of the state benefit system and into privatized provision. Further, the tax system was restructured to help achieve such goals. Hence, for example, the introduction of charitable status for private schools and tax relief for private pensions and health insurance premiums.

As Chapter 2 has indicated, welfare provision was reorganized to mimic markets and the welfare system reshaped to reinforce a flexible labour market. The resulting social inequality was seen as the price of wealth creation. For Hutton, instead of the shift towards privatization, the welfare state needs more democracy and sensitivity to the real needs of people.

What is required is that the welfare system is brought back in line with democratic principles. It should provide boundaries to the operation of mar-kets, underwrite social cohesion and help reproduce the values that sustain co-operation. The postwar welfare state, based on political consensus, was an attempt to strike a balance between welfare, social justice and efficiency. The structures of welfare were never designed to deal with the scale of inequality thrown up by the free market and the abandoning of full employment as a central policy aim of the state.

The end of the welfare state?

So what role is stakeholderism to play in the future provision of welfare? In the mid-1990s the challenge of 'thinking the unthinkable' about restructuring welfare was laid at the feet of Frank Field, Labour MP and then Chair of the Social Security Select Committee. In *Stakeholder Welfare* (1996) he puts forward a case for a radical overhaul of the system to harness self-interest by extending the scope of contributory benefits. Field calls his proposals 'stakeholder welfare' because individuals will own the welfare capital created by their contributions and those of their employers.

The end of the welfare state, as most people know it, seemed much closer on Tuesday 7 May 1996, when both the Conservative and Labour parties released statements outlining their future strategies for state welfare provision. Both offered a vision of the welfare state distant from that which had been known for 50 years. Certainly, it is difficult to see how the post-1945 notion of provision 'from the cradle to the grave' can be set within the parameters of either of the major political parties' plans or ideological stances. Both parties now emphasize the reduction of the state's role as a provider of welfare and give increasing primacy to private insurance. Stephen Dorrell, the then Conservative Health Secretary, put it clearly when he said, the 'principal responsibility for making [that] provision must rest with the individual citizen' (*The Guardian*, 8 May 1996).

New Labour has sought to outline what it sees as a 'radical' definition of the welfare state, including a rejection of the previously held central idea of the state acting as the sole provider. This was made explicit by the then Shadow Social Security Secretary, Chris Smith, when he offered broad agreement to the Conservative agenda outlined above:

> Some argue that it is only the state that can possibly deliver the elements of proper social security. I disagree. Of course there are some things that only the state can do. But the principle must surely be that the state acts as the guarantor of all provision, the regulator of all provision – and the administrator of some. (*The Guardian*, 8 May 1996)

Following the election of New Labour in 1997 such views were given a strong fiscal backing with the commitment that the administration would keep public expenditure well in check. This contrasts directly with previous Labour governments of the 1960s and 1970s, which expanded public expenditure. Indeed, as can be seen from the Table 4.1, New Labour actually reduced public expenditure as a percentage of GDP.

Conservative Party efforts to reform the welfare state showed a turning point in the late 1980s. Up to then, and despite the rhetoric, it is possible to understand most Conservative changes to the welfare state as mere tinkering, largely forced upon them by the need to contain costs and meet self-imposed budgetary constraints. Then came a series of deeply ideologically-driven changes. The Education Reform Act introduced the national curriculum, open school enrolment and provision for schools to opt out of local authority control. State schools would still be free to their users, but the reforms would begin to change the system from one that allocated resources according to the plans of central and (especially) local authorities into one

TABLE 4.1   PUBLIC EXPENDITURE AS A PERCENTAGE OF GROSS DOMESTIC
PRODUCT, 1964–97

Years	Government	Public Expenditure as % of GDP
1964–1970	Labour	39.9
1970–1974	Conservative	41.4
1974–1979	Labour	45.4
1979–1990	Conservative	43.0
1990–1997	Conservative	41.4
1997–	Labour	39.4

Source: *The Guardian*, 25 August 1999

that worked more like an open market, a 'quasi-market', for educational
services. The idea was simple enough: schools (and later higher education
institutions) would compete with each other, and thus, through this rivalry,
standards would rise.

In 1988, the Conservative government also set up a review into the future
of the National Health Service (NHS). This yielded a shake-up that was even
more radical than the one that had just begun in education. Again, the
principle of free provision was not questioned. Instead, another 'internal
market' was to be established. Hospitals could opt out of health authority
control, and many general-practitioner practices would be given their own
budgets to buy services from hospitals or health authorities as they chose.
Again, competition was intended to raise standards, by exposing inefficiency,
weighing the costs of treatment more explicitly and causing resources to be
better employed.

The quasi-market idea was also extended to other areas. In public
housing, for instance, landlords were allowed to bid for control of local
authority housing, with rents shifted closer to market levels and housing
benefits raised to reflect that. The government's policy on 'community care'
also intended that public providers would play a smaller role and private
providers a bigger one, all at taxpayers' expense.

Taken together, these different initiatives suggested the beginning of a
deep transformation of the welfare state. Henceforth, it was argued that even
though public services could continue to be paid for out of general taxation,
they might be almost entirely provided by a variety of competing private
suppliers. According to the ideal type quasi-market model, most, if not all,
schools, hospitals, providers of 'social housing', and so on would one day be
private, as opposed to state-owned and state-run institutions. The government's role would be confined to injecting money, regulating, promoting
competition and monitoring the results. Hence, the current trends are seen as
a mere attempt to reverse changes made under the Conservative administration. According to Michael Heseltine:

We battled to secure individual rights and freedom in the workplace; Labour want to re-establish power for their stakeholders – the Trade Unions. We broke up the old monolithic nationalised industries, privatised them and enabled employees and the general public to purchase their shares in the new companies. Labour resents this attack on the state, their preferred stakeholder. (Conservative Party, *Press Release*, 12 January 1996)

A future for welfare?

There are two crucial questions to ask about the future of the welfare state. The first is how big should the welfare state be? The second is how should it be organized? In seeking to answer these questions about the future of the welfare state, much of the contemporary discourse revolves around another query – how much should it all cost and who should pay for it? Across the advanced capitalist world welfare spending has become a central issue as states cut their social wages in an attempt to make their countries more 'competitive' in the globalized economy.

Much of the New Labour government's plan continues to place responsibility for the endurance of poverty on the poor themselves. Such new 'political realism' means a welfare system in danger of detaching the bottom third, the underclass, from the rest of the working class. If the political logic of New Labour ideology is realized, state provision will become almost a residual category, carrying huge stigma of something reserved only for life's failures. Labour will have succeeded only in fracturing its own base, in making it harder to win and retain majority support. Far from helping people 'out of dependency', the plans to cut child benefit and narrow the remit of state responsibility (notably for pensions) will create the sort of 'no-go areas', the ghettos of hopelessness and alienation, commonplace in many cities in the USA.

In the volatile debate about the future of welfare, it is easy to forget that the modern welfare state emerged within the particular economic and social context of full male employment, family stability and established patriarchal relationships. Beveridge's 'cradle to grave' welfare state was based on full-time, uninterrupted male employment, 'dependent' wife and a relatively short period of retirement, all of which have been transformed. Alongside economic and work changes, there are changes in family patterns, and an emphasis on greater individualization and individual choice. All of these bring new expectations of a welfare state shaped by notions of homogeneity and uniformity.

The connection between economic and social policy has been increasingly recognized in British debates. The Commission on Social Justice (1994) and the 'Rowntree Report on Inequality' put it very much at the heart of their policies. Labour market flexibility, low pay and inequality are unlikely to disappear. The role of welfare has been redefined as needing to find a 'middle path'. In what was an important positioning speech for New Labour, Tony Blair, at the beginning of 1996, outlined part of his vision for a 'New Britain'. It involved:

The creation of an economy where we are investing and producing goods and services of quality needs the engagement of the whole country. It must become a matter of national purpose and national pride. We need to build a relationship of trust not just within a firm but within a society. By trust, I mean the recognition of a mutual purpose for which we work together and in which we all benefit. It is a Stakeholder Economy in which opportunity is available to all, advancement is through merit and from which no group or class is set apart or excluded. This is the economic justification of social cohesion, for a fair and strong society, a traditional commitment of left of centre politics but one with relevance today as it is applied anew to the modern world. (*The Guardian*, 7 January 1996)

We have already encountered New Labour's attempts to define a third way that supersedes both free market and statist approaches (see Blair, 2000; Finlayson, 1999; Garnett, 2001). We shall discuss this in even more detail in Chapter 7. Here, however it is important to point to a whole series of social policy initiatives, such as 'welfare to work' and the New Deal, that the New Labour administration has introduced. All are claimed to 'modernize' the welfare state, and to herald the onset of stakeholders in a 'social investment state' (Powell, 1999, 2000). This, it is argued by supporters of New Labour, marks the onset of something that is in tune with a changing social structure, a radically transformed workforce and a society that is increasingly culturally diverse.

Stakeholding and the new communitarianism

Tony Blair has also heralded the notion of 'stakeholding' in the distinct context of providing the economic justification for 'social cohesion'. A commitment to the stakeholding society it is claimed is one of the tools for the New Labour government to tackle long-term and structural unemployment, and the development of an underclass cut off from mainstream society (*The Guardian*, 8 January 1996).

Dovetailing with the above, the notion of 'communitarianism' has received increasing emphasis from a variety of political perspectives. Roger Scruton, one of Conservatism's leading contemporary thinkers, has, for example, increasingly talked about it in the context of the collapse of 'social feeling' in society, arguing:

No one now doubts the value of economic freedom or the spirit of enterprise; but the exclusive emphasis on these things looks like so much self-serving rhetoric on the part of those whose only interest is profit and whose concern for the community goes no further than the search for customers. (*The Observer*, 9 February 1997)

These ideas, which are becoming more important as a perceived basis for restructuring contemporary society, are identified with the 'new communitarians', and much of its dynamic came from Etzioni's *The Spirit of Community* (1995). As Toynbee and Walker (2001: 37) put it, this new communitarianism rests on a view that implies 'reimposing old lace-curtain social disciplines'. These communitarians, like many of those on the political right (see Chapter 4), take as their starting point an assumed golden age, (usually somewhere around the mid-1950s), when there was an identifiable respectable working class, disciplined by the culture of respectability and deference.

The 'dangerous' categories of the underclass, such as single parents, unmarried mothers, lesbians or working mothers, which have since emerged in the political arena were previously kept in check by 'everybody knowing their place'. Many communitarians seem to be about restoring that tradition of deference. The restructuring (or dismantling) of Britain's manufacturing base left many working-class neighbourhoods without sustaining economies, and fit only for the so-called underclass. The most dominant notion of the underclass has been that promoted by Murray (as discussed in Chapter 6).

While there are communitarians who are unsupportive of Murray's often overt contempt for the survival strategies of the poor, or the notion that the poor reproduce their own poverty, the approaches of many communitarians and underclass theorists nonetheless often merge in contemporary debate.

In pragmatic political responses supporters of both perspectives often focus on a society they regard as dangerous, unmanageable and unruly. Civilization as they know it is falling apart with a generation of disenfranchised youth threatening neighbourhoods. Many point to the rise in the numbers of single parents as the reason.

Many of these views are invoked by Dennis and Erdos (1992). In a tract written for the Institute for Economic Affairs, they focus on 'commonsense' explanations, suggesting that in days gone by fathers passed on to their sons a sense of responsibility for community and property. In the contemporary period, however, particularly following the increased political and ideological support for feminism and Marxism in the 1960s, such central values were lost. The resulting 'fatherless communities' produce the brutal, alienated, anti-social young working-class men of today.

Such views, of course, ignore connections between the social structure of such communities and the major economic restructuring of Western societies. The destruction of the United Kingdom manufacturing base since the mid-1970s demolished the core of thousands of traditional working-class communities. As a result, large factions of the working class were pauperized and marginalized as traditional working-class communities fragmented. The notion of 'golden age' of respectable fathering is also highly questionable. For many, even in the mid-1950s, fathers were visitors to their families.

At some level communitarianism also needs to be understood as an expression of a middle class disorientated by the rapid social, economic and political transformations of contemporary society. By seeking to accommodate such views fully there is little in the New Labour agenda to suggest anything that can be radical in its thinking about the provision of welfare. It is, after all, the middle classes that perceive themselves as having most to lose in any changes in the current levels of welfare provision.

New Labour, through its commitment to third way politics, has largely taken the concept of communitarianism wholesome and unquestioned from the experience of the USA, adopting Etzioni as a guru figure along the way. It promotes communitarianism as the way to return to a golden age, when there were supposedly universalistic moral values. It does so, however, largely by ignoring established class differences, economic differentials and most of the new social movements that provide the basis for many of the political conflicts and differences in the contemporary United Kingdom.

Some conclusions

The search for contemporary community ignores the experiences of many of those, such as the underclass, gays, women and ethnic minorities, who are excluded from much of mainstream politics and society in the United Kingdom. Indeed, at times it is difficult to identify much in the third way beyond that of a strong discourse endorsing realism and modernization. In welfare provision, New Labour has repackaged many of the previous administration's policies and offered an extremely positive response to wider dynamics of globalization.

Further, the philosophy of neoliberalism and the introduction of the concepts of markets, competition and the notion of the citizen as consumer have all remained central to the formulation of contemporary welfare policy. Within the United Kingdom, all of this seems to have remained uncontested by the evolution of New Labour and the ideology of the third way.

DISCUSSION QUESTIONS

- Why have questions surrounding the welfare state and the provision of welfare become such a central focus in contemporary UK politics?
- Has the traditional welfare state been 'dismantled' in the United Kingdom?
- Critically discuss the ways in which relationships between social welfare and the state have changed since the 1980s.
- What case can be made for the state as the major provider of welfare?

5

Northern Ireland, Political Violence and the Politics of Terrorism

Key concepts and issues	Key theorists and writers
• The conflict in Northern Ireland • Ideologies of the conflict • The politics of peace • Political violence and terrorism • Defining terrorism	• Noam Chomsky • John Darby • Walter Laqueur • Valerie Morgan • Rosemary Sales • Jon Tonge • John Whyte

The use of the term 'the Northern Ireland problem', with its implication that a solution lies around the corner for anyone ingenious enough to find it, is misleading. The most recent violence lasted for more than 25 years. The background conflict stretches back at least to the seventeenth century, and some believe the twelfth century; the very choice of date has a political connotation. Today the Northern Irish conflict is a tangle of inter-related questions. (Darby, 1997: 55)

By far the most contested expression of politics and of political identity within the United Kingdom still surrounds that of the six counties of Northern Ireland. During the past three decades, that which has somewhat euphemistically become known as the 'troubles' has seen the regular occurrence of widespread inter-community conflict, violence and bloodshed involving at least 35,000 shooting incidents and some 10,000 explosions. Between 1969 and 1997 the death toll from the conflict amounted to over 3,500 people, including members of paramilitary organizations, the security forces and, of course, civilians (McKittrick et al., 1999).

In the most recent period, however, the 'peace process' has brought about a vast reduction, although certainly not the disappearance, of overt violence and the emergence of the structures for a devolved power-sharing government in the form of the Northern Ireland Assembly. While such events have altered the public face of politics in Northern Ireland, it would be incorrect to suggest that Northern Ireland does not continue to be a deeply divided and conflictual society. It remains highly segregated, both socially and physically. Much political and social life is fettered by sectarian social relations underpinned by antagonistic national identities and the seemingly irreconcilable forces of Irish nationalism and Ulster unionism as central points of political identification and social organization.

So what are the major social and political cleavages in Northern Ireland? The answer may not be as straightforward as many would assume. The fundamental fracture is often claimed to be around religion. Certainly, this feature of Northern Irish society is dominant in populist accounts and remains a key focus for discord. Marriage and family, education, leisure pursuits, patterns of residence and obviously church life, indeed almost all the essential institutions of socialization, are mainly still divided along religious lines.

There is, however, much to suggest that this is an extremely superficial reading of the situation. What really divides those in Northern Ireland are incompatible political values and goals and disharmony around notions of political congruence and equality. This is especially true around core issues such as national and political identity, the partition of the island and the very legitimacy of the Northern Ireland state itself.

Despite many similarities in lifestyle, deep-rooted folk memories and structured patterns of political allegiance help shape distinct and often conflicting groups. The experiences of social and physical segregation remain most intense for working-class Protestants and Catholics. Here, in particular, sectarian consciousness has given rise to self-perpetuating communities, each with different historical reference points, 'readings' and understandings of, and beliefs about, the nature of Irish society.

In Northern Ireland, British unionists and Irish nationalists hold conflicting views on the origins of the conflict, its causes and solutions. History is often recycled to interpret contemporary events and to highlight continuities with the past. Events such as the 'plantation of Ireland', Cromwell's arrival in 1641, the Williamite victory in 1690 or the rebellion of 1798 (to name but a few) are often invoked when discussing contemporary political events.

Further, both Irish nationalists and Ulster unionists draw on these differing interpretations of history and visions of the future to justify and structure their contemporary positions regarding social and political events (see McBride, 2001; Walker, 1996, 2000).

Background to the conflict

So why has politics in Northern Ireland developed in a form so distinctive from the rest of Ireland and the remainder of the United Kingdom? There now exists an extensive literature on Northern Ireland and the origins and subsequent trajectory of the conflict (see Darby, 1997; Dunn, 1995; Tonge, 1998). Obviously, this material involves a wide range of theoretical argument and the recognition of a complex range of factors involved in the Northern Ireland conflict. As Dunn (1995: 7) points out, there is not 'a single Northern Ireland problem', but rather 'a set of interlocked and confused problems'.

So how might we begin to unpack the convoluted and intersecting arguments and representations of events to which Dunn refers? In most developed societies political structure and organization is reinforced by the transmission of a set of reasonably consensual values from generation to generation. For many of Northern Ireland, however, such political socialization is restricted almost exclusively to one's respective community. This reinforces and in turn is reinforced by self-perpetuating discourses, political beliefs and in the reproduction of a whole series of self-generating myths and norms. Traditions are passed on within tightly-knit geographical communities and the 'imagined communities' of Ulster unionism and Irish nationalism. These traditions reflect selective passages from historical events stretching back to at least the seventeenth century. Such partisan readings of history often mobilize and exacerbate the politics of the contemporary.

In the period between 1968 and the paramilitary ceasefires of the mid-1990s, conspicuous violence reinforced these trends and patterns, and has been reinforced by it. As a wide range of biographical accounts demonstrate, socialization into division often begins early (see McCann, 1986, 1993; Taylor, 1989). Indeed, as Connolly and Maginn (1999) demonstrate, it is reasonable to assume that children from about the age of three are able to develop an understanding of the categories of 'Protestant' and 'Catholic' and to apply negative characteristics to the Other.

Such emphasis on sectarian difference is not confined to individual prejudices and beliefs but is manifest in, and reproduced by, peer-group relations, sub-cultures and a whole range of broader social, political and economic structures. Moreover, the expression of sectarianism is rooted in their day-to-day experiences. One of the major ways in which this finds everyday experience is through overt expressions of identity and allegiance within the political arena.

Northern Ireland: a permanent conflict?

Many of the differences in the social, political and sectarian relationships of Ireland were institutionalized at partition. Indeed, one of the main considerations in determining the physical boundary of Northern Ireland was that it included those areas with a Protestant majority. Northern Ireland, however, also contained a substantial Catholic minority of approximately 33.5 per cent within its boundaries (Wichert, 1991: 27).

Thus, the very foundations of the Northern Ireland state were unstable. There were fears expressed from the foundation of the state, from within some sections of the Protestant community, that because of different birth rates and emigration patterns, Catholics might one day constitute a majority.

Equally importantly, the social construction of communal memories of loss, victory and the eternally treacherous and untrustworthy nature of the Other helped structure and maintains both 'Irish/Catholic/nationalist' and 'British/ Protestant/unionist' group identities.

Initially, the lack of commitment many Catholics felt towards Northern Ireland manifested itself in an avoidance of direct engagement with the state, because they feared participation would somehow bestow it legitimacy (Buckland, 1981). In response, the new institutions certainly did little to encourage full participation from the Catholic community and helped create what Burton (1978) calls the *laager* mentality of Ulster Protestants. Indeed, the border came to symbolize the real and supposed peculiarities of the two groups. The polarization of political allegiance along religious lines and unionist hegemony were reflected in the state's intransigence for at least the next 40 years. It also resulted in a near freezing of relationships between the two states in Ireland.

There seemed to be a partial turning point in Irish politics with the passing of Northern Ireland's Premiership from Lord Brookeborough to Terence O'Neill in 1963. This marked an attempt by sections of the unionist leadership to move away from an overtly discriminatory state and towards the notions of political and economic modernity finding expression in the rest of the United Kingdom. Importantly, this was accepted by large fractions of a growing Catholic middle class in Northern Ireland. O'Neill's limited modernization policies, however, caused major tensions within unionism, between those who supported reform and those who strenuously opposed any perceived conciliatory actions.

Against this background in 1964 Belfast experienced its worst riots and street confrontations for over three decades. These events were precipitated by the flying of an Irish Republic flag and brought to centre stage an obscure Protestant cleric, the Reverend Ian Paisley, who, along with his followers, reacted with hostility to a visit of the Prime Minister of the Irish Republic. During 1966 the first political murder for many years took place in Belfast and organized underground loyalist resistance manifested itself in a grouping calling itself the Ulster Volunteer Force (UVF) (see Boulton, 1973; Cusack and McDonald, 1997; P.J. Taylor, 2000).

By 1967 the modernization process provided the opening for the emergence of a new political pressure group, the Northern Ireland Civil Rights Association (NICRA). This increasingly articulated grievances concerning unfair housing allocation and an unjust system of voting rights at local government level. Even though the unionist administration conceded some ground by implementing only the most trifling of reforms, it precipitated a crisis, both within Northern Ireland and between the Northern Irish and British states.

The Northern Irish state reacted strongly, mobilizing the 'B specials', an exclusively Protestant reserve security force organized along paramilitary lines. By mid-1969 the liberal faction had lost its control of the Unionist Party and, following widespread street violence in Derry and Belfast, the Northern Irish Prime Minister called in the British Army to restore order in August.

As the crisis deepened the British Army became more and more centrally involved in 'policing' and the Irish Republican Army (IRA), which had been all but moribund since the mid-1950s, re-emerged in nationalist districts. As the organization developed, it eventually split in December 1969. This was precipitated when the IRA leadership voted to give at least token recognition to the parliaments in London, Belfast and Dublin. Following this, some members walked out of the meeting to form a breakaway grouping, which was to be called the Provisional IRA. The split was confirmed the following month when Sinn Féin held its *Ard Fheis* (annual meeting).

There were now two IRAs: the old Official IRA (the Officials), still dominated by a Marxist-inspired leadership; and the new Provisional IRA (the Provos), promoting a much more militaristic line. As the conflict became overt in the early 1970s, violence escalated on almost a daily basis. The Officials increasingly moved towards 'politics' as the main vehicle for change. The Provisionals, however, initiated a martial campaign, first killing a British soldier in February 1971 and launching a bombing campaign against 'civilian' targets. Loyalist paramilitaries responded, largely through an assassination campaign against equally 'civilian' Catholics.

One consequence was that the British Army's presence increased and ever greater numbers were seen patrolling the streets of Northern Ireland. This phase culminated in the introduction of internment in August 1971, when around 300 people were arrested in dawn raids and held without trial. As a tactic it was fatally flawed. The detentions were over reliant on extremely dated intelligence and resulted in the arrest of only a very few engaged in the contemporary conflict. As a result, rather than curbing the IRA, recruitment to the organization and support for its campaign of wider political violence intensified. There was widespread civil protest, including a rent and rates strike organized by the newly formed nationalist party, the Social Democratic and Labour Party (SDLP).

Five months later nationalist anger was further fuelled by the deaths of 14 people taking part in an anti-internment march in Londonderry. In what has become known as 'Bloody Sunday', paratroopers opened fire on the crowd, asserting that they had come under fire from snipers, a claim that has never been substantiated. The political response led to the winding up of the Stormont parliament and the introduction of direct rule from Westminster in March 1972. From that time, as Quinn (1993: 62) puts it, Unionism's 'lost hegemony has been paralleled by lost harmony'.

Meanwhile, political pressure on the streets was becoming intense. In the early 1970s the local vigilante associations, which had formed in many Protestant districts, began to amalgamate. The resulting Ulster Defence Association (UDA) quickly boasted up to 40,000 members (Flackes and Elliott, 1989: 272–7), many of whom could be, and at times were, mobilized on the streets of Northern Ireland. The deteriorating relationship between the British administration and many loyalists was characterized by illegal marches, industrial stoppages and the setting up of loyalist 'no-go' areas for security forces in response to those in existence in some nationalist districts.

In 1973 there was some glimmer of hope for a solution. A Northern Ireland Assembly was elected as a 'power-sharing' administration between the two communities. Crucially it included members of the mainly nationalist-supported SDLP on its executive body. The Assembly faced widespread resistance, both from sections of the republican movement and many unionists. The opposition of unionists came to a head in May 1974, when the Ulster Workers' Council (UWC), an *ad hoc* organization based largely in the shipyards and power stations, backed by the muscle of loyalist paramilitary groups, called for and organized a 'general strike'. It brought Northern Ireland to an almost complete standstill and forced the executive of the power-sharing Assembly to resign within 14 days.

The period that followed is best characterized by an almost total lack of political initiative and an unrelenting level of both republican and loyalist paramilitary violence (Amnesty International, 1994). In 1975, the report of the Constitutional Convention, set up with a majority of unionist members, demanded a return to the former government at Stormont. Elsewhere, the opposition of many to the violence was mobilized as the 'Peace People' came to prominence. The movement faded, however, unable to reconcile the conflicting visions of the best way forward that emanated from the different communities.

The political stalemate continued. Attempts to set up devolved institutions in 1977 and 1980 both failed, opposed at different times and for different reasons, first by the SDLP and later by the Ulster Unionist Party (UUP). Between 1982 and 1984 a process of 'rolling devolution' was introduced. This allowed for the return of power to local political parties as and when they could agree process, but it too collapsed, boycotted by the SDLP because it did not guarantee 'power sharing'. The next phase culminated with the Anglo-Irish Agreement signed between the British and Irish governments in November 1985. The signing of the agreement did not involve local politicians and was bitterly opposed by unionists, interpreted as it was within as yet another lost battle.

Throughout this time the conflict on the streets remained intense. Any possibility of resolution was made even more difficult by intense divisions throughout all levels of civil society. With the election of Margaret Thatcher in 1979 policies throughout the United Kingdom developed around a hardening rhetoric of 'law and order' (see also Chapter 3). As a result, even the prisons became grounds for political conflict. On the first day of March 1981, an IRA prisoner, Bobby Sands, began a hunger strike which ultimately resulted in death. It was the beginning of a strategy directly to challenge the 'criminalization' policy, which had removed 'prisoner-of-war status' from paramilitary inmates in Northern Ireland's prisons.

In all, ten republican prisoners died in the campaign, seven were members of the IRA and three belonged to the Irish National Liberation Army (INLA). The immediate reaction to the series of deaths was widespread and extended street violence. In broader political terms, however, the refusal of the Thatcher government to accede to the prisoners' demands led to increased support for Irish republicanism. Further, the republican position attracted extensive international media attention, won worldwide support and further strengthened the position of the IRA within its own community.

The Provisional IRA reacted militarily and almost gained a spectacular revenge when it bombed the Conservative Party conference at the Grand Hotel in Brighton in 1984. A timed device exploded in the early hours, killing a number of delegates, but Mrs Thatcher and her cabinet narrowly escaped. In 1991 the IRA again hit directly at the heart of government, firing three mortar bombs at 10 Downing Street while the Prime Minister, John Major, was discussing the Gulf War with cabinet colleagues. Again, ministers escaped injury, but only just.

Equally importantly, however, the republican movement successfully harnessed the subsequent protests, which brought on to the streets hundreds of thousands in support of the republican position. They reorganized and restructured politically. It was this that paved the way for the development of Sinn Féin as a more coherent and organized political movement.

This provided the base for the next stage in the conflict. Although the bombings and shootings continued, and the state responded militarily, both sides were coming to realize that they were locked in a military stalemate. Sections of the republican leadership increasingly believed that they could never force the British government out of Northern Ireland at gunpoint. There was a similar realization by fractions of the British establishment that it could never defeat the IRA. As a result, behind-the-scenes negotiations began to take place to persuade the IRA to declare a ceasefire and to let its political wing, Sinn Féin, come to the negotiating table.

The subsequent search for political settlement in Northern Ireland has revolved around the notion of integrating political representatives from the constitutional parties and both loyalist and republican paramilitaries into a political process (see Mallie and McKittrick, 2001; McGinty and Darby, 2002; Ruane and Todd, 1999; Wilford, 2001).

The politics of peace

The path of the resulting peace process has, however, often been convoluted and tortuously sluggish (see Elliott, 2002; Hennessey, 2000; McKittrick, 1999). When the peace process began is highly contested. Certainly, part of the initial impetus for the strategy came following the arrival of Peter Brooke as Secretary of State for Northern Ireland in July 1989. He utilized the three-stranded framework, developed by John Hume, to set up a new series of talks and to seek to develop relations between the two communities in Northern Ireland. Crucially, the strategy sought also to develop relations between the north and south and the governments in Dublin and London.

The process was temporarily abandoned in July 1991 when, following a meeting of Intergovernmental Conference between the United Kingdom and the Republic of Ireland, unionists made it clear that they were unwilling to continue. While Peter Brooke presented a new formula for talks in December 1991, it was his successor, Patrick Mayhew, who created some space for negotiation when the Intergovernmental Conference was suspended for three months. However, these talks later failed after unionists received a luke-warm reception in Dublin during the second strand of negotiations.

During the later stages of the Brooke and Mayhew initiative, Irish nationalists were pursuing an alternative strategy. The dialogue between John Hume (leader of the SDLP) and Gerry Adams (leader of Sinn Féin), which had started in 1988, was re-established in the early 1990s and was to provide the main stimulus for the 'Downing Street Declaration' of December 1993. Importantly, the Declaration stated for the first time that Britain had 'no selfish, strategic or economic interest in Northern Ireland'. The target audience was Sinn Féin, in a hope of bringing them to the negotiating table and forcing a ceasefire from the IRA. The statement, however, convulsed much of unionism.

Unionist fears were not eased in 1993 when the Downing Street Declaration, jointly announced by the Prime Minister John Major of the United Kingdom and the Irish *Taoiseach*, Albert Reynolds, formally introduced the possibility of Sinn Féin becoming involved in talks. The condition was an ending of violence for at least three months. In recognition of the unionist position the Irish government stated that any constitutional change in the status of Northern Ireland required the support of a majority within Northern Ireland. This set the parameters for much of the negotiation that followed.

A solution appeared tantalizingly close in 1994 when both republican and loyalist paramilitaries called 'ceasefires' in favour of all-party talks. Within 18 months, however, the IRA showed its frustration at a stagnating political process by bombing Canary Wharf in the heart of London's docklands.

A 'talks' process was eventually re-established in 1996. This culminated on Good Friday 1998, when, under the stewardship of the United Kingdom and Irish governments and the guidance of Senator George Mitchell from the USA, the Belfast Agreement was signed by all of the major political parties involved. It initiated a devolved administration in Northern Ireland and provided the framework for developing a pluralistic society in Northern Ireland, based on mutual recognition of opposing traditions.

However, although the Belfast (or Good Friday) Agreement clearly recognizes diversity of identities and traditions, it also affirms the division of the people of Northern Ireland into two mutually exclusive communities. Partly for this reason, the period since then has been fraught. Indeed, it is now extremely difficult to remember with any clarity the feelings of elation and political optimism that followed the signing of the Good Friday Agreement. Even then, there were indications that not all involved the settlement were assured. While in Northern Ireland support was forthcoming from both sides of the political divide and the bulk of Irish nationalists supported the deal, only a small majority of unionists gave backing to the process.

Soon after the referendum, however, optimism rapidly withered amid continuing conflicts involving Orange Order parades and especially circumstances surrounding the disputed annual Drumcree march. Even these concerns rapidly faded, however, in the light of the world's stare following the killing of 28 people by a bomb planted in Omagh by the 'Real IRA' on 15 August 1998.

Thus, when the new Northern Ireland Assembly eventually met, it was against a background of increasing political tension and conflict. Since then the peace process has stuttered and stalled and the institutions it set in place have been subject to a series of resignations by ministers, suspensions by the Secretary of State for Northern Ireland and challenges from its own members. Those elected to the Assembly have largely found themselves embroiled in such divisive issues as the future of policing, whether the Union Flags should be flown over public buildings and the future of paramilitary members released from prison as part of the settlement.

Despite some evidence that the two political blocs could operate on a day-to-day level (McAuley and Tonge, 2001), the broader political agreement finally ran aground on the issue of the decommissioning of paramilitary weapons in October 1998, where it has more or less remained ever since. The peace process has continued to stutter, move on, stall and move on again. While at a structural level the peace process provides a framework for developing a pluralistic society and institutions of political devolution, it also continues to reproduce many of the social and political differences fundamental to Northern Irish society.

Northern Irish society is still best understood in terms of ethno-political divisions that cut across the formation of a common national identity or other shared social identities such as those based around gender or social class. Class politics or a class-based political party have never developed in Northern Ireland along the lines common to the rest of the United Kingdom. Rather, the dominant pattern has been that of a polarized stability between the oppositional politics of 'Catholic Irishness' and 'Protestant Britishness'.

Analysing the conflict in Northern Ireland

Since the outbreak of the current phase of conflict, academic studies of the Northern Ireland problem have accumulated at a prodigious rate. Much of this literature has focused on both the social (see Coulter, 1999; Darby, 1997) and the political (Dixon, 2001; McGarry and O'Leary, 1990, 1995; Ruane and Todd, 1999) aspects of the conflict. A useful starting point remains Whyte's *Interpreting Northern Ireland* (1991), which categorizes eight major frames of explanation. These are: traditional unionist view; traditional nationalist view; mainline Marxist view; neo-Marxist view; religious view; pluralist view; colonialism; and the fragmented society.

The next part of this chapter will explore some of these major theoretical perspectives on the Northern Irish conflict and relate some of them to the broader perspectives of the state discussed in Chapter 1. It is, however, still useful to begin with the basic views which help weave the fabric of the conflict. Ulster unionism and Irish nationalism remain the dominant conflicting ideologies through which politics is understood and much of everyday life is interpreted. These perspectives remain central to any analysis of the Irish conflict.

Unionist and nationalist interpretations

Ulster unionist discourses and understandings take as a starting point the perceived obviousness of two distinct 'peoples' and identities on the island of Ireland. The central claim underpinning unionists' core claim is therefore that those in the north-east of Ireland form a community which differs in decisive ways, culturally, politically and socially from the people of the rest of the island. For unionists there is a clear difference between being objectively part of Ireland and subjectively having a clear self-identity, expressing the strong desire to uphold their 'British way of life' within the United Kingdom. In others words, unionists would argue that there is no singularity between geography and politics.

The essence of the traditional Irish nationalist argument mirrors the above. While Catholics are a minority in Northern Ireland they are in the vast majority on the island. The 'Irish people' form one nation, through a unity of geography, culture and politics. The essential reason for the conflict is partition of the island. The nationalist position thus stresses the interference of Britain in Irish politics, and the resultant disjunction, as the fundamental issue. The classical perspective for Irish nationalists is to regard unionism as only one more manifestation of England's age-old strategy of 'divide and rule'. Fundamentally, the nationalist perspective suggests that the people of Ireland would be united if foreign interference in the shape of Britain had not kept the island divided.

The political manifestation of these positions is far from uniform. It would be wrong to project either unionism or nationalism as homogeneous in character. Indeed, as we shall see, some of the most important dynamics in Irish politics have been motivated by divisions and conflicts within Irish nationalism/republicanism and Ulster unionism/loyalism. Further, both nationalism and unionism have undergone much self-reidentification in recent years.

While the traditional unionist and nationalist understandings outlined above are crucial starting points, there are other key interpretations of the Northern Irish conflict. Here, in particular, we shall consider Marxist, pluralist and feminist interpretations as foundations for understanding events in Northern Ireland. We shall also seek to link some of the material here with the broad theoretical perspectives outlined in Chapter 1.

Marxist perspectives

A constant feature of Northern Irish society since the formation of the state has been its low socio-economic profile. At partition, the economy rested on an outmoded base of agriculture, shipbuilding and linen, the latter two both desperately vulnerable to the fluctuations of the world capitalist economy. Furthermore, shipbuilding, its related engineering works, and the linen industry were extremely geographically concentrated – in and around Belfast. The narrowness of Northern Ireland's industrial base meant it suffered badly in the postwar economic restructuring. By the mid-1950s it was clear to the unionist leadership that an economy based on shipbuilding, textiles and engineering did not have a viable future (Rowthorn and Wayne, 1988).

Attempts to attract external capital in the form of multinational companies proved reasonably successful, but only in the short term. Northern Ireland's economic base was steadily undermined, particularly as recession caused transnational companies physically to relocate elsewhere. As Gaffikin and Morrissey (1990) demonstrate, from 1979 on Northern Ireland found itself subject to the overall process of de-industrialization common to the United Kingdom economy. The decline in manufacturing was partly offset by a rapid rise in service industries (which rose by two-thirds between 1958 and 1980) and a growth in work related to the worsening 'security' situation. Nevertheless, Northern Ireland's regional economy remained extremely weak.

The traditional Marxist analysis of Ireland draws on these economics to follow the broad Marxist perspective outlined in Chapter 1. The partition of the island in 1921 is considered as part of a broader political conspiracy to retain control of as much of Ireland as possible. The Northern Ireland 'state' was, as De Paor (1970: xv) argues, an artificial creation, arbitrarily carved out of the state of Ulster and structured by a 'divide and rule conspiracy' of the British state (Farrell, 1976: 325–6). Much of the strategy at this time rested on an economic and strategic alliance between the unionist bourgeoisie and the British ruling class. Central to this was an attempt to protect imperial markets, and the 'buying off' of the support of Protestant workers through ensuring them relatively 'secure and well paid jobs' (Farrell 1976: 199). Such open discrimination became institutionalized at partition in the form of the 'Stormont State' and the parliament which existed in Northern Ireland between 1921 and 1972.

It was in this context of resistance to, and demands for, reforms of the Northern Ireland administration that the growth of the Northern Ireland Civil Rights Movement in the late 1960s should be seen. Its emergence, and the loyalist reaction to it described above, rapidly transformed the situation into a classical anti-imperialist struggle for national liberation. Thus, Farrell (1976: 330–5) argues that the first step towards revolution was to remove the British presence in Northern Ireland and thus pave the way for a reunited island. This traditional 'anti-imperialist' analysis is also clearly represented in the works of De Paor (1970), Bell (1976, 1984), McCann (1974) and Farrell (1983).

Although there is a later generation of Marxist and neo-Marxist writings which have challenged the established Marxist orthodoxy (see Bew, 1994; Bew and Patterson, 1985, 1987; Bew et al., 1979), the position outlined above represents a classical Marxist interpretation of a political situation. Irish Marxism remains fragmented and marginal, with many of the differences that exist within the broader theoretical frameworks of Marxism (see previous chapters) mirrored in writings from the Left regarding Northern Ireland.

Class difference still represents one of the most important sources of difference in Northern Irish society and directly influences the meanings that people ascribe to their lives (Coulter, 1999: 61–100). Political expressions of class consciousness and organizations of the working class have been largely absent from civil society in Northern Ireland. Class awareness has been sub-sumed within the wider constructions of sectarian ethnic blocs.

Pluralist theories of the conflict

Obviously this situation has meant that many refuse to accept that the basic cleavage in Northern Ireland is class based, or even that there is a primary economic basis for such social divisions. Indeed, McGarry and O'Leary (1995) suggest that the concept of social class can add little to our under-standing of the situation in Northern Ireland. Rather, they suggest that the conflict is based around conflicting cultural identities between ethnonational blocs. Another important set of starting points therefore involve pluralist ideas and see Northern Ireland as a situation where sub-groups differ cul-turally on matters of public concern.

From these perspectives the origins of the problem rest in the failure of two different ethnic groups to integrate. Indeed, much of the official per-spectives from both the British and Irish governments recognizes this, and both have set about introducing policies to bring about a 'pluralist' society in Northern Ireland.

In the meantime, however, it is clear that many Catholics and Protestants have overtly self-proclaimed and mutually exclusive self-identities. Further, it is possible readily to identify high levels of largely voluntary physical and social self-segregation between the two communities. Not only do many Catholics and Protestants obviously go to different churches, most commonly; they still send their children to different schools, read different newspapers, play different games, have different popular ballads, and traditionally have occupied different economic sectors.

Employment patterns therefore represent another vital feature of differ-ence in Northern Ireland. Unemployment rates in Northern Ireland have always been much higher than in the rest of the United Kingdom. In the 1920s, for example, the figure was close to 20 per cent, and in the 1930s it averaged 27 per cent. Even with the onset of the economic 'boom' and a commitment to full employment, as part of the postwar consensus, the unemployment rate in Northern Ireland stood at three times the UK average. The imbalance between rates of employment and occupational levels for Catholics and Protestants, which was a feature of the economy before 1968, is still significant.

In an important early analysis of the contemporary period, Birrell (1972) agues that relative deprivation was a major factor in the conflict in Northern Ireland. These social divisions of labour remain apparent today, although in a diluted form. By the mid-1980s, the unemployment rate stood at 21 per cent compared with a UK average of just over 13 per cent. Overall unemployment rates have disguised markedly different historical employment patterns. One example of this can be seen in comparative unemployment figures, between

Protestants and Catholics. The simplest explanation for the weaker occupational position of Catholic workers is a legacy of discrimination, shown in favour of Protestants, at both an institutional and local level.

In the mid-1980s, Catholic men were 2.6 times more likely to be unemployed. By the early 1990s, this ratio had fallen only to 2.2 (*The Guardian*, 26 June 1993). Employment patterns are, however, changing. In August 2001, for example, the Equality Commission reported that the Catholic share of the workforce had risen from 34.9 per cent in 1990 to 39.6 per cent in 2000 and that the share of employment between Protestants and Catholics is now almost the same as the share of the population.

Despite this, however, sectarian division remains embedded within the social relations of Northern Ireland. Indeed, several reports indicate that the levels of division and sectarianism have increased over the period of the peace process (Shirlow, 2000). Sectarianism is constructed through a history of social division. There are several key markers in identifying the lack of success of an assimilation process in Ireland. These include minimal levels of shared cultural values; a lack of agreement of common past; social self-reproduction; distinct networks of social contacts; and the identification of self and others as distinctive.

Many Catholics and Protestants, as we have seen, experience distinct socialization processes, resting on contrary mythological histories, folk memories and expressions of popular culture. In broad terms both groups are to some extent at least biologically self-perpetuating. There remain throughout Northern Ireland strong cultural constraints opposing cross-community or 'mixed marriages'. Further, there is evidence that each group is socially exclusive. Particularly in urban areas, social interaction is overwhelmingly concentrated within each community (see Burton, 1978; McAuley, 1994a, 1996a, 1996b).

While the extent of residential segregation has not been constant, and there was some degree of mixing between the groups up to 1968, physical segregation has been a feature of Northern Ireland since its inception. Such segregation is largely voluntary, but is often borne out by experiences of physical intimidation. The result is that much of the urban working-class population of Northern Ireland lives in areas surrounded by its 'own kind' (Darby, 1986).

Elsewhere, McKittrick (1999) argues that this geographical separation means that some people can experience lives of near-apartheid. Further, such lives seem natural to them, even although they rarely, if ever, mix or socialize across the religious, cultural or demographic divides. Some 30 years of overt sectarian violence have only served to deepen and widen these existing divisions.

This resonates at an everyday level. Jacobson (2000) shows the importance upon meeting someone of 'placing' them, in terms of religion, through names, addresses, schooling, sports and even knowledge of particular songs. This mirrors Burton's (1978) emphasis on the 'telling' of group membership before individuals engage in social interactions. The work of several social psychologists (see Cairns, 1987, 1994; Trew, 1992) clarifies this position when they suggest that every culture, including Northern Ireland, needs an out-group in times of social change. The purpose of this out-group is to act as a scapegoat for the majority's frustrations. It is defined by stereotypes, which are surprisingly uniform from culture to culture – fecklessness, overbreeding, sexual promiscuity and so on.

Within this framework, identity derives from people's knowledge that they belong to an identifiable social group. Elsewhere, Bruce (1994) suggests that at the core of the conflict is 'ethnic power' and that while religion is not the fundamental difference, it certainly is a major part of it. Hence, in *The Narrow Ground*, Stewart (1977) argues that the current crisis is deeply shaped by patterns of sectarian differences laid down in the past. However, such strong cultural differences do not necessarily result in widespread social and physical conflict. There remain crucial theoretical questions to be asked concerning the emergence and perpetuation of social divisions in Northern Ireland and how and why this has sometimes manifested itself in physical conflict and violence.

The entire peace process in Ireland rests on the provision of a viable framework for developing a pluralistic society in Northern Ireland. It also, however, affirms the division of the representatives of the people of Northern Ireland into communities according to whether they are Catholic or Protestant, nationalist or unionist. While the process legitimizes aspirations of a united Ireland and of a reconfirmation of Northern Ireland's status as part of the United Kingdom, these desires remain contradictory, mutually exclusive and impossible to achieve in political terms.

Women and the conflict

There are other important interpretations of the situation in Northern Ireland. As Coulter (1999: 101–48) rightly points out, the position of women in Northern Irish society has been remarkably under-researched. He concludes (1999: 148) that the position women hold 'remains an essentially subaltern one'.

Increasing the representation of women must also be seen as a core aspect of fostering political pluralism. Jacobson (2000: 191) identifies that the gendered constructions of the public and private in Northern Ireland have led to a 'startling absence of women from all forms of political representation'. Several other writers strongly support this view (see Fearon, 1999; McCoy, 2000; Rooney, 1992, 2000).

Wilford and Galligan (1999) suggest that this confinement to the private arena has led some to draw on deeply rooted stereotypes of women as 'carers' and 'peacemakers' and to suggest that this is their primary role in Northern Irish society. Further, as Sales (1997) highlights, the centrality of the sectarian divide in Northern Ireland obscures the realities of other forms of inequality, including those based on gender. That is not to say that women are not engaged in the conflict (Morgan and Fraser, 1995). As Morgan (1995) demonstrates, to describe women simply as 'peacemakers' in Northern Ireland says little of value. While some women have made a notable contribution to reducing violence (as have some men), others have merely reproduced community divisions. Rather, it is more accurate to regard women as both peacemakers and peace-thwarters.

Throughout the contemporary period, the range of women's attitudes and responses to the conflict in Northern Ireland has been as wide and varied as that of men. It simply does not make sense to draw on some abstraction that suggests a generalized feminine orientation to peacemaking. To understand the different manifestations of women's politicization we must draw on the different historical, social, political and economic roles of women and men as evidence. There is much data to suggest that the deep fractures in Northern Irish society can be best understood as expressions of competing national identities (see Darby, 1997). These differences have been expressed just as clearly and as directly by women as by men.

The politics of identity

Others have sought to explain the situation in Northern Ireland by utilizing the concept of identity. This has been employed within a wide range of social science approaches to Northern Ireland, including politics (see Cash, 1996; Porter, 1996; Walker, 2000), sociology (see Bruce, 1994; McAuley, 1994) and psychology (see Cairns, 1987; Trew 1992, 1998). Indeed, it is increasingly possible to regard identity as the core to understanding the fissures in Northern Irish society (see Cassidy and Trew, 1988; McAuley, 1994, 1997a, 1997b, 1997c).

Competing expressions of identity are represented through the four-fifths of Protestants in Northern Ireland who primarily consider themselves to be 'British' and the 60 per cent of Catholics who regard themselves as 'Irish' (Breen, 1996). A history of grievances derived from these conflicting senses of national identities are expressed and reinforced through a divided political culture, which finds expression in both the public and private areas of life.

This sense of difference thus remains a core social construct, central to the maintenance of political values and social identities across time. Cairns, Lewis and Mumcu (1998) have, for example, examined the relationship between the social construction of memory and ethnic identity using two cohorts of Northern Irish students in 1984 and 1995. They conclude that over the decade there were virtually no differences between both groups in terms of their baseline identity. Throughout the period of research, Catholic participants felt equally strong in their Irish identity and the Protestant participants felt as British as they ever did. This supports McBride's (2001) evidence that in Northern Ireland conflicting communal memories reinforce social divisions based on constructed differences.

Hence, in a society as politically and culturally divided as Northern Ireland, the very validity of the state itself remains a deeply contested issue. Moreover, the direction and form of political culture and political participation remains highly conflictual. In contemporary Northern Ireland this is found in arguments surrounding, for example, the future of the police and policing, and the future of loyalist and republican paramilitary members released from prison under the terms of the Good Friday Agreement.

Contemporary politics for all those living in Northern Ireland remains dominated by the search for a secure and enduring settlement resting on an agreed set of political values and arrangements. However, the evidence of any move towards the stable social relationships upon which any political settlement must rest, remains contradictory. While the level of political violence has been dramatically reduced, events on the street continue to demonstrate the fragility of support for a party political settlement.

Sectarian divisions continue to emphasize and reinforce the persistence of conflictual social and political relations. Central to any possibility of a permanent resolution to conflict in Northern Ireland is the development of some working consensus around future political values. For the moment, however, there remains only an acute awareness of highly conflictual values, which continue to be transmitted from one generation to another in Northern Ireland.

Political violence and terrorism

Many of the issues outlined above, and much of the recent history of armed conflict in Northern Ireland, needs to be set in the context of a broader set of questions. These concern how Western democracies first define and then seek to deal with conflictual questions surrounding politics and the political. The remainder of this chapter therefore engages with a discussion of the definitions of 'terrorism' and the contentious notions surrounding political violence.

For some the answer to these questions is simple, and the categorization of such violence reasonably straightforward. To most unionists in Northern Ireland, for example, all Irish republican violence over the past 30 years can simply be understood as terrorism. To many Irish republicans, however, it is merely the latest phase of a long and legitimate political struggle to remove the British presence from the island.

Events in Northern Ireland need to be viewed against the scale of political violence worldwide. Throughout many contemporary societies, political violence and terrorism remain central to contemporary political events. During the time this book has been written, for example, terrorism has all but decimated the tourist trade in Egypt, and the Russian state has been constantly engaged with groupings such as Chechen separatists which have used political violence to challenge its political legitimacy and authority.

Above all, the USA has for the first time witnessed major acts of external terrorism within its boundaries. Following the devastating attack on the World Trade Center and the Pentagon on 11 September 2001, in which many thousands of ordinary people died, it appears that the entire relationship of political forces in the world may again change in the wake of a terrorist assault.

But what is terrorism? There are multiple definitions (see Barnaby, 1996; Laqueur, 1999). For some, terrorism is defined best by 'process'; for others, it is clarified by studying the 'strategies' involved. Others still have sought to define terrorism as a form of violence that may only be understood in a political framework. A useful working definition of terrorism remains that it is 'the deliberate and systematic murder, maiming and menacing of the innocent to inspire fear for political ends' (Netanyahu, 1979: 9).

Several other key themes emanate from within mainstream interpretations. Thornton (1964) identifies two large categories of terrorism: enforcement terror and agitational terror: the first is used by a dominant group or state to maintain authority; the second is used by those wishing to undermine the dominant group's authority.

Some useful attempts to categorize terrorism may be found in the following examples of types and structures of such organizations (see Harmon, 2000; McLaughlin, 1996; Thornton, 1964; Wilkinson, 1977):

- **Nationalist/separatist terrorism**: such as the Irish Republican Army (IRA), the Liberation Tigers of Tamil Eelam (Tamil Tigers), the Basque Euzkadi ta Askatasuna (ETA), or Al-Fatah, which is within the umbrella of the Palestine Liberation Organization (PLO).
- **Revolutionary or left-wing terrorism**: for example, in the 1970s organizations such as the Rote Armee Frakton (Germany), Action Directe (France) and Brigate Rosse (Italy). More recently, examples include the Partiya Karkeren Kurdistan (PKK) and Devrimci Sol (Dev Sol) in Turkey and Epanastatikos Laikos Agonas (ELA) in Greece.
- **Reactionary or right-wing terrorism**: examples of which are the Ku Klux Klan, Turkish Grey Wolves, Japanese Shield Society, the radical militias in the USA and C18 in the United Kingdom.
- **Individual terrorists**: usually assassins, at best they have some vague obsession which is perhaps remotely socio-political. An example is Alittgca, the young Turk who attempted to assassinate Pope John Paul II in Rome in 1987. Although it was claimed that he had some connections with Grey Wolves, he claimed to be the re-embodiment of Jesus Christ.
- **Single-issue terrorism**: such as anti-abortion campaigners in the USA, and some animal rights campaigners in the United Kingdom.
- **Religious terrorism**: those involved regard the violence they engage in as a response to a God-given religious command. Examples are the Aum group in Japan, and a variety of Islamic fundamentalist organizations, including HAMAS (Islamic Resistance), al-Jihad (Egyptian Islamic Jihad) and al-Qa'ida.
- **State-sponsored terrorism**: a classic example was the sinking of the Greenpeace ship *Rainbow Warrior* in New Zealand by the French authorities in 1985.

Recent decades have witnessed a marked change in the dynamics and structure of terrorism. On the one hand, the existence of Left- or Marxist-motivated terror organizations has dramatically reduced in contemporary

Europe. Organizations such as Baader-Meinhof and Red Army Faction in West Germany, and the Red Brigades in Italy, have either officially disbanded or been expunged. It is only in Greece, with the '17th November' and 'ELA', and in Turkey with 'DevSol' that there is continuing organized political violence from left-wing groupings. In other parts of the world, Left ideology still continues to have some influence. The Shining Path movement in Peru, for example, claims Maoism as its major political influence.

On the other hand, single-issue groups and organizations driven by right-wing ideology are growing sources of political violence. Although issue-group extremists aim at changing specific policies or practices rather than the whole socio-political system, their potential should not be underestimated. For example, in the USA over several years there has been a series of often vicious and sometimes fatal attacks against medical staff, at clinics and hospitals where abortions are undertaken.

The extreme Right has also been responsible for violence within the United Kingdom. During 1992, for example, a section broke away from the British National Party (BNP) claiming that violence was necessary to obtain their goals to 'secure the existence of our people and a future for white children' (*The Guardian*, 22 January 1997). Later, in the mid-1990s, the British neo-Nazi group Combat 18 (C18) revealed itself. The group's name represents the position of Adolf Hitler's initials in the alphabet. It publishes a journal of the same name that contains a vile mixture of ultra-right diatribe, 'hatelists' and articles promoting attacks on 'known' left-wingers, communists and fellow travellers.

The far Right remained central in organizing violence throughout the 1990s. In 1995, Combat 18 was fundamental in organizing the crowd violence that caused the abandonment of the soccer match between England and the Republic of Ireland in Dublin. The trouble was a co-ordinated protest against the 'Anglo-Irish peace process', bringing into sharp relief the alleged links with loyalist paramilitary organizations. Members of Combat 18 have continued to make headlines. In early 1997 they were involved with Danish neo-Nazis in a violent campaign to send 'letter bombs' to leading personalities of 'mixed race' marriages and those they deemed to be left-wing politicians.

More recently, *The Observer* (2 September 2001) revealed coherent plans by far-right extremists, including the BNP, National Front (NF) and C18, to initiate further street conflicts and re-ignite the 'race riots' that swept through several northern English towns during the summer of 2001 (see Chapter 2). Even here, however, it is possible to read a political content to such interventions.

The most recent manifestation of the changing nature of terrorist action came with the unprecedented and tragic events of 11 September 2001. The deliberate crashing of four US passenger planes (one into each tower of the World Trade Center, one into the Pentagon in Washington, and one almost certainly bound for another major target, in a field in Pennsylvania) marked an unprecedented level of terrorist action. The horrifying images carried worldwide of the 'bombing' of the World Trade Center's twin towers imprinted itself forever on the minds of all who saw it.

In the subsequent charge to identify the perpetrators and to target the al-Qa'ida network led by Osama bin Laden the notion of terrorism was used in an all encompassing and uncritical manner (Abu Khalil, 2002). This is perhaps understandable given the feelings of repugnance rightly felt by many. As the works of Chomsky (2001) and the collection of writings by Scraton (2002) all indicate, however, the widespread repulsion at events should not be allowed to obscure a view of the broader political context. In particular, it is important to recognize the importance of the feelings of resistance to the foreign policy and the economic and corporate power of the USA (Sardar and Davies, 2002).

Defining terrorism

Rather, it was the notion of irrational and evil terrorists that was directly invoked to structure what happened after 11 September, as George Bush rallied support for a US-led 'war against terror' worldwide. Yet surely even here there is room for critical assessment of what terrorism is. Indeed, the answer to the question 'what is terrorism?' still seems most often to depend on who is asking it. Likewise, the label terrorist usually depends on who has the power to apply it. Part of the project of the Western-led alliance against terrorism following the events of 11 September has been to reinforce a particular set of political and ideological definitions. While official and governmental definitions of terrorism are by no means based on a coherent set of ideas, a constant theme directed towards those engaged in such actions is that they are denied legitimacy and characterized as essentially unlawful in their behaviour.

It is common for the state to emphasize the simple criminality of those who take up arms against democracy. A good example of this can be found in a statement made by the then Prime Minister of the United Kingdom, Margaret Thatcher, after an incident of paramilitary violence in Northern Ireland. She declared (cited in Schlesinger et al., 1983: 4): 'I hope that when their murderers have been tried and convicted no one will claim that they are entitled to special privileges – which is what political status means – when they serve their prison sentences.'

For Thatcher, and many others, such paramilitary members had no political motivation and, according to her famous adage, a 'crime is a crime is a crime'. It was this ideological position which captured the move to 'criminalize' members of paramilitary organizations in Northern Ireland in the early part of the 1980s (see above). This brings us to one of the core issues in understanding political violence.

Governments in the West have commonly promoted a view of the terrorist as mad and irrational. Terrorism is seen as the activity of criminals, and thus any possible legitimacy or rationality is denied. Also prevalent in large sections of the press is a discourse that suggests each terrorist action is an individual act devoid of any political meaning. Rarely are such events presented as part of an ongoing political struggle with set goals and aims.

The 1980s and 1990s saw the creation of a whole series of folks devils, through which political causes were reduced to the characteristics of one individual presented as mad or evil. Hence, Gerry Adams, Saddam Hussain, Colonel Qaddafi and Osama Bin Laden have, at various times, all been constructed in this way – as the 'dangerous Other', evil leaders of groupings located outside the political, social and moral mainstream of Western, 'civilized' society.

(Re)defining terrorism

Given the above, it is clear that many definitions of terrorism are far from neutral. Any proper definition of terrorism must also focus on the political objectives of terrorism, rather than simply on the affiliation of those involved. By doing this, it is possible to avoid some of the more obvious value judgements regarding terrorism. This is particularly important because of the extremely loose definitions often used by the media and especially by sectors of the popular press.

Gearty (1991, 1997) argues that while terrorism has existed for centuries, the contemporary literature on terrorism can be grouped into three separate categories. At one end of the spectrum are accounts of single acts of violence or histories of violent organizations. At the other end of the spectrum he places works in which the use of the word 'terrorist' indicates a strong moral standpoint. Most importantly, he recognizes 'terrorism' as a term moulded by political interest. Gearty (1991: 4–5) further suggests that at times the words 'terrorist' and 'terrorism' have deteriorated into little more than terms of abuse. He goes on to argue that 'terror' and 'terrorism' 'have come to be regarded as such powerful condemnations that all those looking for a suitable insult have wanted to appropriate them'. Indeed, he questions whether the terms 'terrorist' and 'terrorism' have any real meaning beyond those who oppose the dominant group.

These concerns have led other commentators to attempt to replace the term 'terrorism' with the term 'political violence'. Such violence is calculated to affect the views and behaviour of specific groups. Hence, certain central tenets of the 'official' perspective on terrorism must be challenged. For example, while the instilling of fear may characterize the action of many organizations, it is not necessarily the principal goal of all terrorist acts. Hence, Shultz defines political terrorism as:

> the threat and/or use of extra normal forms of political violence, in varying degrees, with the objective of achieving certain political objectives/goals. Such goals constitute the long-range and short-term objectives that the group or movement seeks to obtain. These will differ from group to group. Such action generally is intended to influence the behaviour and attitude of certain targeted groups much wider than its immediate victims. (Shultz, 1990: 45–6)

Terrorist organizations are diverse but a common characteristic is the political nature of their origin and proclaimed purpose and the claimed political motivation of their membership. It is, of course, possible to identify other shared features, such as the methods they employ and the organizational and command structures they adopt. However, as a form of explanation the term 'terrorism' is normally applied only to political enemies. Thus, for example, state-sponsored terrorism is often given a degree of legitimacy denied to opponents of the state.

Political violence: some conclusions

Despite the horror of events on 11 September, wide-ranging assumptions concerning the psychological characteristics of those involved in political violence must be treated with some scepticism. The development of terrorist organizations can often be located in highly specific social and political circumstances. There are, for example, few, if any, national states that do not have significant ethnic, economic or religious minority groups within their boundaries. In these societies conflict is almost always present but violence is not. However, when the formation or legitimacy of the nation-state is under challenge, violence is often a common response. It is, however, rarely an initial response.

The dominant explanation of the political violence of terrorist organizations remains to dismiss it either as illegitimate in its political form or pathological in its membership, or both. However, no matter how unpalatable it is to many, such violence can also be understood in terms of rational rather than irrational acts.

For many, this is difficult to accept. Further, to make this argument is in no way to condone or support political violence or terrorism. The value-laden nature of the term, and ideological bias in its use, helps explain why finding an acceptable definition has proved so difficult. The wide range of definitions of terrorism indicates how such definitions are set according to when and where the act takes place and who is responsible for it.

By defining terrorism as 'the' problem removes it from the political culture in which it has developed. The process of definition itself is part of a process of ideological and political construction. To fully understand this political violence, it is important to try to understand how the social organization and the political and social structures in which it developed and exists shape its dynamics. Only then is it possible to begin to move to a solution. Surely that is one lesson that may be learnt from the experiences of Northern Ireland.

DISCUSSION QUESTIONS

- **Critically examine the main political problems surrounding the search for 'peace' in Northern Ireland.**

- What are the major causes of the conflict in Northern Ireland?
- Do the terms 'terrorism' and 'terrorist' have any coherent political meaning?
- What is the future of terrorism?
- How may the trends towards globalization affect terrorism?

Section III

The Future of Politics and the State

6

Post-industrialism and the End of Politics?

Key concepts and issues	Key theorists and writers
• Poverty and wealth in the contemporary United Kingdom	• Jean Baudrillard
• Class, politics and social structure	• Daniel Bell
	• Alex Callinicos
	• Francis Fukuyama
• Marx and Weber on class politics	• André Gorz
• The end of class?	• Will Hutton
• The end of politics?	• Fredric Jameson
• The end of history?	• Ernesto Laclau and Chantal Mouffe
• New social movements	• Charles Murray
• Postmodernism and politics	• Alain Touraine
• Post-industrial politics	• Erik O. Wright

A wealthy barrister . . . was keen to play a notoriously exclusive golf course. The Secretary refused him but as he turned to leave he spotted a vaguely familiar figure of a local peer seated in the corner.

Nervously he asked if he might play as the old boy's member. His lordship looked him up and down.

'Church?' 'C of E, Sir.'

'Education?' 'Eton and Oxford, Sir.'

'Athletics?' 'Rugby blue and rowed number four when we beat Cambridge, Sir.'

'Military?' 'Guards, Sir. Military Cross and Knight of the Bath.'

'Campaigns?' 'Dunkirk, El Alamein and Normandy, Sir. Wounded twice.'

His lordship considered long and hard, and then nodded at the Secretary.

'Very Well. Nine holes.'

(*The Dalesman*, June 1995: 49)

The humour in the above story comes from its use of reference points that are common to, and understood by, most with even a passing knowledge of the social structures of the United Kingdom. The structures of class may not be as rigid as once they were. Nevertheless, their pertinence to politics is difficult to ignore. This chapter addresses some major aspects and changes in the social structure of the contemporary United Kingdom and discusses its relevance for politics and the political.

Underlying much of the chapter are debates surrounding the continued usefulness of the concepts of class, gender and ethnicity, and their relevance in explaining the world around us in the twenty-first century. Hence, the chapter will also relate the current conflict over notions such as the 'end of class' and the 'end of history'. Further, it will also engage with some issues concerning the development of ideas surrounding postmodernism, the development of postindustrial society and the 'end of politics'.

Since the end of the Second World War, changes in the social structure have been dramatic. From the severity of life in the immediate postwar period, the UK population, and the working class in particular, soon began to experience the relative affluence of a society based on mass production and consumption. This was in part brought about by the 'long boom' and the white heat of the technological revolution of the late 1950s and the 1960s. During that time some now classical sociological writings were produced to support, and then later strongly contest, the notion of embourgeoisement, and the idea that rapidly rising living standards were transforming the masses into a new middle class.

Throughout the 1950s and 1960s, immigration from the West Indies and the countries of the New Commonwealth rose, largely in an attempt to plug widening gaps in the labour market. At the same time there was an equally sensational expansion of women in the workforce. The traditional male domain of work, while still important, was chipped away. Jobs in the public sector, for example, were growing at a meteoric rate. The entire workforce structure moved away from a distinct manual towards a non-manual one.

As the previous chapters have indicated, the late 1970s brought important changes throughout the capitalist world. Widespread recession created havoc in the United Kingdom's manufacturing base and in the traditional manufacturing regions such as the north and midlands of England and Northern Ireland. Unemployment reached figures not seen since the 1930s and in many cases surpassed them. When there was eventually some glimmer of a recovery in the mid-1980s the picture which emerged was one of an economy based on service jobs, largely concentrated in the south of England, part-time female work and a male economic base which had contracted almost beyond recognition. In addition the Conservative administration from 1979 to 1997 showed little commitment to maintaining, let alone developing, the United Kingdom's traditional manufacturing base. The advancement of the welfare state was halted, with increased emphasis on the private provision of health, and the introduction of the market into welfare provision and education. Further, the cleavages that emerged along the lines of employment, income levels and the accumulation of wealth all highlighted a new culture of individualism and privatized consumption.

What has been the effect of such social change on the politics of the United Kingdom? At its most basic level, for instance, changes in class structure may well affect political alignments. Against this background, there are several key factors that this chapter seeks to further highlight, including the changing social structure and its contemporary composition; the distribution of income, poverty and wealth; and the changing structure and form of consumption and cultural change.

Wealth, income and poverty

One key starting point for all of this is the pattern of distribution of economic resources. Issues such as unemployment, public ownership and the distribution of economic resources have traditionally represented fundamental cleavages in British politics (Heath et al., 1985, 1990). The entire area of discussion surrounding the distribution of wealth and poverty, however, remains a political battlefield. Interpretations, understandings, analyses and, indeed, definitions surrounding such issues vary dramatically and remain intensely contested.

Such debates, however, are far from academic or sterile. A major ideological pillar behind the policies of the Conservative governments of the 1980s and 1990s, for example, was the claim to bring about increased prosperity, both to individuals and to the nation. Indeed, many of those on the political Right would claim to have succeeded in widening the distribution of wealth through council house sales and wider share ownership. Those supporting these views would also suggest that the last three decades have seen a real rise in income for all social classes and perhaps a steady move towards a 'classless society'.

Likewise, for New Labour, the issue of social divisions has been central. Indeed, one way New Labour seeks to represent its contemporary political project is, on the one hand, as a critique of overt neoliberalism and, on the other hand, as an attempt to negotiate a path between *laissez-faire* and state planning. This has been reflected in the shift by New Labour towards the centre of the British political spectrum and in the development of a so-called third way in politics.

The third way, it is claimed, transcends the 'outmoded' divisions which locate politics of a Left–Right spectrum and emphasize class divisions. This understanding is central to key sections of the New Labour project, seeking as it does to appeal to a wider constituency, through 'good' government and 'social justice'. The third way creates a new mixed economy, balancing regulation with deregulation, public with private. The economy is judged in relation to wider social consequences. Government creates a stakeholding business culture through a balance of controls and incentives.

Further, the third way defines a new form of democracy based on devolved power. This democratization involves devolving some responsibility to the regions, such as in Scotland and Wales, and expanding forms of participation, such as referenda and non-orthodox forms of participation. It sets new limits to the boundaries of sovereignty and a changed constitution and a radically reformed welfare state, establishing a new set of relationships between the individual and collective responsibilities (see Chapter 7).

There has, however, been little or no evidence of any widescale commitment to economic redistribution during the New Labour administration. The main dynamic of the welfare state has been to confine and compartmentalize definitions of social problems and to direct highly focused and limited interventions through welfare administration. Certainly, this is the case in identifying target areas of disadvantage and special needs (see below). Overall, however, there is little feel so far from New Labour of an administration seeking to tackle directly the structural and economic imbalances of contemporary UK society (see Chapter 7).

Let us consider such inequality in more detail by assessing the changing patterns of wealth, poverty and disadvantage in the United Kingdom over the past two decades. Oppenheim (1994a, 1994b) provides a useful starting point with some illuminating material, focusing on arguments surrounding the measurement of poverty in the absence of any official 'poverty line'. Another key reference point is the 1993 House of Commons Social Security Committee report, itself based on figures produced by the Institute for Fiscal Studies (IFS) called the Low Income Families Statistics 1979–1989. Some of its major findings indicate that some 11,330,000 people (20 per cent of the population) were living in poverty (on or below income support). Further, of these, 4,350,000 people (8 per cent of the population) were living below the poverty line. In addition, another 16,520,000 (29 per cent of the population) were in or on the margins of poverty (living on up to 140 per cent of income support).

A second level of measurement is that based on the figures from the Households below Average Income. This time Oppenheim takes 50 per cent of the average income after housing costs as a relative marker for the poverty line. Again, there are important conclusions to be drawn. In the United Kingdom in 1988/89, 12 million people were living in poverty (over 20 per cent of the population). This is over double the number in 1979, when the equivalent figure was 5 million (around 9 per cent of the population).

Such broad figures are revealing, but they mask the make-up of those who experience poverty. Here, it is important to consider two distinct groupings, those who are living 'in poverty' and those who are most 'at risk' of being in poverty. Table 6.1 shows the composition of the poor by economic and family status. From these figures it is clear that unemployment is a crucial determinant of poverty, as it tallies with nearly 20 per cent of those in poverty.

The risk of suffering poverty is also very different for distinct social groups. Those at highest peril are the unemployed, where around 70 per cent are in poverty. There is also a high risk for families that are supported by part-time work. Other highly vulnerable groups are single pensioners, where 40 per cent are in poverty, and single parents, where half are living in poverty.

TABLE 6.1 AVERAGE INCOME (£ PER WEEK, APRIL 1993 PRICES)

Family type	1979	1990/91	Change (%)
Couple, no children	244	340	40
Single, no children	213	276	30
Couple, children	179	239	34
Pensioner couple	147	203	38
Single pensioner	140	185	32
Single children	139	153	11
Person type			
Male adult	202	277	37
Female adult	187	252	35
Dependent child	171	218	28
Benefit status of family			
Non-recipient family	195	270	39
Family on income support	111	126	13
All	188	254	35

Source: Nicholson (1994)

Sixty per cent of people of Bangladeshi or Pakistani origin live in poverty. More than half of African-Caribbean and African people live in districts with the highest rates of unemployment (Runnymede Trust, 2000).

Other data for England and Wales shows that in 1997 people in social classes IV and V were more likely to have low birth-weight babies than those people belonging to social classes I to III. The percentage of low birth-weight babies for social classes IV and V stood at around 8.4 per cent as against 6.8 per cent for social classes I to III (Joseph Rowntree Foundation, 1999).

It is also worthy of note that women, indicating their high perilousness in relation to poverty, dominate these groups. Research on low-income households has shown that women who normally manage household budgets develop a number of strategies in order to afford to feed their families. These include shopping frequently to keep food stocks at home at a minimum; hunting for special offers and buying convenience foods that they know their children will eat, to avoid waste. Women will also go without meals and items such as clothing in order to provide for their family (Joseph Rowntree Foundation, 1996). Further, as Sir Donald Acheson's inquiry into health inequalities concludes, benefit rates are too low to allow expectant mothers to purchase a healthy diet. One result is an increasing number of low-weight babies (Acheson et al., 1998).

How have the statistics of poverty altered over the past two decades? Oppenheim (1994a, 1994b) draws the following conclusions concerning the poorest 10 per cent of the population (using after-housing costs statistics). In 1989, pensioners made up a smaller proportion of this grouping, down from 31 per cent to 14 per cent. Couples with children made up a slightly larger proportion (from 41 to 44 per cent). Most striking, however, is the rise in single people without children (from 10 per cent to 22 per cent of the bottom 10 per cent). Much of this increase can be put down to increased unemployment and the changes in benefit rates. Even more startling figures show that the poor have been falling even further behind the rest of society since 1979.

It would be strange of course, if the transformation and restructuring of the British welfare state over two decades of Conservative government had not had profound effects on the number of people in poverty. Poverty is a highly politicized concept. This is true, not only in terms of its definition and the debate over its causes, but also in terms of the overt attempts of recent administrations to redefine the policies and forms of intervention (or not) surrounding it. Government policy directly affects the rates of benefit, which in turn affects the standard of living for many in low-paid jobs. Other factors, such as unemployment rates, are also a direct consequence of policy.

Pond (1989) demonstrates that after several decades where inequality in the United Kingdom decreased, it increased noticeably during the 1980s. While increased home ownership may have slightly widened the distribution of wealth, the overall patterns remain best characterized by stability rather than any radical change.

Poverty in the contemporary United Kingdom remains widespread. Further, as Alcock (1993) and Walker and Walker (1987) highlight, there are direct links between poverty and gender, racism, ageing and disability: women, blacks, the old and the disabled suffer disproportionately from poverty. Alcock concludes that the position of the most disadvantaged groupings in contemporary Britain is a function of the majority of society, who regard poverty as a problem of, and for, the poor themselves, rather than of society as a whole. The negative and destructive effects on those living in long-term poverty has been clearly show in several studies (see Cohen et al., 1992; Seabrook, 1985).

The gap between the richest and poorest sections of society is getting wider. At the start of the 1970s the incomes of the richest 10 per cent were three times higher than the poorest 10 per cent. In the 1990s they were four times higher. The distribution of wealth has altered little in the past 20 years and is now even more unevenly shared. In 1996, 1 per cent of the population owned 20 per cent of the wealth – approximately £388 billion. Around 10 per cent of the population owned over 50 per cent of the total wealth. The wealthiest 50 per cent, however, owned 93 per cent of the wealth (*The Guardian*, 11 May 2000).

Between 1979 and 1999, the numbers living on a low income (that is below half of the average income) in the United Kingdom increased from 5 million (9 per cent of the population) to over 14 million (26 per cent of the population). This means that 7.5 million people are so poor that they cannot afford to engage in what are considered by most of the rest of the population as 'normal' social activities such as Christmas, birthdays, visiting relatives in hospital, and so on. Over two million British children go without at least two things they need: three meals a day, and toys or adequate clothing (Joseph Rowntree Foundation, 2000). Moreover, this section of society cannot afford one or more essential household goods in their homes, such as a fridge, a telephone, or carpets for the living areas (*The Independent*, 11 September 2000).

Further, the Joseph Rowntree Foundation, in a report entitled *Income and Wealth* (1995), warned that the gap between rich and poor in the United Kingdom was at its widest for 50 years. They reported that income inequalities have widened further in the United Kingdom than in almost any comparable country. The report also suggested that between 1979 and 1992, the poorest 20 to 30 per cent of the population failed to benefit from economic growth. Indeed, the poorest 10 per cent were worse off in 'actual' as well as relative terms. In the mid-1970s only 6 per cent of the population had incomes below half the national average. By 1990, however, more than one in five were in that category.

The distribution of wealth in the United Kingdom also remains vastly unsymmetrical in pattern. Up until the 1980s, wealth inequalities had narrowed rapidly. They then became fixed, with the gap much wider than for income. The Child Poverty Action Group (CPAG) claimed that in 1989 there were 12 million people living in poverty. Further, Britain showed the sharpest rise in poverty in any country in the EC between 1980 and 1985 (*The Observer*, 23 November 1994).

More people are now living in poverty than at any other time in the past 20 years. Of the 56 million Britons, about 15 million or 26 per cent of the population live without what many would regard as the basic necessities of life (*The Scotsman*, 11 May 2000). There is still more evidence. In late 1998, Sir Donald Acheson, a former government chief medical officer, warned of a growing gap between rich and poor, claiming that it was now impossible for many poor families to buy a nutritious diet.

It has also been reported (*The Independent*, 15 October 1998) that during the past 20 years the difference in life expectancy between those at the top and the bottom of the social structure has widened. Death rates throughout that time have fallen by 40 per cent among social classes I and II, by 30 per cent among classes III and IV. In the lowest class category, however, the equivalent figure is only 10 per cent. Beyond this, men in social classes I and II live an average of five years longer than those in classes IV and V, while women live, on average, three years longer. The poor also suffer illness disproportionately. One in five professional men aged 45–64 has longstanding illness, compared with half of unskilled men. The gap between the rich and poor continued to grow throughout the 1990s (*The Guardian*, 11 May 2000). The *Office of National Statistics Report* (2000) confirmed that during the 1990s the rate of growth of incomes of the top 10 per cent continued to outstrip improvements at the bottom.

The gendered pay gap is also apparent from the *ONS Report*. The average earnings of men in full-time work are around 42 per cent higher than the average earnings of women. Between 1961 and 1998 the proportion of households headed by a lone parent rose from 2 per cent to 7 per cent. A quarter of all black families is made up of a lone parent with dependent children.

There are distinctly identifiable geographical aspects to these patterns of deprivation. Some of the areas of 'worst health' include parts of Glasgow, Liverpool, Manchester, Salford, Tyne Bridge, Southwark North and Bermondsey. In contrast, the areas of 'best health' can be found mainly in southern England, East Anglia and the West Country.

Despite what the New Labour government would have us believe, however, the poor are not necessarily concentrated in identifiable geographical pockets of deprivation. As Denny (2000) points out, in 1997, two-thirds of all unemployed people lived outside the 44 most deprived districts, as identified by the Social Exclusion Unit. Nor is there any crude north–south divide in evidence.

The consequences for the one million people dwelling in one of the 'worst health' areas in the United Kingdom are dramatic. In 1991 they were 2.8 times more likely to report suffering from a long-term, limiting illness than were those in areas of 'best health'. People living in the 'worst health' constituencies were 2.6 times more likely to die prematurely than those living in the 'best health' localities (Shaw et al., 1999).

The growing prominence of the poor has set in motion a fierce political debate. Following on from arguments in the USA, there is now controversy as to whether sections of the United Kingdom's inner-city communities have reached the point where it is possible to describe them as an underclass, that is a stratum in society comprising the long-term unemployed, those who have never worked and those who are fully dependent on social security and state provision for their living standards. The underclass is that section of the working class that has most directly experienced the spread of unemployment and job insecurity, the move away from traditional, male, full-time employment towards part-time, largely female work. They have also experienced the continuing gap between state benefits and average earnings.

Notions of the underclass

Underlying much of the discussion regarding Britain's new poor is the ideological positioning around whether they are victims of broader structural features of society or merely feckless and workshy individuals who have excluded themselves from the mainstream economy. Further, if an underclass exists within the United Kingdom, will it have the desolating effect on British society that it seemingly has done in many cities and regions in the USA?

The origins of the contemporary usage of the term 'underclass' lie in the USA. Here, it was used to describe a group of people entirely reliant on state handouts, or the proceeds of illegal or informal work. Their social position was marked by an extremely low degree of mobility out of this group into any another. It was argued that disadvantage was generational in that one generation's poverty was passed on to the next. Hence, disadvantage becomes almost pathological. Wilson (1987) argues that an underclass composed of those below the stable employed working class has come into existence in the USA.

The notion of an underclass and the parameters of much of the contemporary debate on both sides of the Atlantic has, since the publication of his controversial bestseller, *Losing Ground* (1984), been dominated the writings of Charles Murray. It was in a series of feature articles published in *The Sunday Times* that Murray (1989) first expanded his views regarding a United Kingdom underclass. He predicted that, within a decade, Britain's underclass would become proportionately as large as that of the United States.

In a more recent work, Murray (1994a, 1994b) examines Britain's social problems and claims to identify the emergence of a British underclass, defined not only by its poverty but also by its behaviour. He concentrates on three 'signals' of the rising underclass: rising levels of violent crime; economic inactivity among working-aged men; and 'illegitimacy', the number of children born outside marriage. He provides 'evidence' to support his thesis. Between 1987 and 1992 property crime in England and Wales increased by 42 per cent. By 1992 the risk of being burgled in England and Wales was more than double that in the USA. The violent crime rate increased by 40 per cent, so that the rate in England and Wales in 1992 was the same as in the USA in 1985. In 1987, some 23 per cent of births in England and Wales occurred outside marriage. By 1992 this figure had risen to 31 per cent.

Murray uses this material to defend his claim that the welfare state has had unintended and perverse effects, actually making matters worse, at least for its supposed beneficiaries. Indeed, in his more recent writings (*Sunday Times*, 13 January 2000) he widens his focus and calls for a return to the liberal ideals of limited government, local autonomy and control over one's own destiny.

The works of Murray have certainly not gone unchallenged. From various perspectives, Brown (1996), Deakin (1996), Mann (1994) and Walker and Walker (1996) all reject the usefulness of Murray's notion of underclass. Field (1989) suggests the term is only of some use if the notion is constructed with precision. While clearly identifiable differences between the 'new poor' and the traditional working class have led some to classify the former as an underclass (Dahrendorf, 1982), Field has pointed out that the underclass and the poor are not synonymous.

What distinguishes the underclass from others on low income is that they are cut off and isolated from mainstream society, drawn, for example, from the long-term unemployed, single parents and very old pensioners. Field highlights four major reasons for the construction of what he terms the contemporary underclass. First, the nature of social mobility. For many years 'bright' working-class children rose to well-paid middle-class jobs. To some extent Murray recognizes that this trend continues. What is new is that the contemporary social structure forces those who previously held respectable working-class jobs into the underclass. Secondly, throughout the 1980s and 1990s income and wealth was pushed towards those at the top. Thirdly, throughout the same period, an ever-widening gap in living standards was an 'official objective' of Conservative governments, abandoning any commitment to paternalistic Conservatism. Finally, he points to a major shift in public attitudes. This has led to the psychological and political separation of the poorest sections of society. Importantly, the concept of solidarity within the working class has been undermined.

The term 'underclass' is also be used in a way to blame the poor for the position they occupy (Walker and Walker, 1996). At its extreme it suggests that the situational disadvantage of such people makes them unemployable. Reflecting the earlier notions of Lewis (1961), it is argued that these individuals create a culture of deprivation which, when transmitted to their children, forms part of a 'cycle of deprivation'. For Murray, this has produced a culture which erodes any distinction between the 'deserving' and 'undeserving' poor. Throughout his recent writings, he is particularly keen to apply the above to black youth in America and to explain the withdrawal of black youth from the voluntary labour market.

Murray (1984) has also argued that in the USA several important social changes occurred during the 1960s. In particular, the idea that a man should be the family 'breadwinner' and cater for his wife and children was directly undermined. For Murray, this was largely because explanations and understandings of the situation shifted away from an emphasis on individual characteristics and behaviour and towards structural factors such as poverty and unemployment. One result, it is argued, is that notions of 'self-sufficiency' and individual responsibility were undermined, eroding the moral obligations of healthy adults. This in turn helped remove any 'stigma' of receiving public assistance and welfare, making this section of the population more and more willing to live off the welfare provision of the state and further increasing dependency.

Politics and the underclass

For Murray (1990: 2), perhaps the only major difference between the USA and the United Kingdom is that the 'United States reached the future first'. Within the United Kingdom such ideas have been readily adopted and applied by several neoconservatives. Mount (cited in Loney, 1987: 11), for example, makes his distaste for the poor overt when he claimed that the rich 'admire the poor less and less, partly because the poor are not as poor as they used to be, but also because the poor fritter their money on such trash – video cassettes and cars with fluffy mice that joggle in the back window'.

Marsland (1994: 14–17) is another who makes his position clear on such issues. He believes that the state provision of welfare has 'inexorably corrupted the whole nation'. It is simply not needed because of the rising living standards of the whole population, because it cannot be afforded and simply does not work. More specifically, the underclass or, as he would term them, those minority who are temporarily incapable of self-reliance, are in the position they occupy because of their own failings.

From such perspectives, the welfare state has thus only succeeded in creating dependency and 'sustaining a self-excluding underclass'. Marsland's (1994: 16) thoughts on the homeless are typical: in his view a large proportion are 'mentally ill and handicapped people who were much better and more economically served in asylums. Others are young people who left home inappropriately and unnecessarily in the expectation that the state will provide what their own prudence has not.' This viewpoint is representative of that ideology which seeks to extend its account to link widescale unemployment, family break-down, increasing crime rate and other social problems directly to the construction of a culture of dependency and the concept of the underclass.

The idea of an underclass whose composition is determined by genetic or cyclical inferiority has not gone without criticism. As Bagguley and Mann (1992) point out, the term 'underclass' has increasingly been used to blame victims for their own deprivation. Part of this, for Bagguley and Mann, takes the form of a classic moral panic around the notions of illegitimacy, violent crime and fecklessness, hence the construction of the distinct image of members of the underclass as 'idle thieving bastards'. They further argue that this constructed myth is best understood as an instrument of ruling-class ideology, obscuring the core processes that perpetuate social inequalities.

Further, as McNicol (1987) highlights, the concept of an underclass as a sub-stratum group that falls outside an otherwise cohesive and integrated society has a remarkably longstanding and tenacious history. Despite much recent widespread attention, the concept remains hazy, involving biological arguments and moral judgements as well as arguments about the effects of a changing class structure, inadequate socialization and a continued deviant sub-culture.

What holds the definitions together is a political desire to criticize certain groups in society as failing and a burden on the 'successful'. As Morris (1994) demonstrates, Murray's arguments have become central in setting the context of the underclass debate on both sides of the Atlantic. Hence, in the United Kingdom the spotlight has in particular been directed towards high rates of illegitimacy among 'never-married mothers' and high dependency among the unskilled manual working class.

The '30–30–40' society

With much of the above in mind, Hutton (1995b) categorizes the United Kingdom as a '30–30–40 society'. His model is based on recent social fissures of the working population. Here, he defines the underclass in slightly different terms. The first 30 per cent, he calls *the disadvantaged*. Central to this grouping are the four million who are out of work and unemployed, including unemployed women and those women who cannot work because the loss of their husband's income support would not make this financially viable.

The second 30 per cent are made up of the *marginalized* and *the insecure*. Those in this category are defined not so much by income but by their relation to the labour market. Working as they do in insecure working conditions, they are marginal to the mainstream. There are more than five million people in the contemporary United Kingdom, working part-time, of whom around

80 per cent are women. There are others, those with full-time but insecure employment. Their position in the labour market is unprotected. They are increasingly under threat, through the growth of casual employment and short- and fixed-term contracts at work.

Finally, there is that 40 per cent which comprises *the privileged*. The market power and strength of this segment has increased since 1979. It is made up of several important groups – those full-time employees and the self-employed who have held their jobs for over two years, and those part-timers that have held their position for over five years. The 31 per cent of the workforce who remain members of trade unions and have a high degree of workplace representation usually fall within this category.

According to Hutton, the above break-down of the labour market is restructuring Britain for the worse, creating 'a new and ugly shape of British society'. This draws him to some startling conclusions. As he puts it:

> The fact that more than half the people in Britain who are eligible to work are living either in poverty incomes or are in insecure work has had dreadful effects on the wider society. Britain has the highest divorce rate and the most deregulated labour markets in Europe and these two facts are closely related. The impact of inequality is pervasive, affecting everything from the vitality of the housing market to the growth of social security spending. (Hutton, 1995b)

Class, politics and social structure

So how can the social structure of the contemporary United Kingdom best be understood? In considering theories of social class in social theory we enter a debate where clashing interpretations, models and schemes seem to have no end. What all of these have in common is the attempt to make sense of the social world. After all, what are termed 'class', 'class relations', 'class conflict' and so on are products of humans attempting to order the chaotic manifestations of the world around them. First of all, therefore, it is useful to consider some general issues such as how to classify objects in the social historical world.

The world is, in part at least, constructed by our social practices, by our narratives, our stories, myths and language, by our social understanding, and our social theories, formalized or otherwise. In this sense, we have to consider 'social class' as a rhetorical term. Existing groups redefine themselves, perceive themselves in new ways, present new faces to the outside world, divide and fuse and are formed out of a practice of struggle where definitions and identities are constituted by a complex web of representation and characterizations. Clearly, however, the definition of class is not just subjective, but also reflects 'real' changes in an existing social structure.

This immediately draws us to other questions, such as how such groups form, and what holds them together? Obviously, homogeneity is not a necessary and sufficient condition for cohesion. A group that manages itself together in its existence, and establishes formal representative institutions, constitutes, in some respects at least, an objective entity.

Any subsequent discussion of this, however, depends on how class is defined. That there is no agreed theoretical position on how class is defined is a breathtaking act of understatement. It is, however, possible to identify two broad approaches, deriving from the works of Marx and Weber. Let us begin, therefore, by considering in rather more detail these two major perspectives, drawing as they do on class in different ways as a core organizing principle of society.

Contemporary Marxism and class

Although Marx is inevitably seen as the most detailed theorist of class, it is now a well-documented paradox that he never made a consistent statement on the matter (see Wright, 1985). There is, however, plenty in Marx's writings to indicate strongly the direction of his thinking. At a general level of Marxist analysis, class in capitalist society can be defined as follows: in any capitalist society the class of wage earners has nothing to sell but its labour power. This it sells to a class of employers, which owns all capital assets and resources.

This is the relational theory of class with which most are familiar, that places two basic classes in a dichotomous relation of antagonism or struggle. It is important, however, not to think that Marx's major works form some seamless web on the issues of class. Indeed, it is in his more journalistic writings, such as *The Class Struggle in France* [1895] 1969), where Marx identifies a more complex model of class, which has been adapted by several more recent Marxist writers.

One understanding of contemporary class structure derived from Marxist writings can be found in the work of Wright (1978), who has argued that while class remains central, it is necessary to introduce the further concept of 'domination'. Previously, ownership of property meant control over investment, physical capital, such as plant, and control of labour. In modern economies, however, legal ownership is often separated from investment and production and from direct control of the labour process. Ownership of companies ranges across individuals and institutional shareholders. The 'top' management retains control of the use of assets, but the control of day-to-day production is delegated to junior managers, who in turn delegate control of the workforce to supervisors.

For Wright, all of this means that many people find themselves in contradictory class positions: managers control without ownership; the petty bourgeoisie may own, but not actually employ labour; many craft workers have control over the labour process, but they of course remain employees. Wright also believes that the petty bourgeoisie are 'outside' the capitalist mode of production, although they clearly exist as an identifiable grouping within capitalist societies.

TABLE 6.2   ASSETS, EXPLOITATION AND CLASSES

Type of class structure	Principal asset unequally distributed	Mechanism of exploitation	Classes	Principal contradictory location
Feudalism	Labour power	Coercive extraction of surplus labour	Lords and serfs	Bourgeoisie
Capitalism	Means of production	Market exchanges of labour power and commodities	Capitalists and workers	Managers/ bureaucrats
Statism	Organization	Planned appropriation and distribution of surplus based on hierarchy	Managers/ bureaucrats and non-management	Intelligentsia/ experts
Socialism	Skills	Negotiated redistribution of surplus from workers to experts	Experts and workers	

Source: Wright (1985)

Wright's work has led to criticisms and has resulted in another fundamental reassessment by Roemer (1982) of Marxist class theory. He believes that by emphasizing aspects of control, Wright had made a misjudgement, particularly as this separated domination from exploitation. His is a complex argument surrounding the rejection of control of the labour process and the appropriation of surplus value.

Further, Roemer argues that it is necessary to generalize Marx's notion of exploitation to make it applicable to socialist, feudal and capitalist societies. He seeks to show that different forms of exploitation are characteristic of different types of society. Roemer's fundamental argument is that property relations are the key to exploitation, not social relations at the point of production, and that 'democratic control' of the surplus, not of the workplace, is the real necessity for social transformation. Roemer attempts to escape from talking only about capitalism. He wanted to abstract from actually existing capitalism as much as possible, to construct a general theory that could be used to discuss exploitation under socialism as well.

In response to Roemer's largely theoretical approach, however, Wright (1985) revised much of his work on contradictory class locations, formulating a scheme of modes of production (see Table 6.2). For Wright, there is no inevitable movement towards socialism and communism, but rather struggle between exploiters and exploited. For him, all the previous major transitions, from feudalism to capitalism, and from capitalism to state socialism, have been marked by the previous contradictory class becoming dominant. For example, in the French Revolution it was the bourgeoisie who were central in restraining the power of the monarchy and aristocracy. Likewise, in the Russian Revolution, power was centralized with state functionaries who controlled production and labour.

What both Roemer and Wright are seeking to do is to demonstrate, while remaining within the essential framework of Marxism, that there are multiple strands of exploitation within contemporary capitalist society. Others have sought to reformulate Weber's classical view on social classes. The relationship between the two perspectives is not necessarily a directly oppositional one. It is useful to remember that, although essentially conservative in his politics, Weber's writings reflect not only a clear opposition to the emerging socialist movements in Europe at the time, but also a healthy intellectual respect for Marx's theoretical position.

Weber and class

The starting point for many subsequent criticisms of Marx's concept of class can be found in Weber's 'Class, Status and Party' in his massive volume *Economy and Society* (1978). In particular, the interpretation, which argues that Marx treated 'class' as a purely economic phenomenon and, moreover, regarded class conflict as in some way the inevitable outcome of clashes of material interest, has been central to many Weberian and neo-Weberian arguments.

Such critics point out that the divisions of economic interest which create classes do not necessarily correspond to sentiments of collective identity which constitute differential 'status'. Thus status which depends upon subjective evaluation is a separate dimension of stratification. It differs from class, and the two may vary independently. There is yet a third dimension, so the argument continues, which Weber recognized as another independently variable factor in stratification, that of power.

Another dimension of Weber's work on class, which has been identified by Giddens (1994), is that Weber's viewpoint 'strongly emphasises a pluralistic conception of classes'. For example, the class position of the property-less is differentiated in relation both to the types and degree of 'monopolization' of 'marketable' skills that they possess. Most importantly, there are various types of middle class which stand between the 'positively privileged' classes (the propertied capital asset owners) and the 'negatively privileged' classes (those who possess neither property nor marketable skills).

Clearly this is a more complex cartography of class than the orthodox interpretation of Marx would suggest. A Weberian reading of class points to the working class 'segmented' into several different categories. For those coming from a Weberian perspective, class is best understood in terms of social status and skills. Within these, occupation is the key determinant of class. Different jobs can be ranked in a hierarchical order of status as the key indicator.

Although in Marx's terms these groups are separated from the ownership of the means of production, they cannot be said to occupy the same location as the traditional working class. While, on the one hand, there are strong arguments supporting the view that Marx's and Weber's concept of class are not contradictory in their essence, there are, on the other hand, counter-perspectives, especially from more orthodox Marxists, that these views of class differ fundamentally. Certainly this is correct, in respect that Marx sees privileges originating in the sphere of production relations, while Weber concentrates on relations of distribution and circulation.

Contemporary Marxist and Weberian models: towards convergence?

One of the main challenges offered by neo-Weberians to the Marxist analysis is that Marxism cannot account for the increasingly fragmented class relations in contemporary society. Weberians are also highly critical of the idea of an aggregated consciousness originating from workplace relationships which will lead to collective action. A refutation of such Marxist tenets can classically be found in the works of Lockwood (1958, 1966). In classical Weberian vane, he emphasizes that consciousness has many sources, some of which generate individualized and privatized consciousness which may actually move against collective identity and action by working people.

Dahrendorf (1959, 1982) is another who has produced a clear neo-Weberian critique. For him, the Marxist analysis is increasingly outmoded and outdated, and simply cannot account for the complexity of contemporary class relations. In the case of the bourgeoisie, this has involved a clear separation of ownership of capital (which is increasingly in the hands of shareholders) from the control of capital (which is ever more in the hands of managers). The proletariat, far from becoming more homogeneous, has become increasingly fragmented, especially as technological advances have widened social divisions and cleavages rather than solidified them.

The issues outlined above have led some to pursue a synthesis of the views of Marx and Weber to produce a partly converged model. Later neo-Marxist writings have stressed the different fractions within classes and, in partly seeking to accommodate the Weberian model, have thus suggested that conflict is possible within classes as well as between them.

One continued difference between the two approaches is that most neo-Marxists still advocate the centrality of class struggle as a transforming force in society. There are, however, increasingly apparent overlaps between the two understandings of class. Bradley (1992: 15) summarizes the main points of comparison and contrast of both Marxist and Weberian perspectives (see Table 6.3). Despite this, there are many that believe that class is no longer a focal point in the understanding and organization of society. One crucial

TABLE 6.3   NEO-MARXIST AND NEO-WEBERIAN POSITIONS ON CLASS

Neo-Marxist	Neo-Weberian
Class divisions generated by relations of production, especially by the mechanism of exploitation	Class divisions generated by the operation of the market
Unifying effect of exploitation emphasized	Classes are seen as subject to growing processes of fragmentation
The existence of 'fractions' and conflicts within classes acknowledged but seen as less important than the conflicts between classes	Divisions and conflicts within classes seen as just as significant as conflicts between classes
Middle classes seen as linked to one of the two major classes or as 'structurally ambiguous'	Middle classes seen as an autonomous grouping and considered as socially significant as the propertied or working class
Consciousness arises from relations of production	Consciousness has many different sources
Dominant ideology accounts for the failure of the working class to develop a critical class consciousness	Fragmentation, social mobility and growth of democratic political structures inhibit the growth of class consciousness
Revolutionary potential of the working class remains	Class revolution is improbable

Source: Bradley (1992: 15)

question in the development of contemporary politics, therefore, is what pertinence, if any, do notions of class have for the lives of ordinary people?

The end of class?

It is now a common proposition that social class is no longer as important as it was (Clark and Lipset, 1991; Compton, 1996). At its extreme, it is claimed that 'class is dead'. Much of this proposition rests on the view that the definition and classification of class has become increasingly complex and elaborate, to the point where it has become so nebulous as to be meaningless. Those who strongly support the 'decline of class thesis' even go beyond this, to suggest that class is no longer a vital determinant of social and political identity. People, it is claimed, simply do not identify with a particular class in the way that they once did, nor can class be seen as the key determinant in life chances and experiences.

   Much of what we have encountered so far, including debates about 'a classless Britain', the 'end of ideology', the 'end of history' and the widespread popular usage of terms such as 'postmodernism' and 'postfeminism', have led some to hail a new epoch for politics within the United Kingdom. Central here is the notion that society is moving beyond the 'old' social divisions, based on class, gender and ethnicity, to a new form of post-class politics, based on differing identities around, for example, sexual orientation or the environment (see Evans, 1993, 1999). Fundamental to all of this is the emergence of the new politics that finds expression through the new social movements, such as those identified later in the chapter.

Miliband (1991: 19), for example, notes that 'an extraordinary degree of confusion and obfuscation attends the discussion of class in relation to capitalist societies'. While he recognizes the growing importance of the new social movements, such as feminism, anti-racism and sexual liberation, he still believes that primacy must be given to the labour movement, which remains 'by far the most important movement in any transformation (of society)' (1991: 96).

While, for some, Miliband's perspective is extremely restricted, for others the death of class has been wildly exaggerated. The concept is still seen to be of direct and continuing relevance. Compton, for example, argues that capitalist industrial societies

> are still stratified, and theories of social class still provide us with essential insights into the manner in which established inequalities in wealth and power associated with production and markets, access to educational and organisational resources, and so on have systematically served to perpetuate these inequalities over time. (Compton, 1993: 206)

Further, as Marshall et al. (1988: 11) suggest, although parts of the decline of class thesis may have some validity, there is no obvious lack of class awareness among the population of modern Britain as a whole, which 'remains a capitalist class society, and the various attempts to identify 'post-industrial' (and post-capitalist) features in the developments of recent years are not at all convincing'.

Debates around the reformulation of class therefore remain central to interpretations and understandings of politics. Crucial here are arguments concerning the extent to which the major organizational categories of society outlined in much of this book, namely, class, gender, ethnicity and race, have been broken down or fragmented to the point where they no longer retain the organizational strength they once did. Indeed, for some, it is extremely difficult, if not impossible, to speak of group and political identities based on these classifications. One source for such thinking was the emergence of an analysis from a section of the British Left in the latter part of the 1980s.

New Times for class

Around the late 1980s there was another attempt from the Left to redefine politics and the political. This involved many of those seeking to understand contemporary politics through a series of theoretical positions: post-Fordism; postmodernism; globalization; and the politics of identity and citizenship. The focus for much of this was the magazine *Marxism Today*, and it was given momentum by the Communist Party, which quickly adopted the *Manifesto for New Times* as a central tenet of its policy. It is useful to identify the starting point for the New Times analysis. From this perspective (*New Times*, 1989: 17), a core feature of contemporary society is 'the proliferation of the sites of antagonism and resistance, and the appearance of new subjects, new social movements, new collective identities – an enlarged sphere for the operation of politics, and new constituencies of change'.

It was recognized that these are not easy to organize into any collective political will and that there is no 'inevitable political trajectory' to society. Hence, *New Times* suggests both the break-down of class narratives and the traditional opposition of Left and Right. The new image, it suggests, is one of fluid identities, whereby, for example, a woman can be a lesbian, a mother, an ecological consumer, a political activist, a community leader, a voter, and so on.

This series of identities is meaningful in a way that simply being 'working class', or seeking to organize as working class, was not. This takes us to another hugely important current perspective regarding the nature and vigour of contemporary politics – the idea that other forms of social movements mobilize and drive politics. The expansion of the definition of politics beyond the party political, the diminished role of the state, the ever-increasing importance of globalization and social fragmentation mean that the centrality of class can no longer be sustained.

New social movements

If class is no longer a central organizing force in society, what does provide the political dynamic in contemporary society? One explanation lies in the growing prominence of 'new social movements' and the differing patterns of radicalism and political values expressed through such groupings (Diani, 1992; Laraña et al., 1994; Melucci, 1980).

A useful starting point to understand the development of such groupings is found in events in the USA in the late 1960s and 1970s. This period saw the emergence of a wide variety of movements, such as those agitating for civil rights, black power and the politicized sexuality of the women and the gay liberation movements. Most of all, however, it manifested itself in the students' movement. In part such movements were a direct response to specific events, particularly the USA's involvement in the Vietnam War.

At times, issues of concern to the student and anti-war movements overlapped with other developing 'separatist' movements, such as the black civil rights movement and the women's and gay liberation movements. Importantly, all these movements developed and were organized outside the existing class-based political structures of the Left.

The structures of new social movements are complex and often involve unplanned, spontaneous actions. The tactics of new social movements may include sit-ins, demonstrations, and perhaps even collective expressions of violence such as rioting. They may also include, however, meetings, fund-raising, lobbying or petition campaigning (see Lofland, 1985; Marwell and Oliver, 1984). New social movements may be characterized as anti-statist, promoting more informal and non-hierarchical forms of participation and organization.

So how is it possible to understand the significance of this transformation from the 'old politics' to the 'new'. Here, Inglehart (1977a, 1977b, 1980, 1981, 1987) provides a useful starting point in identifying what he terms as a 'silent revolution'. This involves the shift from the old politics of materialism towards the new of post-materialism. He suggests that the focus of politics has now radically altered, from a concern with material issues and economic resources towards post-material values and quality-of-life issues. The central issues within old politics were economic growth and distribution, military and social security and social control. At its core were the values of freedom and security of private consumption and material progress. Old politics dominated from the end of the Second World War until around the early 1970s. During this time, there was a sharp separation between those organizations representing societal interests and the political parties concerned with winning votes and office. Collective bargaining and representative government was regarded as the exclusive legitimate mechanisms for resolving political and social conflict. Post-materialist values tend to emphasize senses of belonging, self-expression and issues surrounding the quality of life. Examples include the environment, human rights, peace, personal autonomy and identity. These are forms of politics that can be regarded as neither public nor private. It is a politics that is perceived as having little to do with the class relationships that used to dominate politics.

So how is it possible to understand the roles of new social movements? Such movements often seek to politicize civil society in ways that are not constrained by existing political structures, institutions and political parties. Further, new social movements usually contain several identifiable features, including mass mobilization (at least occasionally), a tendency towards loose organizational structure, spasmodic activity, working (in the past at least) outside established instructional framework, and central aims which are either about bringing social change or preserving the existing social order.

It is possible to argue that the momentum for the growth of new social movements is provided by the development of post-industrial society. Here, crucially, class is displaced as the central location of conflict in society. It is patterns of consumption, rather than of production, which provide the key to unlocking this new society. As Touraine (1971: 9) puts it, the cleavage is now between the 'structures of economic and political decision-making and those who are reduced to dependent participation'. Given this, the workers' movement can no longer be seen as the central social movement in society.

Touraine (1981, 1983) further distinguishes two types of society, the industrial versus post-industrial, with two corresponding forms of social movement. Workers' movements are characteristic of social movements in industrial societies, whereas new social movements are characteristic of post-industrial societies. The aim of post-industrial social movements is not directly to seize power or integrate directly into the political decision-making process. Rather, they seek to represent those non-class-based interests centred around gender, peace, race, ethnicity, ecology, sexuality and so on (see Carter, 1992; Cohen and Rai, 2000; Jordan and Maloney, 1997; Pakulski, 1990; Yearly, 1992; Young, 1990). In the past decade one of the major locations of the new social movements has involved the environmental movement and the emergence of 'eco-warriors' involved in direct action. In particular, this has manifested itself in protests against airport expansion and road-building programmes (see McKay, 1998).

As Doherty (2001) points out, these anti-road protests differed from what had gone before in three crucial ways. First, those involved used direct action, consciously bypassing formal consultation processes. Secondly, activists engaged in promoting a counter-culture, often centred upon anarchistic ideals and values. They were also critical of long-standing environmental organizations, such as Greenpeace, which they saw as having become part of the establishment. Thirdly, protesters utilized particular tactics. These often involved 'headline grabbing' schemes such as occupying trees in areas to be cleared for road-building or digging tunnels under areas marked for airport runway expansion.

The end of history?

Whether the forces representing new social movements can transcend their marginal political position to create a new political paradigm remains to be seen. The notion that society has moved into a new political paradigm is also revealed in Fukuyama's *The End of History and the Last Man* (1992). Here he argues that the fall of the Soviet bloc has brought about a global triumph and the final victory of 'liberal democracy' as there is no longer any counter-vailing ideology left to serve as an antithesis. For Fukyama, the dominant Western free market juggernaut prevails and effectively ends the conflict and friction that generate historical events and shape the flow of history.

Hence, unlike Hegel or Marx, Fukuyama believes that history ends not with the evolution of a classless society of communism, but rather with the triumph of 'democratic capitalism'. Fukuyama sees history developing through a series of stages, the result of economic progress, internal contra-dictions and political struggle. Indeed, the result is what Fukuyama calls a Marxist approach in an effort to reach a 'non-Marxist' conclusion.

Fukuyama claims that it is liberal democratic capitalism which is most 'in tune' with human nature and its related aspirations. For him, it is liberal-democratic capitalism that goes furthest in satisfying the needs of citizens, through the ability to vote and the rights that are acknowledged by the modern liberal state. The material desires of all humans, their capacity for reason and spiritual aspirations, have all gradually developed through the various stages of history.

In most societies these desires and aspirations have been restrained but with the advent of the Enlightenment and the English, French and American Revolutions these have come to fruition with the triumph of the bourgeoisie over its feudal rivals. Following Hegel, Fukuyama claims that once the bourgeois democratic system was initially established it was only a matter of time before it, first, was perfected in the West, and secondly, spread outwards to engulf the globe.

Commentators from across a broad political spectrum have found it difficult to ignore Fukuyama's basic message that there is now no ideological alternative to universal liberal-democratic capitalism. Fukuyama further argues that history is at an end. This is not history in the sense of everyday happenings or political events. Rather, it is history with a capital 'H' that is over. By this he largely means the struggle between ideologies and the systems they represent. This trend has, however, produced individuals who are solely pre-occupied with their 'private lives'.

People are increasingly focused on individual pursuits and individualized lifestyles, such as shopping, keeping fit, listening to personal stereos, watching television and so on. These are selfish individuals, who no longer engage in ideological warfare or in the struggle for ideas.

In a later work, Fukuyama (1995) addresses what he sees as the cultural variations within societies at the end of the twentieth century. Here Fukuyama argues that the successful operation of capitalism can best be achieved by nations with high cultural assets, the most important of which is trust (or cohesion) with civil society. An ability to extend trust throughout a society is essential for the smooth running of modern corporate capitalism. Hence, America, Japan and Germany have high levels of trust, while other societies such as France, Italy and China have low levels.

For Fukuyama, while the free market is essential, it can only account for part of the story. The rest involves a degree of cultural cohesion, which lies at the heart of the economic and social requirement. This new argument from Fukuyama suggests some recognition that even if the broad universal ideological arguments are over, there are still huge variations and tensions within the capitalist nations that need to be understood and analysed.

In *Trust* (1995) Fukuyama tries to address the issue of social problems by indicating that certain forms of economic and social arrangements and liberal-democratic governments are more successful than others in dealing with these. While Fukuyama's ideas have raised much criticism (see below), it is clear that he is engaged in explaining some very real changes in contemporary society. For this reason, it is necessary to consider other perspectives on politics and the postmodern condition.

Fukuyama's works suggest that all societies must now progress towards modernity. That there is nothing to which societies can evolve beyond liberal democracy and free markets. Hence, the end of history. In a recent work, Fukuyama (2001) suggests that society remains at the end of history because 'there is only one system that will continue to dominate world politics, that of the liberal-democratic west'. Those conflicts that remain consist of a series of rearguard actions by those societies whose traditional existence are threatened by modernization.

So while Fukuyama may not now claim that there are no major social divisions to be overcome at the 'end of history', he still clearly believes that these issues can still only be addressed within the framework of the primacy of the structures and demands of liberal-democratic capitalism. The main thrust of his ideas must be seen as being very much of their time. In the United Kingdom in the late 1990s, for example, Thatcher was still claiming to be waging war on socialism. The fall of the Communist bloc in 1989 provided an increasing dynamic for Fukuyama's views. The economic and political position of the United Kingdom meant that many could simply not envisage anything other than an energetic consumer-led economy, driven by the forces of neoliberalism.

Any 'final victory' of liberal democracy, however, must be seen as an extremely shallow one. The period of the 'end of history' has revealed far too much continuity to be the end of anything. The West has continued to find its position under threat from a wide variety of sources. Capitalism has shuddered and oscillated along its 'inevitable road' and the realities of economic difference have become stark. The World Health Organization (WHO) reports that severe poverty is now the earth's biggest killer (Harman, 1995: 7). The differences in the economies of the developed and developing worlds do not seem to lessen. Moreover, the central ideological liberal democracy faces ongoing challenge. The growth of political Islam, radical nationalisms, the bloody battles in and around the Balkans and the former Soviet states, and the events following the attacks on 11 September 2001 in the USA continue to undermine Fukuyama's supposed consensus.

The end of politics?

As Grossberg (1992: 89) points out, by the beginning of the 1990s it was increasingly difficult to gain a handle on 'the rapidly changing political alliances, positions and struggles of contemporary life'. Certainly, knowledge and politics anchored in modernity have been subject to a severe crisis in confidence and has become increasingly fragmented in its response. What remains are competing identity politics and fluid political alliances, which are often formed at the micro level. These alliances, by their nature, are unpredictable in their formation and continuance. So, for example, it is possible to find Marxists, feminists and gays and eco-warriors in complete unison on one issue and at total loggerheads on another.

If we continue with this line of thinking, we come to an alternative position that we are experiencing a dramatic change in the nature of politics itself. There are even some who characterize the contemporary period as heralding the end of politics (see Boggs, 2000; Mulgan, 1994). This builds on recent analyses overflowing with the notion that the old order has come to an end. We have, for example, already encountered Fukuyama's (1992) notion of 'the end of history'. Baudrillard's (1998a, 1998b) celebration of difference and concept of 'the end of the social' reflects a parallel theme.

For those supportive of postmodernism, the politics of 'the Nation', 'the People' or 'the Party' are to be doomed for their totalizing aspirations. So, too, must be the idea of a coherent political self. According to its advocates, the political has become the cultural. Politics now operates through a multitude of groups and identities in civil society and the expression of a wide variety of individual issues.

Politics it is argued must adapt to a new 'mix-and-match' society, where it has become increasingly less relevant to people's identities and priorities. This is reflected in the rising level of disillusionment expressed at the common level regarding politics and politicians. There are many examples of this in the public arena. In the last European elections, fewer than one in four of those eligible voted in the United Kingdom. In the 1997 devolution elections for the Scottish Parliament and Welsh Assembly, turnout was also remarkably low. Indeed, in the Leeds Central by-election of the same year, the turnout, at 19.6 per cent, was the lowest since the Second World War.

In the May 1997 UK general election only 71 per cent voted, the lowest number since the war. The pattern was reinforced in the 2001 general election, when the turnout was even lower with around 16 million of those eligible choosing not to vote. The turnout of 59.1 per cent meant that only one in four voters backed the newly re-elected New Labour government. Across much of the Western world polls reveal large numbers of citizens who endorse the view that their country's government cannot be trusted, and that their nation's economy is being mismanaged.

For some commentators, this turn away from the ballot box undermines the legitimacy of state institutions and perhaps the entire political system. The notion of the end of politics is addressed directly by Boggs (2000), who questions the 'triumph' of liberal democracy and free market capitalism. Rather, he laments the loss of civic participation in the contemporary USA, and argues that the new political sphere fails to include broad participation, generally operating only on behalf of corporate interests. While recognizing the multiple grassroots organizations throughout the country, he suggests that such organizations are increasingly disconnected from wider national and global issues.

Indeed, Boggs argues further that such organizations are depoliticized by our increasingly corporate-dominated culture, ensuring an end of politics which has lost its visionary and empowering qualities. This depoliticized culture results in an anti-political climate, and occurs when individual interests surpass any notion of a commitment to collective values or the collective goals of society. These processes of corporatization, depoliticization and anti-politics have all thrown the public sphere into deep crisis. From this perspective, politics simply has not kept in step with the new organizing principles of society, based largely around individualism and egalitarianism.

If one adds to this the seemingly dramatic decline in the role of the state and the dissolving of the legitimacy and authority of politicians, then the traditional arena of politics is seen as incapable of directly confronting the real issues of contemporary society. Such arguments continue to find resonance in the everyday. At one level, recent political manifestos, the smooth-running 'soundbite' and professionally staged party conferences give credence to the belief that the categories of Left and Right have become increasingly problematic in the politics of the United Kingdom. As Hertz puts it:

> Ideology competes with ice-cream. Politicians become salespeople, offering more and more: lower tax, better schools, more funding for the NHS. It is a double switch: politics has entered commerce; consumerism has entered politics. Unless politicians provide the same levels of service in hospitals and schools, the same quick response to our concerns and make the same effort to meet our needs as do Tesco and Sainsbury's, they will forfeit our custom. Corporations, realising how fickle our vote is, have to become even more conscientious, responsible and accountable, or face our defection. (Hertz, 1999: 105)

At any level it would be strange if the sociological changes outlined in this book had not resulted in political transformations. The core question is just how far political culture has been altered and what continuities may be identified? Corporations are certainly much more powerful than they used to be, but is there a danger of under-estimating the remaining powers of governments and the state? Global financial markets may constrain, but the state in the United Kingdom still allocates the spending of a large percentage of the GDP. How then should we understand the changes outlined above?

Postmodernism and politics

Postmodernism offers one set of explanations for many of the contemporary changes in society. It differs from other cultural forms by its emphasis on the fragmentation of the subject. Postmodernism rejects as irrelevant all existing metanarrative explanations such as Marxism or feminism. Hence, individualism is seen to replace collective loyalties such as class, religion, ethnicity or gender.

Within this perspective there is a loss of the centre, and history is without a core subject (Ashley, 1997). Postmodernist works are often characterized by a lack of depth and are concerned with surface, not substance. Individuals are no longer seen as anomic because there is nothing from which one can sever ties. This is not to say that the cultural products of the postmodern era are utterly devoid of feeling, but rather that such feelings are now free-floating and impersonal. Also distinctive of the late capitalist age is the recycling of old images and commodities, for example in the works of Andy Warhol.

Jameson (1984, 1985, 1998) refers to this cultural recycling as historicism: the random cannibalization of all styles of the past. It is demonstrated by the increasing primacy of the 'neo' and a world transformed into sheer images of itself. The organic tie of history to past events is lost. All of these cultural forms are indicative of postmodernism, late capitalism, or what Jameson calls 'present-day multinational capitalism'.

Considering such developments, several key contemporary Marxist writers (see Callinicos, 1991; Geras, 1987, 1995) have been at best negative, at worst downright hostile to the development of postmodern thought. Rather than regarding it as having emancipatory qualities, they see it as largely reactionary in nature. Hence, despite the so-called triumph of liberal-capitalist democracy, there continues to be strong defenders of neo-classical Marxism.

Callinicos, for one, believes that Marxism retains its integrity despite the weakening appeal of communism around the world. Hence, in *The Revenge of History* (1991) Callinicos argues that the liberal-democratic state has broken its major promises in three main ways: first, involving participation; secondly, the promise of control from below; and thirdly, the supposed freedom to protest and reform. Liberal-capitalist democracy fails, he argues, on all three counts and there are substantial constraints on state action, in particular on the possibility of reform of capitalism: 'the flight of capital is a habitual threat to elected governments with strong programmes of social reform' (Callinicos, 1991: 109).

Given this failure and the inability to solve the problems generated by capitalism, Callinicos attempts strongly to defend classical Marxism. In his opinion, an alternative to liberal-capitalist democracy can be found if we look to Soviet 'democracy' prior to Stalinism. Callinicos sees Stalinism as a counter-revolutionary force that created a 'state capitalist' regime in which the state bureaucracy fulfilled the role once performed by the bourgeoisie. Events between 1989 and 1991 cannot, therefore, be understood in Fukuyama's terms as the defeat of Marxism. Rather, it marked defeat for what was a mutilation of Marxism, resulting in authoritarian Stalinism.

The period of the late 1980s and early 1990s witnessed not a victory for 'democracy' but rather a triumph for 'unregulated capitalism'. For Callinicos, what the revolutions in the old Eastern bloc largely achieved was a political re-organization of the Eastern ruling classes, which allowed them to integrate their economies into the global market. In a series of debates with Fukuyama, Callinicos asserts that the latter's 'capitalist utopianism' fails to recognize the problems of poverty and exploitation which capitalism is incapable of overcoming because they are inherent in the system itself.

From another critical perspective, Jameson (1984, 1985, 1998) is also derogatory of the postmodern project, highlighting the differences in culture between the modern and postmodern periods. He also devotes much time to the effects of these changes on the individual, concerned as he is with the cultural expressions and forms of aesthetics associated with the different systems of production. Indeed, Jameson draws across the fields of architecture, art and other culturally expressive forms to illustrate his beliefs, arguing that it is essential to grasp postmodernism as a dominant cultural form of late capitalism.

These perspectives are underscored by Mandel's thesis (1975) that there have been three fundamental moments in capitalism, each one marking a dialectical expansion over the previous stage. These are market capitalism, monopoly capitalism and, what our own period most correctly called multi-national capitalism (and in Mandel's view wrongly labelled as postindustrial). Mandel's proposition is that late or multinational or consumer capitalism, far from being inconsistent with Marx's great nineteenth-century analysis, on the contrary constitutes the purest form of capital yet to have emerged, marking a monumental expansion of capital into hitherto uncommodified areas.

Following on from this, Jameson claims that there has been a radical shift in the material world and in the ways in which it works. It is therefore appropriate to distinguish several generations of technological revolution within capitalism. Fundamental revolutions in technology thus often appear to be the determinant movements in revolutions in society as a whole. Jameson (1985, 1998) argues that by eradicating older forms, the contem-porary mode has extended into all aspects of life. What Jameson (and others) seek to do is to highlight the cultural and political consequences of this. Not all, however, seek to do so within the parameters of classical or neo-classical Marxism.

Reformulating politics

Indeed, whether or not we accept the validity of the postmodern argument, it is clear that there are difficulties with the relevance of the traditional Marxist model. Not least of these is those growing number of challenges to the contemporary political order, and political mobilizations, which are not easily accounted for in class terms. The significance of such non-class issues should not be underestimated, or the fragmentation of political identity it involves (see Bradley, 1996; Laclau and Mouffe 1985; Mulgan, 1994). While the assault on social democracy led by Thatcher and Major has been resisted by key sections of the electorate and populist mobilizations, they have succeeded in establishing the legitimacy of their central principles – the individual and the market.

For Laclau (1993) classical socialism was based on increasing social homogeneity. Traditionally, socialism has been thought of as the social management of the economic process, Marxism regards the state as an instrument of class domination. The discourse of both classical socialism and Marxism is based on the homogenization of the social structure, and the development of a class that is able to manage socially the productive pro-cesses. Importantly, for Laclau, Marxism ignores the rest of society.

In seeking to explain this, Laclau promotes what he calls 'radical democracy'. Laclau (1993: 6) claims that the present crisis of the Left is not so much linked to the failure of concrete policies. Rather, it is the fact that 'both communism and social democracy, the two classical imaginary horizons of the left, have ceased to galvanise the imagination of the masses and are no longer viable languages for the expression of radial social demands'.

Alternatively, radical democracy starts from the 'irreducible idea of social plurality'. It rests on the argument that late capitalist society, far from

becoming homogeneous, is 'going in the direction of proliferation and fragmentation of antagonisms'. This means that there is no 'essential unity' of
classes. From this perspective, there are alliances that need to be identified and
then politically constructed. In trying to account for this perceived shift in
emphasis away from workers' movements, several writers have been forced to
ask if it is still useful to talk of politics in terms of a Right–Left political divide.

The answer is certainly 'no', according to Laclau and Mouffe (1985),
who argue that traditional socialist demands have been replaced by more
nebulous demands for 'freedom', 'democracy'. They further argue that those
modern social movements, such as feminism, the peace and anti-nuclear
movements, are autonomous and remain incapable of any final synthesis.
What is called for is a 'democratic revolution' where the Left actively and
consciously establishes links with the new social movements rather that
seeking any imposition of Marxist ideology.

Let us consider what some see as the transition from modernity to
postmodernity and the consequences for politics. From the perspective of
postmodernism, the attempts of Laclau and Mouffe to construct post-
Marxism is merely recognition of the decline of Marxism as a 'grand narra-
tive'. Another perspective comes from Gorz (1994), who argues that throughout the 1970s and 1980s the Left led social democracy into a cul-de-sac. With
the world economic crisis competition grew stronger, and economic and
social development was increasingly determined by the strategies of global
capitalism. Hence, individual nation-states found it increasingly difficult to
control their own destiny in socio-economic terms. Unrestricted competition
on the free market meant that many economic decisions remained outside the
parameters of politics. In the West, the dismantling of the advanced welfare
state increased social inequality.

One response has been in the already identified 'new social movements',
such as the Green and ecology movements, which demand changes in the
nature of 'radical' politics. As Gorz (1994) puts it, the established parties of
the Left are programmed for statist politics, for the administration of a system
and for securing votes, so they cannot make a fresh start. The Old Left, which
consists largely of the working class, tends to emphasize economic growth,
redistribution and technological progress. As Offe (1985) argues, however,
wage labour can no longer be taken as a point of departure for 'political
associations and collective identities'. Hence, only an alliance between the
new social movements and the traditional Left, comprising the unionized
working class and elements of the new middle class, can lead to an effective
and successful challenge of the old paradigm of politics.

Post-industrialism, politics and the state

The dramatic changes in the structures of the advanced world, some of which
have been described in this book, involving new technologies, new values,
ideologies, changing lines of social conflict and social contestation, has led to
the popular use of the term post-industrialism to describe the contemporary

world. This highlights the declining dependence of some societies on manu-facturing industry and the rise of service industries, and an emphasis on consumption and leisure.

In seeking to explain this, the term 'capitalism' is retained by some theorists of post-industrialism and abandoned by others. So, for example, sometimes the term 'post-industrial capitalism' is used to denote the idea that post-industrial society remains fundamentally capitalist. At other times, however, the term 'post-industrial' is used to convey the idea that society is also post-capitalist. This makes the debate sometimes difficult to follow at times, but worth considering in rather more detail.

Post-industrialism – an optimistic gaze

It was with Bell that the term 'post-industrialism' came into its contemporary usage and it is with his works that we shall begin this discussion. Bell (1973) sought to go beyond those existing theories that sought to classify advanced societies as 'industrial'. Manufacturing employment is seen as in major decline (factories producing commodities are increasingly displacing labour with the introduction of new technologies). Service employment is seen as a major growth area, especially in relation to collecting, processing and distri-buting information. This transition must be viewed against the background of economic theory that has a tripartite division by kind of work: first, the primary sector, in agriculture and the extraction of raw materials; secondly, the secondary sector, in which goods and commodities are manufactured; thirdly, the tertiary or service sector, in which everything else not included in the other two categories is lumped.

Using these categories, it is clear that the primary sector has declined dramatically and the majority of those employed are not involved in the production of tangible goods. The manual and unskilled worker class gets smaller and the class of knowledge workers becomes predominant. The character of knowledge also changes and an emphasis is put on theoretical rather than empirical knowledge. Theoretical knowledge is the impetus of innovation and growth. Because of this, universities will become central institutions and prestige and status will be rooted in the intellectual and scientific communities.

Another feature of the post-industrial society is the speeding up of the 'time machine', so those intervals between the initial forces of change and their application have been dramatically reduced. Technocracy is thus defined as a political system in which the determining influence belongs to technicians of the administration and of the economy. A technocrat is a person who exercises authority by virtue of his or her technical competence. Within the technocratic mindset, the emphasis is on the logical, practical, problem-solving, instrumental, orderly, and disciplined approach to objectives, and a concept of a system (Bell, 1973: 348–9).

This does not necessarily mean, however, that the technocrats themselves will become a dominant class. In post-industrial societies, the stratum of scientists will have to be taken into account in the political process. In addition, the scientific ethos will predispose scientists to act in a different fashion, politically, from other groups. Class denotes not a specific group of persons, but a system that has institutionalized the ground rules for acquiring, holding and transferring differential power and its attendant privileges.

Society has become rational, that is, government, rather than the market, makes crucial decisions. It has also become communal, that is, more groups now seek to establish their social rights through the political order. The politics of the future will not involve quarrels between interest groups over economic resources, but the concerns of a communal society, particularly the inclusion of disadvantaged groups.

There are difficulties with this sort of classification, not least the highly diverse kind of employment it brings together into the single category of 'services'. This can be highlighted by a simple example, whereby an employee in a fast-food restaurant is included in the same category as a computer programmer.

Bell tends to ignore such objections by identifying 'services' with the professions and credentialization. The increased part played by science in the productive process, the rise to prominence of professional and technical groups, plus the introduction of 'information technology', all bear witness to a new 'axial principle', the 'energising principle of the new social formation is the centrality of theoretical knowledge' (Bell, 1973: 52).

For Bell, science and theoretical knowledge is the key resource in post-industrial society. It replaces the 'game against fabricated nature' (the work of transformation of matter on the assembly line or workshop) with that of a 'game involving persons' (the relationship of the professional to client) and the production of information.

This new social assemblage has been captured and understood differently by others. Most do not share Bell's view of the benefits of the new social order. Indeed, while there are many who agree with the view that new technologies mean that mass manufacturing employment is at an end, they take a much more pessimistic view of the contemporary world and that society may become more rational and communal in its direction.

Post-industrialism – a pessimistic gaze

The writings of Jean-François Lyotard (1979) provide a useful starting point for this perspective. He argues that the status of knowledge is altered as societies enter what is known as the post-industrial age and cultures enter what is known as the postmodern age. This transition has been under way since at least the end of the 1950s. Indeed, in broad terms, this view of the transformation from industrial society to post-industrial society is in line with Bell's. However, the political implications of Lyotard's ideas are quite different. While Bell is in essence a neoconservative, who argues that the conflicts of capitalist industrial society are over, Lyotard argues that such conflicts will be reconstructed.

For Lyotard, it is knowledge that has become the principal force of production over the last few decades. This has had the noticeable effect on the composition of the workforce of the most highly developed countries and constitutes a major bottleneck for the developing countries. In this scenario, the 'metropolis' will maintain its hold over the 'periphery' by monopolizing information and technologies.

To highlight the fact that post-industrial society is characterized by conflict, Lyotard argues that knowledge is already, and will continue to be, central in the worldwide competition for power. For him, it is fully conceivable that nations will one day battle for the control of information, just as in the past they struggled for access and control of raw materials and cheap labour. A new field is opened up for industrial and commercial strategies, on the one hand, and political and military strategies on the other.

For some postmodern thinkers this world of information technology produces a situation where social relations are converted into electronic signs. To the fore of this set of beliefs is Baudrillard, who argues that this has led to what he calls a totally hyperreal and simulated world, which has imploded in on itself, leading to the collapse of all the classical reference points, such as class, proletariat and objective conditions.

Baudrillard (1998a, 1998b, 1993, 1996) thus suggests that the only point of reference which still functions is that of the silent majority. All contemporary systems function on this entity – no longer social, but statistical. His vision of post-industrial, postmodern society is one that is dominated by electronic images, computer matrices and the all-enveloping media event. There are clear examples, especially the USA, which is seen as the first hyperreal country. It operates on the level of the sign and of the symbols which are more and more obviously seen in the representations of Coca-Cola, McDonalds and so on.

Further, Baudrillard outlines what he sees as the dramatic ways in which post-industrial technologies will affect our culture and ways of imagining and thinking. Again, unlike Bell, who is optimistic about these technologies, Baudrillard takes a much more pessimistic reading regarding new technologies as 'machines for destroying meaning'. Baudrillard's image of society is one where the vast majority will largely be consumers of images, such as video, advertising, montages of pop songs and so on.

Post-industrialism – post-Marxist and postfeminist perspectives

Others believe that the version of post-industrialism associated with Bell gives too much emphasis to the causal qualities of changing technologies. Indeed, Jameson (1984, 1991) has written that technology from the Marxist gaze must be seen as 'the result of the development of capital, rather than some primal cause in its own right'. Hence, apart from the optimism of Bell, and the somewhat pessimistic views of Baudrillard, there is also a third perspective within post-industrialism theorizing. This can be seen as both radical and post-

Marxist and is associated with such writers as Gorz (1980, 1982, 1985, 1989, 1994), Bahro (1982, 1983, 1986) and Touraine (1971, 1981, 1983).

Touraine, for example, adopting a 'post-Marxist' position, argues that the characteristic feature of post-industrial society is that the central investments are now made at the level of production management, and not at the level of the work-based organization, as in the case of industrial society. Class domination consists less of organizing work and more in managing the production and data-processing apparatus, that is, ensuring the control of the supply and processing of a certain type of data, and hence of a way of organizing social life. Thus, it is not the struggle between representatives of capital and labour which is now central, but the difference between various kinds of consumers and those who identify with particular consumer brands.

Political action in post-industrial society is all-pervading. It enters into the health service, into sexuality, into education and into energy production and so on. For Touraine, the workers' movement is no longer the key dynamic factoring society. The lines of social contestation are more between the technocracy and the new social movements, based on new values and ideas, which have been called post-materialist by writers such as Jürgen Habermas and Clauss Offe.

Unlike Bell, however, Touraine also believes that society is still based on conflict. This line of analysis has been further developed by Gorz, who has argued that post-industrial development, such as the introduction of 'new technology', will lead to a massive displacement of labour (unemployment and under-employment) and the formation of a mass of people on part-time work and short-term contracts. They will form part of a 'flexible' workforce that can be drawn in and out of the labour market to suit the requirements of the employer.

These people form what Gorz calls a class of 'non-workers', who have no identification with the traditional proletarian and form a core identity far beyond that which originates in the workplace. As Gorz (1994: 72) asserts, the 'criticism of capitalism and socialist sensibility are not to be derived from their working lives or their class consciousness but, rather, from the discovery they make as citizens, parents, consumers, residents of a neighbourhood or town, of capitalist development dispossessing them of their – social and natural – lifeworld'.

Elsewhere, Gorz articulates the vision of a post-Fordist and post-Thatcherite world. Clear divisions have opened up between, on the one hand, a labour aristocracy of tenured primary workers with jobs, who are 'functionally flexible' and on the other hand, a marginalized and peripheral class of workers employed irregularly and on a part-time basis and which are located in secondary labour markets. From this view, post-industrial society means an ever-expanding and increasingly marginalized grouping – an underclass.

Some have sought to explain such events within postmodern frameworks, in the sense that they seek to create distance from beliefs concerning truth, knowledge, power, the self, and languages that are taken for granted within. It is possible to see here the concerns of both postmodernism and feminism as to some extent interrelated. Both contemporary feminists and postmodernists have sought to develop their own paradigms of social criticism that essentially challenge the founding writers of social and political theories, such as those outlined in Chapter 1.

Some conclusions

As this chapter has indicated, there are many different views on the existence, nature and form of the new politics in society. New social movements, for example, seek to achieve their effects in a variety of ways. First, they exert cultural influence. This can be seen, for example, in 'style' through impact on gender relations, new values and lifestyles. In other words, new social movements often change the cultural values within which politics operates.

Secondly, social movements have a more direct effect on politics and decision-making through absorption of their central prerequisites. There are also cases of overlaping demands between social movements. In the 1980s, for example, the anti-nuclear protests at Greenham Common saw clear overlaps between the feminist and broader peace movements. By challenging the boundary between state and civic society, definitions of what constitutes a political issue can be altered. Social movements work within civil society and interact with the state.

Thirdly, social movements are not defined simply by ideology but also by the organizational features of the resources they command. Most social movements have identifiable 'life-cycles'. They begin with high levels of mobilization around specific issues and end with the incorporation of the movements into mainstream decision-making organizations.

Some of the strongest critiques of contemporary society have come from postmodernist and feminist perspectives. Both sets of theories offer new and useful tools for looking at relationships between politics and power. Some postmodernists, for example, have sought to 'decentre' the modern subject in a radical way, arguing that people are created through discourses which are culturally and historically specific and generally unconscious. Thus, there is no all-powerful subject capable of manipulating discourse. Such perspectives clearly suggest that the dynamic of contemporary politics has moved a long way from traditional political formations and has heralded the onset of a new politics. We shall consider the idea that a new politics is in formation more fully in the final chapter.

DISCUSSION QUESTIONS

- **Critically examine sociological contributions to an understanding of the nature of power in post-industrial societies.**
- **Discuss the idea that class politics has completely given way to a politics based in new social movements.**

- What do contemporary feminist perspectives add to our understanding of politics and society?
- Does postmodernism provide the evidence to enable us to understand the move towards more fragmented and pluralistic societies?
- Are we experiencing the end of politics?

7

Politics in the New Millennium: Globalization and the End of Social Democracy?

Key concepts and issues	Key theorists and writers
• Globalization	• Manuel Castells
• Politics beyond Right and Left	• Anthony Giddens
• The politics of New Labour	• Noreena Hertz
• The end of social democracy?	• Paul Hirst
• The future of politics and the political	• Eric Hobsbawn
	• Naomi Klein
	• George Monibot

> A new political synthesis is taking shape. After a period of stasis and confusion, a modernised centre left has won power in much of the western world. Yet its victory does not mark a simple swing of the pendulum. Instead, the centre-left has had to come to terms with a period of profound social, geopolitical and economic change that has undermined many of its assumptions. It has had to accept some of the right's agenda, while also returning to some of its own historical roots to find ideas more relevant to present and future challenges. (Hargreaves and Christie, 1998: 1)

This concluding chapter highlights some of the more important arguments identified in the book and puts these in a broader contemporary context. It sets some indications of future issues and the possible parameters of forthcoming debates concerning political sociology and the state at the beginning of the twenty-first century.

At several places this book has highlighted those many people who now live at the margins of UK society. Life expectancy for some groups in contemporary Britain has actually worsened for the first time in 50 years. Indeed, the most deprived areas in the north of England show mortality rates for some groups which are as bad as in the 1940s (*The Guardian*, 29 April 1994). These divisions are extremely apparent in the issues of income and wealth, but there is also much evidence to suggest that many are, and importantly feel, excluded from key social and political processes.

There is little evidence to suggest the validity of the dominant ideology of the 1980s of 'trickle-down' from rich to poor, even though it is still promoted by sections of New Labour, albeit with a somewhat more developed social conscience. Millions continue to perceive themselves as having little or no stake in the future economic or social development of the United Kingdom. These include the long-term unemployed and those solely dependent on state benefits, but also incorporates large sections of young people and key sections of ethnic minority groups, who lack the basic skills to occupy any meaningful place in the labour market. In part this must be seen as a response to globalization, which has exerted the powerful political pressures of neo-liberalism on the politics of the United Kingdom.

Globalization and the nation-state

One part of the conventional wisdom that has developed surrounding global-ization rests in the belief of that the growth of the global economy marks the decline of the era of the nation state. Hence, it can be argued that the political sociology of the contemporary United Kingdom can only be understood in terms of much broader changes in historical and international circumstances. The arguments surrounding globalization are multi-fold and complex (see Falk, 1999; Featherstone, 1990; Garrett, 1998; Held and McGrew, 1993; Hertz, 2001; Miliband and Panitch, 1994; Panitch and Leys, 1997; P.J. Taylor, 2000).

Much of the contemporary debate concerning globalization has to do with the argument that McGrew (1992: 26) identifies that there now exists a 'multiplicity of linkages and interconnections that transcend the nation-states (and by implication the societies) which make up the modern world system'. This certainly is the view, albeit in different ways, taken by some of the writers we are about to encounter, such as Castells (1996, 1997, 1998), Hobsbawn (1995), Hirst and Thompson (1996) and Giddens (1998).

So is it that we can best understand contemporary politics only by adopting a much longer vision? Hobsbawn (1995), for example, argues that by the outbreak of the First World War, nineteenth-century liberal bourgeois capitalism had collapsed. After that there were 30-odd years of what he calls the 'Age of Catastrophe'. After the Second World War, however, liberal bourgeois society was dramatically restructured, as it entered an extra-ordinary phase of rapid expansion. This period, which roughly lasted between the late 1940s to the early 1970s, is what Hobsbawn refers to as the 'Golden Age'. It was during this time certain Western advanced industrial countries benefited most, but there were very few countries in which things did not improve, including the Soviet Union. However, in the early 1970s, nations passed into the 'crisis decades'.

The third part of Hobsbawm's book therefore deals with this period, which takes us up to the present, and in fact gazes into the future. At the end of the 1980s, the world was clearly in crisis, highlighted by the collapse of the socialist economies and societies. But this disintegration coincided with what was the most serious crisis in the Western capitalist economy since the 1930s. The 'collapse of socialism' precipitated a world crisis that affected capitalism mainly through the rise of the new transnational economy and was largely outside the control of governments. All the old problems of mass unemployment and economic slumps reappeared. At the same time there were massive regional shifts within capitalism, notably away from the Atlantic and towards the Pacific. It was this that caused a crisis in the first generation of industrial states.

There is not only an economic crisis but also a political and ideological crisis, marked by the failure of the emphasis on the market. There is crisis in social democracy and a crisis in state socialism, but no creditable alternative approach is on offer. The major issue in the future is not going to be how to get the world economy to grow. It will be how to distribute the product of the world economy in the absence of the old mechanisms that ensured this. If we no longer need workers, then how do they get a living? In the past it was possible to predict with some certainty that the economy was going to expand at a sufficient rate to generate more jobs. It is no longer possible to make those assumptions, certainly in the developed industrial countries, and probably not in many of the developing nations.

So far there has been only one adequate mechanism for redistributing the national product and that is the state, or other forms of public control. It cannot and will not be done by market forces. It was the collapse of the communist bloc that marked the real crisis point in the world economy. The Cold War had created stability for all economies and political systems and its removal precipitated the inability of the countries involved to manage without it. One result has been that world markets have subsumed all other kinds of markets to the point where most can only understand politics in the context of the globalization of world economic markets.

It is now clear that world capitalism has been undergoing a profound reorganization and restructuring since the mid-1970s. There now seems to exist, almost as received wisdom, the notion that national markets have disappeared, and global market forces, particularly in areas such as finance, manufacturing and services, have come to be dominated by enormous transnational companies that are beyond any form of effective regulation by individual states.

There are two main reactions to this. The first regards it as highly positive. The new millennium is seen to usher in the final victory over the political Left and those ideologies that promote political regulation and the interventionist role of the state. Through a variety of popular cultural forms, we are told that we live in a 'global village', where global communications will allow multinational companies ever more easily to buy and sell goods in a global market.

The brand names of products such as Sony, Sega, Coca-Cola, McDonalds, Mercedes, Nike and so on, are recognized and desired by consumers all over the world. People from Huddersfield to Hong Kong, Belfast to

Beijing and Manchester to Montréal, can all enjoy the same music or games on minidisc or CD, or view the latest movie, all released into the same chain of shops on the same day. Increasingly, people in the West can use the Internet to acquire such commodities without even leaving their homes. They inhabit the world of 'cyberspace', where they communicate through personal computer networks, e-mail and the Internet to bring about yet another brave new world based on the strength of individualized consumption.

The second set of reactions to globalization are, however, not so positive. Large numbers of the world's population are excluded from such aspects of life. Even in the West the process is uneven, witness the underclass debates and those identified above as economically excluded from mainstream society. In February 1997, for example, there were widespread redundancies at Ford's Halewood Plant as work was moved to Spain and Germany. Throughout the late 1990s, downturns in the Far Eastern financial markets resulted in extensive redundancies in the microelectronics component production industry across the entire United Kingdom.

In January 2001, thousands of car workers and their supporters were forced on to the streets to protest against General Motors' decision to end Vauxhall car production at Luton. In April of the same year, the USA mobile phone giant Motorola announced the closure of its Bathgate plant in Scotland with the loss of more than 3,000 jobs. The decision was blamed on disappointing demand for mobile phones worldwide (*The Guardian*, 25 April 2001).

These are but random examples of what has become an almost weekly set of occurrences in the globalized market. Globalization has clear and widespread social and political implications (Berndston, 2000). For some, free enterprise and the development of the global marketplace means the possibility of democracy and prosperity for the world's millions. In this view, state intervention in the economy in anything but its most limited form is likely to stunt development and encourage dictatorship. If the world economy really is globalized then it will not succumb to intervention by an individual national state. If this is the case, those who support free market views must be right.

Further, the traditional project favoured by the Left and by Keynesians, of regulating capitalism through state intervention, is futile. Indeed, if the global market is in place, then individual governments cannot be blamed for the failures of national economies. Instead, the problem lies with wider economic forces and the worldwide recession.

So in what form does globalization exist? Certainly many supporters of neoliberalism and others on the political Right believe that globalization has so transformed society that it can no longer be divided into the old categories of business and labour. Society has achieved a positive new order, where old theories based on ideas formulated in the nineteenth century have no purchase. Globalization has dissolved national frontiers and nation-states, industrial processes are post-Fordist, dynamic ideas are postmodern and societies are multicultural. The collectivism of the past has been replaced by a new individualism, and the social democracy of the postwar period has become unworkable and unfeasible. It is now taken as read in large sections of the media that the world is being taken over by huge multinational corporations, accountable to no one, with governments reduced to playing a secondary role to big business.

Pilger (2002) disputes this, arguing that it is folly to believe that big business alone is shaping the new world order. To accept this is to allow the arguments surrounding globalization to be depoliticized. Most crucially, it misses the point that state power in the West is actually accelerating, rather than being decreased. He argues that the illusion of a weakened state is merely a smokescreen thrown in place by the designers of modern, centralized power. In the United Kingdom, for example, New Labour has merely continued the trend set by Thatcher in concentrated executive power, while claiming the opposite.

It is, however, in the USA where this trend is most clearly seen. The notion that the state is submissive to big corporations is naive. Rather, the two go hand in hand. Pilger argues that large oil companies, weapons manufactures and big agribusiness have always been among the occupants of the White House and the US government. Indeed, the groupings are interchangeable. It was the triumphant American state that fashioned the present global economy at Bretton Woods in 1944, so that its military and corporate arms would have unlimited access to minerals, oil, markets and cheap labour. The World Bank and the International Monetary Fund (IMF) were invented explicitly to implement this strategy.

This project continues, although the IMF has now succeeded in projecting itself in more temperate terms, promoting dialogue with 'moderate' non-governmental organizations (NGOs) opposed to globalization. Following the protests against the World Trade Organization (WTO) in Seattle (see below), more than 1,200 groups and organizations from around 85 countries called for a moratorium on the further liberalization of trade and an audit of WTO policies. One thing that did not happen, however, was a direct challenge to the very legitimacy of the WTO itself. Yet, 'this secretive, entirely undemocratic body is the most rapacious predator devised by the imperial powers' (Pilger, 2002).

Hirst and Thompson (1996) also question the populist understanding of globalization. They argue that globalization is a myth developed and spread in order to support the thesis that national economies are ungovernable and better left to the unfettered forces of the global competitive markets. It is a myth because what is commonly called globalization is nothing more than a continuation of inter-national economic trends that are not very different from what has been happening for the last century. As they further demonstrate, contemporary globalization is best understood as a return to the *status quo*. Indeed, the world economy of the late nineteenth century was, if anything, more global than today. Borders were more open to migration; capital flows in relation to GDP were greater; the gold standard imposed tighter constraints on national economic autonomy than does the exchange rate regime of today. The trade barriers and competitive devaluations of the interwar years were a response to the break-down of the late nineteenth-century order.

For Hirst and Thompson, it is the rhetoric and discourses surrounding globalization that is at least as important as the reality. Such rhetoric is seen as a powerful weapon in the intellectual armoury of the neoliberals. What, however, of that reality? Increasingly, state intervention is necessary to offset the impact of falling profitability. Despite the rhetoric of free markets, the reality is that the state has found numerous ways to keep 'free enterprise' going, through many kinds of subsidy, curbing competition and directly running large sections of the economy. Their conclusion is therefore that governance is desirable and possible at the national and international level and that contemporary patterns of globalization should be no obstacle to this.

Elsewhere, Petras and Veltmeyer (2001) characterize contemporary globalization as little more than a new form of imperialism. They argue that the 'inevitability' of globalization and the adjustment of societies to free market capitalism depends on the capability of the dominant classes to convince people that the interests of ordinary citizens and the ruling group are the same. The trend towards internationalization is an attempt by capitalists to try to overcome the barriers to national development at a global level.

This manifests in different ways. Much foreign direct investment, like Honda's involvement in Rover in the United Kingdom, is undertaken to guarantee capitalism a foothold in large foreign markets that might otherwise be protected. The results of this on a worldwide scale are startling. A recent report by the United Nations Development Programme indicates, for example, that the richest 20 per cent of the world's population account for 86 per cent of global consumption. The poorest 80 per cent of the world's population struggle to survive on just 14 per cent of its total spending on consumption (Danaher, 2001).

These processes of globalization are, however, increasingly challenged. Part of the objection is intellectual. Central here are the writings of Klein (2001a, 2001b), Hertz (2001) and Monbiot (2000). In broad terms, these writers suggest that existing democratic systems are being eroded and individual choice limited by mass-marketed 'mono-culture'. Monbiot (2000) focuses on events in Britain to offer a critique of multinational corporations and what he regards as the subversion of Britain's democratic institutions. He suggests that large corporations destroy public life and threaten democracy, and warns of a new form of social control through corporate power.

It is Klein's *No Logo* (2001a) that has become an unofficial manifesto of much of the anti-globalization movement. It documents the popular backlash against the increasing economic and cultural reach of multinationals and argues that politicians and big business ignore the anti-globalization movement at their peril. Hertz (2001) also supports the view that governments' surrender to 'big business' is the greatest threat facing democracy today. Her book also traces in detail some of the major confrontations between the protest movements and multinational corporations.

Another manifestation of the objections to globalization takes a more physical form. Recent years have seen widespread and co-ordinated street protests, largely directed at the meetings of those organizations which are seen to control the world economy, such as the International Monetary Fund

(IMF), the World Bank, or the leaders of the most powerful nations in the developed world (G8). Increasingly, it is argued that these institutions are coming under the control of transnational corporations and promote continued exploitation across large parts of the world.

In the popular consciousness this part of the movement was 'born' in 1999 when thousands gathered in Seattle to protest at the WTO meeting promoting free trade and the movement of transnational capital. The protest mobilized a wide range of organizations from environmental groups like Rainforest Action Network and Greenpeace, Left, socialist-orientated groups and trade unionists to a heterogeneous variety of anarchists and aligned groupings, most notably the Direct Action Network. Indeed, Hertz (2001) demonstrates just how eclectic the anti-corporate and anti-capitalist movement (brought together as it is through the media, the underground press, the Internet, and by word of mouth) can be.

While much media reportage focused on confrontations between sections of the protesters and police and attacks on multinational outlets, there are other important aspects. The events in Seattle included the largest-scale civil disturbances seen in the USA since the anti-war protests of the 1960s. Nonetheless, it also witnessed widespread peaceful and non-violent demonstrations located in an unprecedented coalition of trade unionists, environmental activists and a whole range of people unhappy with globalization and the exploitation of the developing world.

The global free market economy has inspired a vibrant counter-movement. It is represented in part by a burgeoning series of social movements, all of which are anti-capitalist, anti-corporate and anti-globalization in nature. The exact shape, or indeed coherence, of this movement is, however, still to be determined.

The main division in the theoretical analysis of the anti-globalization movement centres on whether globalization is reversible. There is agreement that globalization, driven by the free market, is on a clear path leading to a growing concentration of economic and political power and to an eco-catastrophic development. Sections of the Left believe that globalization can be reformed. Others, however, are of the view that only by developing a new mass anti-systemic movement can the process be halted. It is argued that such an alternative globalization should be based on a new 'democratic world order' that is founded on the equal distribution of political and economic power between nations and their citizens, irrespective of gender, race, ethnicity or culture.

Politics beyond Right and Left

For many, the core of contemporary politics rests, therefore, on identity politics and what is often termed the 'postmodern condition'. This suggests that those universalizing ideologies, as characterized in the time of the Cold War, have lost coherence and in many cases have been dissolved. What has replaced them is a diversity of political identities and demands formulated around different sites of antagonisms. These involve, for example, gender or sexual orientation, environmental issues, ethnicity and cultural values. Such a perspective has important consequences for the nature of politics because, from within the postmodern perspective, society and the individual become centreless networks which can never be fully represented.

Phrases such as 'post-industrial society', 'postmodernity' and 'globalization' have all been used in this book to describe society at and beyond the turn of the twentieth century. All raise important questions concerning the political relationships within society and between society and technology. It is frequently assumed, particularly in popular culture for example, that technology will increasingly determine the structure and form of society. It is difficult, however, to see new technologies fully governing the shape and form of society because it happens as the result of human decisions and action.

An extension of this argument, that social class is no longer a key determinant, has led to the suggestion that the terms 'Right' and 'Left' are no longer meaningful in understanding contemporary society. This argument draws on several different themes. One strand suggests that Thatcher and the New Right succeeded in transforming the nature of British politics and in initiating 'the great moving right show'. Hence, all contemporary politics, including that of New Labour, reflects deeply-engrained Thatcherite values (see Gamble, 1994b; Novak, 1998; Panitch and Leys, 1997).

Analysing New Labour and the Third Way

Another analysis is that New Labour is 'post-Thatcherite'. Its major political direction reflects continuity with Thatcherite commitments to free trade, flexible labour markets, sound money and individual self-help, rather than any clear break from it. New Labour has taken on board the main tenets of neoliberalism. Alongside this, however, the New Labour administration has added the distinctive notions of communitarianism and inclusion (see Driver and Martell, 1998, 2000; Kenny and Smith, 1997; Perryman, 1996; Savage and Atkinson, 2001). New Labour is thus seen to reflect both continuity with neoliberalism and a break from it. In a slightly different interpretation, Gould (1999) suggests that while New Labour is not necessarily neoliberal in direction, it certainly does not seek to maintain perpetuity with the traditions of Labour.

Walker (1998: 19) has given several pointers to the contours of the contemporary debate surrounding New Labour. The third way is New Labour's description of a political movement that supposedly rejects both the neoliberalism of the New Right and the social democracy of the Old Left. According to its supporters, the third way is about reasserting traditional values in a world dramatically changed by globalization, new technologies and a government that can no longer undertake a major redistributive role. Hence, New Labour is about a reworking of core values surrounding individual liberty, social justice, equal worth, opportunity, responsibility and community. The theory can be seen in the practicalities of New Labour policy formation such as the New Deal and the minimum wage. It is also reflected in the development of public and private partnerships, and the government's commitment to reviving a community spirit through a discourse of inclusion.

It is Giddens (1994, 1998) who has provided the strongest theoretical base for third-way politics. He openly argues that old-style socialism (by which he means both communism and social democracy) is now finished forever. Social democracy relied on the state to redistribute wealth through nationalization or taxation and placed emphasis upon the role of the state in generating both solidarity and equality. Since the 1970s, however, this was put into reverse. In response to the challenges of contemporary neoliberalism, Giddens (1994; 1998; 1999) argues that politics based on the old divide between Left and Right is incapable of addressing modern social problems. Rather, it is the political centre that holds the solution and in its development rests the political future. The politics of the third way involves abandoning collectivism in the search for new relationships between the individual and the community. Central to this is a redefinition of the rights and obligations of the citizen. Giddens (1994; 1998; 1999) seeks to clarify where this new path is leading, introducing the conceptual basis for notions such as 'democratizing democracy', 'devolution of the regions', and the making of government more accountable and relevant to the people.

So is the third way simply an adjustment of social democracy to the contemporary values of the free market and globalization, as highlighted above? It is still sometimes difficult to grasp much of the coherence of New Labour ideology. Indeed, it may well be that the third way will eventually be best understood as a form of political pragmatism rather than as any con-gruous political theory.

The main differences, however, between the previous administrations of the Thatcher and Major governments and New Labour appear to be the promotion by New Labour of a politics involving:

- an increased democratization of the British state, particularly through devolution of the 'celtic fringe' of Scotland, Wales and Northern Ireland;
- a limited form of state intervention, such as a minimum wage and trades union recognition if the majority of the workforce want it;
- a changed 'internationalist' foreign policy, overtly more pro-European, although New Labour is still very attached to old bonds with the USA (a relationship reinforced after the attacks of 11 September and the development of an anti-terrorist alliance); and
- a central direction in politics between Right and Left which is perceived as an essential basis for the 'modernization' of the contemporary United Kingdom.

Third-way politics is also projected as an attempt to control the free market and to prevent the inequality and excesses of unfettered capitalism. According to this part of third-way thinking, the only alternative to free market capitalism is regulated capitalism. Each national economy must therefore develop an accord between the public and private sectors, which harnesses the market but puts the public interest to the fore. The government's core role is therefore to achieve a balance between regulation and deregulation of the market.

For some, however, New Labour's rejoinder to neoliberalism is to continue to reorganize the major function of the state as guarantor rather than provider. People must provide for education, health-care, pensions and unemployment benefits, and the state will intervene only if structures of personal provision fail. It seems that, as currently constructed, the economics of the third way retains a marked continuity with some core beliefs of Thatcherism and neoliberalism (see Hay 1999; Heffernan, 1999).

This is also seen if we consider the direction of New Labour's social policy. This reveals a clear failure to promote progressive taxation or increased spending by the state. The centrepiece of its welfare programme has been the New Deal, and the most prominent of the new schemes has been the working families tax credit scheme, which involves combining taxes and personal allowances in such a way as to benefit families in households with low-income earners. While, on the one hand, the government has introduced schemes to target particular deserving groups, on the other hand, it has attacked what it regards as a 'something for nothing' culture and proposed that benefits should only go to those whom they define as 'most in need'.

New Labour and the end of social democracy

So how should we understand New Labour? A positive interpretation is that New Labour is a modernized politics for contemporary times; that New Labour does indeed mark a clear attempt to carve out a distinctive path which recognizes some of the important sociological and social structural changes outlined in this book. From this perspective, the politics of New Labour is crucially located within the collapse of traditional divisions between public and private, labour and capital, and the state and the market (see Callaghan and Tunney, 2001; K. Coates, 1996; MacIntyre, 2000; Mandelson and Liddle, 1996).

Within this understanding, traditional social democracy is therefore simply no longer relevant to contemporary times. What New Labour is seeking to do is to 'adapt' its traditional values, regarding social justice, equal opportunity and collective community, to these new social and economic circumstances. From the perspective of many of its supporters, the third way aims to help citizens navigate a path through the major social and political transformations and crises of our time. These include globalization, the growth of individualism, the emergence of ecopolitics, the changing nature of family structure and the end of traditional notions of the political Left and Right (see Blair, 1996, 1998).

A more negative reading is that Blairism marks a clear and profound break from the traditional core values of social democracy. It refrains from any direct recognition of class divisions in society, or any articulation of an engagement with class politics (see Barratt Brown and Radice, 1996;

Coddington and Perryman, 1998; Ludlam and Smith, 2001). For example, as Alasdair Blair (2000: 6) highlights, the current relationships between New Labour and the trades union movement are lukewarm. Indeed, New Labour is increasingly suspicious of any enhanced role for the trade unions in industrial or economic policy-making. Certainly New Labour does not seek to extend public ownership, and rejects the overt redistribution of wealth, or even any notion of progressive taxation. Further, even when the New Labour administration announced that public spending was due to rise to 42 per cent of GDP by 2005–06, this was a figure exceeded in all but two of the 18 years of the last Conservative government. In addition, the current average across the European Union is 46 per cent (*New Statesman*, 22 July 2002).

By highlighting the non-redistributive role of the state, New Labour fully accepts the capitalist economy, while attempting to govern with a social conscience. In broad economic and fiscal matters, however, the New Labour agenda differs little from the neoliberalism of the Thatcher era. Indeed, on most major economic issues, New Labour has accepted the validity of Thatcherism and neoliberalism. Overall, the third way does indeed seem to mark more of a break with the social democratic past than to highlight any continuity.

Politics in a globalized world

Another core thesis of third-way politics states that the international free market must be controlled. It argues that excessive economic power must be countered by 'transnational systems of governance', by which Giddens (1994, 1998) means the setting-up of international controls aimed at regulating the world's economy, attacking global economic inequalities and controlling ecological risks. It is difficult to see how this part of third-way theory has been realized. Indeed, what has emerged within the Labour Party corresponds directly with globalization and the expansion of transnational corporations.

Throughout Blair's leadership, it has been claimed that it is the Labour Party that can most 'successfully' manage the UK economy in the new globalized world, where no one nation is immune from vast economic and social change. Indeed, it is almost an article of faith for New Labour that the global market and transnational corporations are now all-powerful and that their political influence cannot be resisted. For New Labour, any possibility of reforming capitalism has given way to an agenda of how best to manage capitalism. This has been a key claim of New Labour manifestoes and is apparent in its support for public–private partnerships, flexible working and the development of a wide range of new low-paid and often part-time jobs.

Some final thoughts

There have been significant changes in economic, political, cultural, techno-logical and theoretical levels of society in the last 30 years. Many of these changes have been highlighted in one form or another in this book. For the most part, contemporary politics seeks to justify the emergence of the present neoliberal form of modernity through the universalization of liberal democracy and the market as the overriding organizational principles of the economy and society.

Against this background, one task facing politics in the new millennium is to re-engage people with politics. This is no simple task. How will politics connect the micro and macro levels of society, the local with the global, to allow people to express deeply-felt political identities in a positive way? In recent times, for example, almost all the dynamic political and social movements have been negative in their ethos, based on protest – anti-globalization, anti-government, anti-politics, and campaigns against road-building, airport expansion, global warming and so on. It is, however, difficult to distinguish a thriving social movement based on positive progressive change.

Further, people are simply not engaging with traditional forms of politics in ways that they once were. In the United Kingdom general election of 2001, for example, around 16 million of those who were eligible did not vote. A turnout of 59.2 per cent (Buckley, 2001: 4) meant that only one in four voters backed the re-elected New Labour administration. Even more importantly, some two-thirds of young people did not vote, while in many seats the majority of working-class voters stayed at home.

So is this the end of politics? Certainly many writers (see Boggs, 2000; Mulgan, 1997; Schedler, 1997) have seriously addressed the increasingly conventional wisdom that politics is at an end, unable to stimulate or inspire, and incapable of providing the basis for solutions to social and economic problems.

We clearly live in times of massive upheaval in almost every part of our existence: in economics, in lifestyle, in gender roles, in the nature of the state, and in the definition of society. Further, many of us now find that our personal lives are directly linked to the global world through advanced communications systems, and that global political events and multinational organizations have much more relevance to our personal experiences that ever before.

One result is seen in the growing disillusionment with formal politics and the distrust of elected representatives. As a reaction to this, we may well witness the development of more active, reflexive citizens who will engage in the political world around them. As the processes of globalization continue to erode politics and political structures, this may create new points of resistance and political organizations opposed to the dominance of such global forces. While traditional politics for many is ever less meaningful, the political is increasingly more important.

DISCUSSION QUESTIONS

- **How convincing is the argument that the categories of Left and Right are no longer meaningful in contemporary politics?**

- Is there a 'third way' in the politics of the United Kingdom?
- Discuss the proposition that globalization means the end of the nation-state.
- Have we come to the end of social democracy in the United Kingdom?
- Are we at the end of politics?

References

AbuKhalil, A. (2002) *Bin Laden, Islam and America's New 'War on Terrorism'*. New York: Seven Stories Press.

Acheson, D., et al. (1998) *Report of the Independent Inquiry into Inequalities and Health*. London: Department of Health.

Alcock, P. (1993) *Understanding Poverty*. London: Macmillan.

Ali, T. and Livingstone, K. (1984) *Who's Afraid of Margaret Thatcher?* London: Verso.

Almond, G.A. and Verba, S. (1963) *The Civic Culture*. Princeton, NJ: Princeton University Press.

Almond, G.A. and Verba, S. (eds) (1981) *The Civic Culture Revisited*. Boston, MA: Little Brown.

Alter, P. (1989) *Nationalism*. London: Arnold.

Althusser, L. (1971) *Lenin and Philosophy and Other Essays*. London: New Left Books.

Althusser, L. (1977) *For Marx*. London: New Left Books.

Althusser, L. (1984) *Essays on Ideology*. London: Verso.

Amnesty International (1994) *Political Killings in Northern Ireland*. London: Amnesty International.

Anderson, B. (1983) *Imagined Communities: Reflections on the Origin and Spread of Nationalism*.

Anthias, F. and Yuval-Davis, N. (1982) *Racialized Boundaries: Race, Nation, Gender, Color and Class and the Anti-Racist Struggle*. London: Routledge.

Ashley, D. (1997) *History Without a Subject: The Postmodern Condition*. Oxford: Westview Press.

Atkins, F. (1986) 'Thatcherism, Populist Authoritarianism and the Search for a New Left Political Strategy', *Capital and Class*, 28: 25–48.

Bagguley, P. and Mann, K. (1992) 'Idle Thieving Bastards: Scholarly Representations of the Underclass', *Work Employment and Society*, (6) 1: 113–26.

Bahro, R. (1982) *Socialism and Survival*. London: Heretic Books.

Bahro, R. (1983) *From Red to Green: Interviews with New Left Review*. London: Verso.

Bahro, R. (1986) *Building the Green Movement*. London: Heretic Books.

Barnaby, F. (1996) *Instruments of Terror*. London: Vision.

Barratt Brown, M. and Radice, H. (1996) *Democracy versus Capitalism: A Response to Will Hutton with Some Old Questions for New Labour*. Nottingham: Spokesman.

Barry, N. (1994) 'Justice and Liberty in Marriage and Divorce', in C. Quest (ed.), *Liberating Women . . . From Modern Feminism*. Choice in Welfare Series No. 19. London: Institute of Economic Affairs, Health and Welfare Unit.

Baudrillard, J. (1998a) *America*. London: Verso.

Baudrillard, J. (1998b) 'The Masses: The Implosion of the Social in the Media', in *Selected Writings*. Ed. M. Poster. Cambridge: Polity Press.

Baudrillard, J. (1993) *Symbolic Exchange and Death*. London: Verso.

Baudrillard, J. (1996) *Cool Memories II 1987–1990*. Cambridge: Polity Press.

Beck, U. (2000) *What is Globalization?* London: Blackwell.

Beechy, V. (1982) 'Some Notes on Female Wage Labour in Capitalist Production', in M. Evans (ed.), *The Woman Question: Readings on the Subordination of Women*. London: Fontana.

Bell, Daniel (1962) *The End of Ideology: On the Exhaustion of Political Ideas in the Fifties*. New York: The Free Press.

Bell, Daniel (1973) *The Coming of Post-Industrial Society*. New York: Basic Books.

Bell, Desmond (1990) *Acts of Union: Youth Culture and Sectarianism in Northern Ireland*. Basingstoke: Macmillan.

Bell, G. (1976) *The Protestants of Ulster*. London: Pluto Press.

Bell, G. (1984) *The British in Ireland: A Suitable Case for Withdrawal*. London: Pluto Press.

Belsey, C. and Moore, J. (eds) (1997) *The Feminist Reader*. Basingstoke: Macmillan.

Benston, M. (1969) 'The Political Economy of Women's Liberation', *Monthly Review*, 21 (4): 13–27.

Berndtson, E. (2000) 'Globalization as Americanization', in H. Goverde, et al. (eds), *Power in Contemporary Politics*. London: Sage.

Beveridge, W.H. (1942) *Social Insurance and Allied Services*, Cmd. 6404. London: HMSO.

Bew, P. (1994) *Ideology and the Irish Question*. Oxford: Oxford University Press.

Bew, P., Gibbon, P. and Patterson, H. (1979) *The State in Northern Ireland*. Manchester: Manchester University Press.

Bew, P. and Patterson, H. (1985) *The British State and the Ulster Crisis: From Wilson to Thatcher*. London: Verso.

Bew, P. and Patterson, H. (1987) 'The New Statement: Unionism and the Anglo-Irish Agreement', in P. Teague (ed.), *Beyond the Rhetoric: Politics, the Economy and Social Policy in Northern Ireland*. London: Lawrence and Wishart.

Bircham, E. and Charlton, J. (2001) *Anti-Capitalism*. London: Bookmarks.

Birrell, D. (1972) 'Relative Deprivation as a Factor in Conflict in Northern Ireland', *Sociological Review*, 20 (3): 317–40.

Blair, A. (2000) 'New Labour: New Social Policy?', *Talking Politics*, 13 (1): 4–8.

Blair, T. (1996) *New Britain, My Vision of a Young Country*. London: Fourth Estate.

Blair, T. (1998) *The Third Way: New Politics for a New Century*. London: Fabian Society.

Bogdanor, V. (2001) *Devolution in the United Kingdom*. Oxford: Oxford University Press.

Boggs, C. (2000) *The End of Politics: Corporate Power and the Decline of the Public Sphere*. New York: Guilford.

Bottomore, T. (1979) *Political Sociology*. London: Pluto Press.

Boulton, D. (1973) *The UVF 1966–1973*. Dublin: Torc Books.

Boyd, J. (1985) *Out of My Class*. Belfast: Blackstaff Press.

Bradley, H. (1992) 'Changing Social Divisions: Class, Gender and Race', in R. Bocock and J. Thompson (eds), *Social and Cultural Forms of Modernity*. Cambridge: Polity Press.

Bradley, H. (1996) *Fractured Identities: Changing Patterns of Inequality*. Oxford: Polity Press.

Breen, R. (1996) 'Who Wants a United Ireland? Constitutional Preferences Among Catholics and Protestants', in R. Breen, P. Devine and L. Dowds (eds), *Social Attitudes in Northern Ireland*. Belfast: Appletree Press. pp. 33–48.

Brittan, S. (1975) 'The Economic Contradictions of Democracy', *British Journal of Political Science*, 5 (2): 129–59.

Brittan, S. (1977) 'Can Democracy Manage an Economy?', in R. Skidelsky (ed.), *The End of the Keynesian Era*. Oxford: Martin Robertson.

Brivati, B. and Bale, T. (eds) (1997) *New Labour in Power: Precedents and Prospects*. London: Routledge.

Brown, J.C. (1996) 'The Focus on Single Mothers', in R. Lister (ed.), *Charles Murray and the Underclass*. London: Institute of Economic Affairs.

Bruce, S. (1994) *The Edge of the Union: The Ulster Loyalist Political Vision*. Oxford: Oxford University Press.

Bryson, V. (1992) *Feminist Political Theory: An Introduction*. Basingstoke: Macmillan.

Bryson, V. (1999a) *Feminist Debates, Issues of Theory and Political Practice*. Basingstoke: Macmillan.

Bryson, V. (1999b) '"Patriarchy": A Concept Too Useful to Lose', *Contemporary Politics*, 5 (4): 311–24.

Buckland, P. (1981) *A History of Northern Ireland*. Dublin: Gill and Macmillan.

Buckley, J. (ed.) (2001) 'Stirring up Apathy', in 'The British: Who Do They Think They Are?', *Understanding Global Issues*, 102.

Burrows, R. and Loader, B. (eds) (1994) *Towards a Post-Fordist Welfare State?* London: Routledge.

Burton, F. (1978) *The Politics of Legitimacy: Struggles in a Belfast Community*. London: Routledge and Kegan Paul.

Cairns, E. (1987) *Caught in Crossfire: Children and the Northern Ireland Conflict*. Belfast: Appletree Press.

Cairns, E. (1994) *A Welling Up of Deep Unconscious Forces: Psychology and the Northern Ireland Conflict*. Coleraine: University of Ulster.

Cairns, E., Lewis, A. and Mumcu, O. (1998) 'Memories of Recent Ethnic Conflict and Their Relationship to Social Identity', *Peace and Conflict: Journal of Peace Psychology*, 4 (1): 13–22.

Callaghan, J. and Tunney, S. (2001) 'The End of Social Democracy?', *Politics*, 21 (1): 63–72.

Callinicos, A. (1987) *Making History*. Cambridge: Polity Press.

Callinicos, A. (1991) *The Revenge of History*. Cambridge: Polity Press.

Callinicos, A. (2001) *Against the Third Way*. Cambridge: Polity Press.

Campaign Against Racism and Fascism (2000) 'Asylum Policy: Made in Europe', *Campaign Against Racism and Facism*, 54 (February/March): 8–13.

Carter, A. (1988) *The Politics of Women's Rights*. London: Longman.

Carter, A. (1992) *Peace Movements: International Protest and World Politics since 1945*. London: Longman.

Cash, J.D. (1996) *Identity, Ideology and Conflict*. Cambridge: Cambridge University Press.

Cassidy, C. and Trew, K. (1988) 'Identities in Northern Ireland: A Multidimensional Approach', *Journal of Social Issues*, 54 (4): 725–40.

Castells, M. (1996) *The Information Age: Economy, Society and Culture. Volume 1: The Rise of the Network Society*. Oxford: Blackwell.

Castells, M. (1997) *The Information Age: Economy, Society and Culture. Volume 2: The Power of Identity*. Oxford: Blackwell.

Castells, M. (1998) *The Information Age: Economy, Society and Culture. Volume 3: End of Millennium*. Oxford: Blackwell.

Cawson, A. (1982) *Corporatism and Welfare: Social Policy and State Intervention in Britain*. London: Heinemann Educational.

Cawson, A. (1986) *Corporatism and Political Theory*. Oxford: Blackwell.

Chomsky, N. (2001) *9–11*. New York: Seven Stories Press.

Clark, T.N. and Lipset, S.M. (1991) 'Are Social Classes Dying?', *International Sociology*, 6: 397–410.

Clarke, J. (ed.) (1993) *A Crisis in Care? Challenges to Social Work*. London: Sage.

Clarke, J. and Cochrane, A. (1994) 'Introduction: Reconstructing Welfare', *Social Problems and Social Welfare*, Block 4, D211, *Readings*. Milton Keynes: The Open University.

Clarke, J. and Langan, M. (1993) 'The British Welfare State: Foundation and Modernisation', in A. Cochrane and J. Clarke (eds), *Comparing Welfare States: Britain in International Context*. London: Sage.

Coates, D. (1989) *The Crisis of Labour: Industrial Relations and the State in Contemporary Britain*. London: Philip Allen.

Coates, D. (1994) *The Question of UK Decline: Economy, State and Society*. London: Edward Arnold.

Coates, D. (1995) *Running the Country*. London: Hodder & Stoughton.

Coates, D. and Lawler, P. (eds) (2000) *New Labour in Power*. Manchester: Manchester University Press.

Coates, K. (1996) *New Labour's Aims and Values: A Study in Ambiguity*. Nottingham: Spokesman.

Coates, K. (ed.) (1999) *The Third Way to the Servile State*. Nottingham: Spokesman.

Cochrane, A. (1992) 'Is There a Future for Local Government?', *Critical Social Policy*, 35: 4–19.

Coddington, A. and Perryman, M. (eds) (1998) *The Moderniser's Dilemma: Radical Politics in the Age of Blair*. London: Lawrence and Wishart.

Cohen, R. and Rai, S.M. (eds) (2000) *Global Social Movements*. London: Athlone Press.

Cohen, R., et al. (1992) *Hardship Britain*. London: Child Poverty Action Group.

Commission on Social Justice (1994) *Social Justice: Strategies for National Renewal*. London: Vintage.

Compton, R. (1993) *Class and Stratification*. Cambridge: Polity Press.

Compton, R. (1996) 'Farewell to Social Class?', *Discussion Paper in Sociology*, No. S96/7, University of Leicester: Department of Sociology.

Connolly, P. and Maginn, P. (1999) *Sectarianism, Children and Community Relations in Northern Ireland*. Coleraine: Centre for the Study of Conflict, University of Ulster.

Conservative Party, News Press Office (1996) 'Blair's Stakeholder Economy is Dangerous Nonesense', *Press Release 32/96*, 12 January.

Coole, D. (1994) *Women in Political Theory: From Ancient Misogyny to Contemporary Feminism*. Hemel Hempstead: Harvester Wheatsheaf.

Coulter, C. (1999) *Contemporary Northern Irish Society*. London: Pluto Press.

Curtis, L.P. (1997) *Apes and Angels: The Irishman in Victorian Caricature*. Washington, DC: Smithsonian Institution Press.

Cusack, J. and McDonald, H. (1997) *UVF*. Dublin: Poolbeg.

Dahl, R.A. (1956) *A Preface to Democratic Theory*. Chicago, IL: University of Chicago Press.

Dahl, R.A. (1961) *Who Governs? Democracy and Power in an American City*. New Haven, CT: Yale University Press.

Dahl, R.A. (1966) *Political Opposition in Western Democracies*. New Haven, CT: Yale University Press.

Dahl, R.A. (1982) *Dilemmas of Pluralist Democracy*. New Haven, CT: Yale University Press.

Dahl, R.A. (1989) *Democracy and Its Critics*. New Haven, CT: Yale University Press.

Dahrendorf, R. (1959) *Class and Class Conflict in Industrial Society*. Stanford, CA: Stanford University Press.

Dahrendorf, R. (1982) *On Britain*. London: BBC Books.

Dahrendorf, R. (1989) *Whose Europe?: Competing Visions for 1992*. London: Institute of Economic Affairs.

Danaher, K. (2001) 'The New Protest Movement – It's about Demanding a Say in the Future of the Planet', *The Observer*, 29 April.

Darby, J. (1986) *Intimidation and the Controls on Conflict in Northern Ireland*. Belfast: Appletree Press.

Darby, J. (1997) *Scorpions in a Bottle: Conflicting Cultures in Northern Ireland*. London: Minority Rights Publications.

De Paor, L. (1970) *Divided Ulster*. Harmondsworth: Penguin.

Deakin, N. (1996) 'Mister Murray's Ark', in R. Lister (ed.), *Charles Murray and the Underclass: The Developing Debate*. London: Institute of Economic Affairs.

Denfeld, R. (1995) *The New Victorians: A Young Woman's Challenge to the Old Feminist Order*. New York: Warner Books.

Dennis, N. (1992) *Rising Crime and the Dismembered Family*. London: Institute of Economic Affairs.

Dennis, N. (1997) *The Invention of Permanent Poverty*. London: Institute of Economic Affairs, Health and Welfare Unit.

Dennis, N. and Erdos, G. (1992) *Families without Fatherhood*. London: Institute of Economic Affairs.

Denny, C. (2000) 'The Twilight Zones', *The Guardian*, 12 January.

Denver, D. (1997) 'The 1997 General Election in Scotland: An Analysis of the Results', *Scottish Affairs*, 20: 17–33.

Diani, M. (1992) 'The Concept of Social Movement', *The Sociological Review*, 40: 1–25.

Dixon, P. (2001) *Northern Ireland: The Politics of War and Peace*. Basingstoke: Palgrave.

Doherty, D. (2001) *Ideas and Actions in the Green Movement*. London: Routledge.

Donnison, D. (1982) *The Politics of Poverty*. Oxford: Martin Robertson.

Driver, S. and Martell, L. (1998) *New Labour: Politics after Thatcherism*. Cambridge: Polity Press.

Driver, S. and Martell, L. (2000) 'Left, Right and the Third Way', *Policy and Politics*, 28 (2): 147–61.

Dunleavy, P. and O'Leary, B. (1987) *Theories of the State: The Politics of Liberal Democracy*. Basingstoke: Macmillan.

Dunn, S. (1995) 'The Conflict as a Set of Problems', in S. Dunn (ed.), *Facets of the Conflict in Northern Ireland*. New York: St Martin's Press.

Durham, M. (1991) *Sex and Politics: the Family and Morality in the Thatcher Years*. Basingstoke: Macmillan.

Eagleton, T. (1991) *Ideology: An Introduction*. Oxford: Blackwell.

Edgar, D. (1983) 'Bitter Harvest', *New Socialist*, October.

Edgell, S. and Duke, V. (1991) *A Measure of Thatcherism*. London: Macmillan.

Elliott, M. (ed.) (2002) *The Long Road to Peace in Northern Ireland*. Liverpool: Liverpool University Press.

Engels, F. ([1884] 1967) 'The Origin of the Family, Private Property and the State'. Reprinted in K. Marx and F. Engels, *Selected Works*. Moscow: Progress Publishers.

English, R. and Kenny, M. (eds) (2000) *Rethinking British Decline*. Basingstoke: Macmillan.

Etzioni, A. (1995) *The Spirit of Community: Rights, Responsibilities and the Communitarian Age*. London: Fontana.

Evans, B. and Taylor, A. (1996) *From Salisbury to Major: Continuity and Change in Conservative Politics*. Manchester: Manchester University Press.

Evans, G. (1993) 'The Decline of Class Divisions in Britain?: Class and Ideological Preferences in the 1960s and the 1980s', *British Journal of Sociology*, 44: 449–71.

Evans, G. (ed.) (1999) *The End of Class Politics? Class Voting in Comparative Context*. Oxford: Oxford University Press.

Evans, M. (1997) *Introducing Contemporary Feminist Thought*. Oxford: Polity Press.

Ewing, K.D. and Gearty, C.A. (1990) *Freedom Under Thatcher: Civil Liberties in Modern Britain*. Oxford: Clarendon Press.

Falk, R. (1999) *Predatory Globalization: A Critique*. Oxford: Polity Press.

Farrell, M. (1976) *Northern Ireland: The Orange State*. London: Pluto Press.

Farrell, M. (1980) *Northern Ireland: The Orange State*. London: Pluto Press.

Farrell, M. (1983) *Arming the Protestants: The Formation of the Ulster Special Constabulary and the Royal Ulster Constabulary*. London: Pluto Press.

Faulks, K. (1999) *Political Sociology: A Critical Introduction*. Edinburgh: Edinburgh University Press.

Fearon, K. (1999) *Women's Work: The Story of the Northern Ireland Women's Coalition*. Belfast: Blackstaff Press.

Featherstone, M. (ed.) (1990) *Global Culture: Nationalism, Globalization and Modernity*. London: Sage.

Field, F. (1989) *Losing Out: The Emergence of Britain's Underclass*. Oxford: Blackwell.

Field, F. (1996) *Stakeholder Welfare*. London: Institute of Economic Affairs.

Finlayson, A. (1999) 'Third Way Theory', *Political Quarterly*, 70 (3): 271–9.

Firestone, S. (1979) *The Dialectic of Sex*. London: Paladin Press.

Flackes, W.D. and Elliott, S. (1989) *Northern Ireland: A Political Directory*. Belfast: The Blackstaff Press.

Flax, J. (1990) *Psychoanalysis, Feminism and Postmodernism in the Contemporary West*. Berkeley, CA: University of California Press.

Foucault, M. (1977) *Discipline and Punish: The Birth of the Prison*. New York: Vintage Books.

Foucault, M. (1979) *The History of Sexuality, Vol. I*. Harmondsworth: Penguin.

Foucault, M. (1980) *Power/Knowledge*. Brighton: Harvester.

Foucault, M. (1985) *History of Sexuality, Vol. II: The Use of Pleasure*. London: Allen Lane.

Friedan, B. (1963) *The Feminine Mystique*. Harmondsworth: Penguin Books.

Friedman, M. (1962) *Capitalism and Freedom*. Chicago, IL: University of Chicago Press.

Friedman, M. and Friedman, B. (1980) *Free to Choose: A Personal Statement*. Harmondsworth: Penguin.

Fukuyama, F. (1989) 'The End of History?', *The National Interest*, 16 (Summer): 3–18.

Fukuyama, F. (1992) *The End of History and the Last Man*. London: Hamish Hamilton.

Fukuyama, F. (1995) *Trust: Social Virtues and the Creation of Prosperity*. London: Hamish Hamilton.

Fukuyama, F. (2001) 'The West Has Won', *The Guardian*, 11 October.

Gaffikin, F. and Morrissey, M. (1990) *Northern Ireland: The Thatcher Years*. London: Zed Books.

Galligan, Y., Ward, E. and Wilford, R. (eds) (1999) *Contesting Politics: Women in Ireland, North and South*. Oxford: Westview Press.

Gamble, A. (1981) *Britain in Decline*. Basingstoke: Macmillan.

Gamble, A. (1985) *Britain in Decline: Political Strategy and the British State*. Basingstoke: Macmillan.

Gamble, A. (1991) 'The Weakening of Social Democracy', in M. Loney, et al. (ed.), *The State of the Market*. London: Sage.

Gamble, A. (1994a) *The Free Economy and the Strong State. The Politics of Thatcherism* (2nd revised edition). Basingstoke: Macmillan.

Gamble, A. (1994b) 'Loves Labour Lost', in M. Perryman (ed.), *Altered States: Postmodernism, Politics, Culture*. London: Lawrence and Wishart.

Garner, R. (1996a) *Contemporary Movements and Ideologies*. New York: McGraw-Hill.

Garner, R. (1996b) *Environmental Politics*. London: Harvester Wheatsheaf.

Garnett, M. (2001) 'The Blair Essentials', *Politics Review*, April: 8–11.

Garrett, G. (1998) *Partisan Politics in the Golden Age*. Cambridge: Cambridge University Press.

Gearty, C.A. (1991) *Terror*. London: Faber and Faber.

Gearty, C.A. (1997) *The Future of Terrorism*. London: Phoenix.

Gellner, E. (1983) *Nations and Nationalism*. Oxford: Basil Blackwell.

George, V. and Wilding, P. (1976) *Ideology and Social Welfare*. London: Routledge and Kegan Paul.

George, V. and Wilding, P. (1994) *Welfare and Ideology*. London: Harvester Wheatsheaf.

Geras, N. (1987) 'Post-Marxism?', *New Left Review*, 163 (May/June): 40–82.

Geras, N. (1995) *Solidarity in the Conversation of Humankind*. London: Verso.

Giddens, A. (1979) *Central Problems in Social Theory: Action, Structure and Contradiction in Social Analysis*. London: Macmillan.

Giddens, A. (1985) *The Nation State and Violence*. Cambridge: Polity Press.

Giddens, A. (1994) *Beyond Left and Right: The Future of Radical Politics*. Stanford, CA: Stanford University Press.

Giddens, A. (1998) *The Third Way: The Renewal of Social Democracy*. Cambridge: Polity Press.

Giddens, A. (1999) *Runaway World: How Globalisation is Reshaping Our Lives*. London: Profile Books.

Gilroy, P. (1987) *'There Ain't No Black in the Union Jack': The Cultural Politics of Race and Nation*. London: Hutchinson.

Gilroy, P. (1992) *'There Ain't No Black in the Union Jack'*. London: Routledge.

Ginsburg, N. (1992) *Divisions of Welfare*. London: Sage.

Goldberg, S. (1977) *The Inevitability of Patriarchy*. London: Temple Smith.

Gorz, A. (1980) *Ecology as Politics*. Boston, MA: South End Press.

Gorz, A. (1982) *Farewell to the Working Class: An Essay in Postindustrial Socialism*. London: Pluto Press.

Gorz, A. (1985) *Paths to Paradise: On the Liberation from Work*. London: Verso.

Gorz, A. (1989) *Critique of Economic Reason*. London: Verso.

Gorz, A. (1994) *Capitalism, Socialism, Ecology*. London: Verso.

Gough, I. (1979) *The Political Economy of the Welfare State*. London: Macmillan.

Gould, P. (1999) *The Unfinished Revolution: How the Modernisers Saved the Labour Party*. London: Abacus.

Gramsci, A. (1968) *Prison Notebooks*. London: Lawrence and Wishart.

Gramsci, A. (1971) *Selections from the Prison Notebooks*. London: Lawrence and Wishart.

Gray, F. (1989) 'Steered by the State', in M. Ball, F. Gray and L. McDowell (eds), *The Transformation of Britain. Contemporary Social and Economic Change*. London: Fontana.

Green, D.G. (1987) *The New Right: The Counter-Revolution in Political, Economic and Social Thought*. London: Harvester Wheatsheaf.

Green, D.G. (1990) *Equalising People*. London: Institute of Economic Affairs.

Green, D.G. (1993) *Reinventing Civil Society: The Rediscovery of Welfare Without Politics*. London: Institute of Economic Affairs.

Green, D.G. (1996) *Community Without Politics. A Market Approach to Welfare Reform*. London: Institute of Economic Affairs.

Greer, G. (1971) *The Female Eunuch*. St Albans: Paladin.

Greer, G. (1999) *The Whole Woman*. London: Doubleday.

Griffin, R. (ed.) (1995) *Fascism*. Oxford: Oxford University Press.

Grossberg, L. (1992) *We Gotta Get Out of this Place: Popular Conservatism and Postmodern Culture*. London: Routledge.

Grosz, E. (1990) 'Contemporary Theories of Power and Subjectivity', in S. Gunew (ed.), *Feminist Knowledge: Critique and Construct*. London: Routledge.

Grosz, E. (1994) *Volatile Bodies: Toward a Corporeal Feminism*. Sydney: Allen & Unwin.

Habermas, J. (1987a) *The Theory of Communicative Action*, Vol. 1. Translated by T. McCarthy. Cambridge: Polity Press.

Habermas, J. (1987b) *The Theory of Communicative Action*, Vol. 2. Translated by T. McCarthy. Cambridge: Polity Press.

Habermas, J. (1987c) *The Theory of Communicative Action*, Vol. 3. Translated by T. McCarthy. Cambridge: Polity Press.

Habermas, J. (1988) *Legitimation Crisis*. Translated by T. McCarthy. Cambridge: Polity Press.

Habermas, J. (1989) *The Structural Transformation of the Public Sphere*. Translated by T. Burger. Cambridge: Polity Press.

Hall, J.A. and Ikenberry, G.J. (1989) *The State*. Milton Keynes: Open University Press.

Hall, S. (1984) 'The State in Question', in G. McLennan, D. Held and S. Hall (eds), *The Idea of the Modern State*. Milton Keynes: Open University Press.

Hall, S. (1988) *The Hard Road to Renewal: Thatcherism and the Crisis of the Left*. London: Verso.

Hall, S. (1993) 'Moving On . . .', Full, edited transcript of a lecture. London: Democratic Left.

Hall, S. (1997) 'Culture and Power: Interview with Peter Osborne and Lynne Segal', *Radical Philosophy*, 86 (November/December): 24–41.

Hall, S. (2000) 'A Question of Identity: What is Britain?', *The Observer*, 15 October.

Hall, S. and Jacques, M. (eds) (1983) *The Politics of Thatcherism*. London: Lawrence and Wishart.

Hall, S. and Jacques, M. (1989) *New Times. The Changing Face of Politics in the 1990s*. London: Lawrence and Wishart.

Hall, S. and Jacques, M. (1997) 'Blair: Is He the Greatest Tory since Thatcher?', *The Observer*, 13 April.

Hargreaves, I. and Christie, I. (eds) (1998) *Tomorrow's Politics: The Third Way and Beyond*. London: Demos.

Harman, C. (1995) *Economics of the Madhouse Capitalism and the Market Today*. London: Bookmarks.

Harmon, C.C. (2000) *Terrorism Today*. London: Frank Cass.

Harris, J. (1977) *William Beveridge: A Biography*. Oxford: Oxford University Press.

Harvey, D. (1989) *The Condition of Postmodernity: An Enquiry into the Origins of Cultural Change*. Oxford: Basil Blackwell.

Hay, C. (1996) *Re-Stating Social and Political Change*. Buckingham: Open University Press.

Hay, C. (1997) 'Divided by a Common Language: Political Theory and the Concept of Power', *Politics*, 17 (1): 45–52.

Hay, C. (1999) *The Political Economy of New Labour: Labouring Under False Pretences?* Manchester: Manchester University Press.

Hayek, F. (1944) *The Road to Serfdom*. London: Routledge.

Hayek, F. (1949) *Individualism and Economic Order*. London: Routledge.

Hayek, F. (1960) *The Constitution of Liberty*. London: Routledge and Kegan Paul.

Heath, A., Curtice, J. and Jowell, R. (1985) *How Britain Votes*. Oxford: Pergamon.

Heath, A., Curtice, J. and Jowell, R. (1990) *Understanding Political Change: The British Voter 1964–1987*. Oxford: Pergamon.

Heath, A., Jowell, R. and Curtice, J. (2001) *The Rise of New Labour. Party Policies and Voter Choices*. Oxford: Oxford University Press.

Hechter, M. (1975) *Internal Colonialism: The Celtic Fringe in British National Development, 1536–1966*. London: Routledge and Kegan Paul.

Heffernan, R. (1999) *New Labour and Thatcherism: Exploring Political Change in Britain*. Basingstoke: Macmillan.

Held, D. (1984) 'Power and Legitimacy in Contemporary Britain', in G. McLennan, D. Held and S. Hall (eds), *State and Society in Contemporary Britain: A Critical Introduction*. Oxford: Polity Press.

Held, D. (1992) 'The Development of the Modern State', in S. Hall and B. Gieben (eds), *Formations of Modernity*. Oxford: Polity Press.

Held, D. and McGrew, A.G. (1993) 'Globalisation and the Liberal Democratic State', *Government and Opposition*, 28 (2): 261–88.

Hennessey, T. (2000) *The Northern Ireland Peace Process*. Dublin: Gill & Macmillan.

Hertz, N. (1999) 'Better To Shop Than To Vote', *New Statesman*, 21 June.

Hertz, N. (2001) *The Silent Takeover: Global Capitalism and the Death of Democracy*. London: Heinemann.

Hickman, M. (1998) 'Education for Minorities: Irish Catholics in Britain', in G. Lewis (ed.), *Forming Nation, Framing Welfare*. London: Routledge.

Hirst, P. (1989) *After Thatcher*. London: Collins.

Hirst, P. and Thompson, G. (1996) *Globalization in Question: The International Economy and the Possibilities of Governance*. Cambridge: Polity Press.

Hite, S. (1993) '"Medieval" Tory Values', *New Times*, 27 November.

Hobsbawm, E.J. (1992) *Nations and Nationalism since 1780*. Cambridge: Canto.

Hobsbawm, E.J. (1995) *Age of Extremes: The Short Twentieth Century, 1914–1991*. London: Abacus.

Hounshell, D. (1984) *From the American System to Mass Production*. Baltimore, MD: John Hopkins University Press.

Hutton, W. (1995a) *The State We're In*. London: Jonathan Cape.

Hutton, W. (1995b) 'The 30/30/40 Society', *The Guardian*, 21 January.

Hutton, W. (1997) *The State to Come*. London: Vintage.

Hutton, W. (1999) *The Stakeholding Society Writings on Politics and Economics*. Ed. David Goldblatt. Cambridge: Polity Press.

Hutton, W. and Giddens, A. (eds) (2001) *On the Edge. Living with Global Capitalism*. London: Vintage.

Inglehart, R. (1977a) *The Silent Revolution*. Princeton, NJ: Princeton University Press.

Inglehart, R. (1977b) *Modernization and Postmodernization: Cultural, Economic, and Political Change in 43 Societies*. Princeton, NJ: Princeton University Press.

Inglehart, R. (1980) *Culture Shift in Advanced Industrial Society*. Princeton, NJ: Princeton University Press.

Inglehart, R. (1981) 'Post-Materialism in an Environment of Insecurity', *American Political Science Review*, 75: 880–900.

Inglehart, R. (1987) 'Value Change in Industrial Societies', *American Political Science Review*, 81 (4): 1289–1303.

Inglehart, R. (1989) 'Observations on Cultural Change and Postmodernism', in J.R. Gibbins (ed.), *Contemporary Political Culture*. London: Sage.

Inglehart, R. and Rabier, J.R. (1986) 'Political Realignment in Advanced Industrial Society: From Class-based Politics to Quality-of-Life Politics', *Government and Opposition*, 21: 456–79.

Jacobson, R. (2000) 'Women and Peace in Northern Ireland: A Complicated Relationship', in S. Jacobs, R. Jacobson and J. Marchbank (eds), *States of Conflict*. London: Zed Books.

Jagger, A. (1983) *Feminist Politics and Human Nature*. Brighton: Harvester.

Jameson, F. (1984) 'Postmodernism or the Cultural Logic of Late Capitalism', *New Left Review*, 146: 52–92.

Jameson, F. (1985) 'Postmodernism and Consumer Society', in H. Foster (ed.), *Postmodern Culture*. London: Pluto.

James, F. (1991) *Postmodernism, or, the Cultural Logic of Late Capitalism*. Durham, NC: Duke University Press.

Jameson, F. (1998) *The Cultural Turn. Selected Writings on the Postmodern, 1983-1998*. London: Verso.

Jenkins, P. (1987) *Mrs Thatcher's Revolution: The Ending of the Socialist Era*. London: Jonathan Cape.

Jessop, B. (1982) *The Capitalist State*. Oxford: Martin Robertson.

Jessop, B. (1989) 'Conservative Regimes and the Transition to Post Fordism', in M. Gottdiener and N. Komninos (eds), *Capitalist Development and Crisis Theory: Accumulation, Regulation and Spatial Restructuring*. London: Macmillan.

Jessop, B. (1990) *State Theory: Putting Capitalist States in Their Place*. Oxford: Polity Press.

Jessop, B. (1992) 'From Social Democracy to Thatcherism: Twenty-five Years of British Politics', in N. Abercrombie and A. Warde (eds), *Social Change in Contemporary Britain*. Cambridge: Polity Press.

Jessop, B., Bonnett, K., Bromley, S. and Ling, T. (1988) *Thatcherism: A Tale of Two Nations*. Cambridge: Polity Press.

Jessop, B., Bonnett, K. and Bromley, S. (1990) 'Farewell to Thatcherism? Neo-liberalism and New Times', *New Left Review*, 179: 81–102.

Johnson, C. (1991) *The Economy Under Mrs Thatcher, 1979–1990*. London: Penguin Books.

Johnson, P. (1980) *The Recovery of Freedom*. Oxford: Basil Blackwell.

Jordon, B. (1985) *The State: Authority and Autonomy*. Oxford: Basil Blackwell.

Jordan, G. and Maloney, W. (1997) *The Protest Business? Mobilising Campaign Groups*. Manchester: Manchester University Press.

Jowett, M. (2000) 'New Feminism in Contemporary Britain', *Politics Review*, February.

Kavanagh, D. (1987) *Thatcherism and British Politics: The End of Consensus?* Oxford: Oxford University Press.

Keesing, R. (1981) *Cultural Anthropology*. New York: Holt, Rinehart & Winston.

Kenny, M. (1994) 'The Family: A Matriarchal Institution', in C. Quest (ed.), *Liberating Women . . . From Modern Feminism*. London: Institute of Economic Affairs, Health and Welfare Unit.

Kenny, M. and Smith, M.J. (1997) '(Mis)understanding Blair', *Political Quarterly*, 68: 220–30.

Kessler, T. (2001) 'Disunited Kingdom? What's Really Happening on the Streets of Britain', *New Musical Express*, 28 July.

Kidd, W., Kirby, M., Koubel, F., et al. (1998a) *Readings in Sociology*. Oxford: Heinemann.

Kidd, W., Kirby, M. Koubel, F., et al. (1998b) 'Introduction: Reading the Sociology of Power and Politics', in W. Kidd, M. Kirby, F. Koubel et al. (eds), *Readings in Sociology*. Oxford: Heinemann, pp. 529–59.

King, A. (1976) *Why Is Britain Becoming Harder To Govern?* London: BBC Books.

Kitchen, M. (1976) *Fascism*. Basingstoke: Macmillan Press.

Klein, N. (2001a) *No Logo*. London: Flamingo.

Klein, N. (2001b) 'Reclaiming the Commons', *New Left Review*, 9 (May/June): 81–9.

Knuttila, M. (1996) *Introducing Sociology: A Critical Perspective*. Toronto: Oxford University Press.

Kundnani, A. (2001) 'From Oldham to Bradford: The Violence of the Violated', extracted from *The Three Faces of British Racism*. London: Institute of Race Relations.

Laclau, E. (1993) 'Radical Democracy Not a Bluprint', *New Times*, 29 May.

Laclau, E. and Mouffe, C. (1985) *Hegemony and Socialist Strategy: Toward a Radical Democratic Politics*. London: Verso.

Laqueur, W. (1999) *The New Terrorism: Fanaticism and the Arms of Mass Destruction*. London: Phoenix Press.

Laraña, E., Johnston, H. and Gusfield, J. (1994) *New Social Movements: From Ideology to Identity*. London: UCL Press.

Le Grand, J. (1998) *Quasi-Markets and Social Policy*. Bristol: Policy Press.

Lenin, V.I. ([1917] 1981) 'The State and Revolution', in *Collected Works*. Moscow: Progress.

Levin, M., Paul, E.F., Conway, D., Papps, I., Taylor J. and McElroy, W. (1992) *Equal Opportunities: A Feminist Fallacy*. London: Institute of Economic Affairs.

Lewis, O. (1961) *The Children of Sachez*. New York: Random House.

Leys, C. (1983) *Politics in Britain: An Introduction*. London: Heinemann.

Lockwood, D. (1958) *The Blackcoated Worker*. London: Unwin.

Lockwood, D. (1966) 'Sources of Variation in Working-class Images of Society', *Sociological Review*, 14 (2): 249–67.

Lofland, J. (1985) *Protest: Studies of Collective Behaviour and Social Movements*. New Brunswick, NJ: Transaction.

Loney, M. (1986) *The Politics of Greed: The New Right and the Welfare State*. London: Pluto Press.

Loney, M. (1987) 'A War on Poverty or on the Poor?', in A. Walker and C. Walker (eds), *The Growing Divide: A Social Audit 1979–1987*. London: Child Poverty Action Group.

Lorde, A. (1992) 'Age, Race, Class and Sex: Women Redefining Difference', in H. Crowley and S. Himmelweit (eds), *Knowing Women: Feminism and Knowledge*. Cambridge: Polity Press.

Lovenduski, J. and Randall, V. (1993) *Contemporary Feminist Politics: Women and Power in Britain*. Oxford: Oxford University Press.

Lowe, R. (1993) *The Welfare State in Britain Since 1945*. Basingstoke: Macmillan.

Ludlam, S. and Smith, M.J. (eds) (2001) *New Labour in Government*. Basingstoke: Macmillan.

Lukes, S. (1974) *Power: A Radical View*. Basingstoke: Macmillan.

Lyotard, J.F. (1979) *The Postmodern Condition: A Report on Knowledge*. Manchester: Manchester University Press.

MacArthur, B. (ed.) (1993) *The Penguin Book of Twentieth-Century Speeches*. London: Penguin.

MacIntyre, D. (2000) *Mandelson and the Making of New Labour*. London: Harper Collins.

Mallie, E. and McKittrick, D. (2001) *Endgame in Ireland*. London: Hodder & Stoughton.

Mama, A. (1995) *Beyond the Masks: Race, Gender and Subjectivity*. London: Routledge.

Mandel, E. (1975) *Late Capitalism* (revised edition). London: New Left Books.

Mandelson, P. and Liddle, R. (1996) *The Blair Revolution: Can New Labour Deliver?* London: Faber & Faber.

Mann, K. (1994) 'Watching the Defectives: Observers of the Underclass in the USA, Britain and Australia', *Critical Social Policy*, 41: 79–99.

Mann, M. (1986) *The Sources of Social Power, Volume 1*. Cambridge: Cambridge University Press.

Mann, M. (1988) *States, War and Capitalism: Studies in Political Sociology*. Oxford: Blackwell.

Mann, M. (1993) *The Sources of Social Power, Volume 2*. Cambridge: Cambridge University Press.

Marshall, G. et al. (1988) *Social Class in Modern Britain*. London: Hutchinson.

Marsland, D. (1994) 'The Use and Abuse of State Welfare', *Sailsbury Review*, June: 14–17.

Marwell, G. and Oliver, P. (1984) 'Collective Action Theory and Social Movement Research', *Research in Social Movements, Conflicts and Change*, 7: 1–27.

Marx, K. (1963) [1852] *The Eighteenth Brumaire of Louis Bonaparte*. New York: International Publishers.

Marx, K. ([1985] 1969) *The Class Struggle in France*, translated by the Institute of Marxism-Leninism. Moscow: Progress Publishers.

Marx, K. (1970) [1867, 1885, 1894] *Capital* (vols 1–3). London: Lawrence and Wishart.

Marx, K. and Engels, F. (1967) [1848] *The Communist Manifesto*. Harmondsworth: Penguin.

Marx, K. and Engels, F. (1970) [1846] *The German Ideology*. Translated by W. Lough, C. Dutt and C.P. Magill. London: Lawrence and Wishart.

Marxism Today (1998) Special Issue, November/December.

McAuley, J.W. (1991a) 'Cuchulainn and an RPG–7: The Ideology and Politics of the UDA', in E. Hughes (ed.), *Culture and Politics in Northern Ireland*. Milton Keynes: Open University Press.

McAuley, J.W. (1991b) 'The Protestant Working Class and the State in Northern Ireland since 1930: a Problematic Relationship', in S. Hutton and P. Stewart (eds), *Ireland's Histories*. London: Routledge.

McAuley, J.W. (1994) *The Politics of Identity: a Loyalist Community in Belfast.* Aldershot: Avebury Press.

McAuley, J.W. (1995) '"Not a Game of Cowboys and Indians" – the Ulster Defence Association in the 1990s', in, A. O'Day, (ed.), *Terrorism's Laboratory: The Case of Northern Ireland.* Dartmouth: Aldershot.

McAuley, J.W. (1996a) 'From Loyal Soldiers to Political Spokespersons: A Political History of a Loyalist Paramilitary Group in Northern Ireland', *Etudes Irlandaises*, 21, 1.

McAuley, J.W. (1996b) '(Re)Constructing Ulster Loyalism: Political Responses to the "Peace Process"', *Irish Journal of Sociology*, 6: 165–82.

McAuley, J.W. (1997a) 'Flying the One-Winged Bird': Ulster Unionism and the Peace Process' in P. Shirlow and M. McGovern (eds), *Who Are 'The People'?*

McAuley, J.W. (1997b) 'The Ulster Loyalist Political Parties: Towards a New Respectability', in P. Joannon (ed.), *Le Processus De Paix En Irlande Du Nord, Etudes Irlandaises*, 22 (2): 117–32.

McAuley, J.W. (1997c) 'Divided Loyalists, Divided Loyalties: Conflict and Continuities in Contemporary Unionist Ideology' in C. Gilligan and J. Tonge (eds), *Peace or War?*

McAuley, J.W. (1998) 'Surrender?: Loyalist Perceptions of Conflict Settlement' in *(Dis)Agreeing Ireland.* James Anderson & James Goodman (eds), London: Pluto Press.

McAuley, J.W. (1999) 'Very British Rebels': Politics and Discourse within Contemporary Ulster Unionism', in *Transforming Politics: Power and Resistance.* Paul Bagguley & Jeff Hearn (eds), Basingstoke: Macmillan Press.

McAuley, J.W. and Tonge, J. (2001) 'The Roles of the Extra-constitutional Parties in the Northern Ireland Assembly'. Final Report to Economic and Social Research Council.

McBride, I. (ed.) (2001) *History and Memory in Modern Ireland.* Cambridge: Cambridge University Press.

McCann, E. (1974) *War and an Irish Town.* Harmondsworth: Penguin Books.

McCann, E. (1986) 'The Protestant Working Class', *Socialist Worker Review*, 89.

McCann, E. (1993) *War and an Irish Town.* London: Pluto Press.

McCoy, G. (2000) 'Women, Community and Politics in Northern Ireland', in C. Roulston and C. Davies (eds), *Gender, Democracy and Inclusion in Northern Ireland.* Basingstoke: Palgrave.

McCrone, D. (1992) *Understanding Scotland: The Sociology of a Stateless Nation.* London: Routledge.

McGarry, J. and O'Leary, B. (1995) *Explaining Northern Ireland: Broken Images.* London: Blackwell.

McGinty, R. and Darby, J. (2002) *Guns and Government: The Management of the Northern Ireland Peace Process.* Basingstoke: Palgrave.

McGrew, A. (1992) 'A Global Society?', in S. Hall, D. Held and A. McGrew (eds), *Modernity and its Futures.* Cambridge: Polity Press.

McKay, G. (ed.) (1998) *DiY Culture: Party & Protest in Nineties Britain.* London: Verso.

McKittrick, D. (1999) *Through the Minefield.* Belfast: Blackstaff Press.

McKittrick, D., Kelters, S., Feeney, B. and Thornton, C. (1999) *Lost Lives: The Story of the Men, Women and Children Who Died as a Result of the Northern Ireland Troubles*. Edinburgh: Mainstream Publishing.

McLaughlin, E. (1996) 'Political Violence, Terrorism and Crimes of the State', in J. Muncie and E. McLaughlin (eds), *The Problem of Crime*. London: Sage.

McLennan, G. (1995) 'The Power of Ideology', in *Politics and Power*, Block 4, Unit 17, D103, *Society and Social Science: A Foundation Course*. Milton Keynes: The Open University.

McNicol, J. (1987) 'In Pursuit of the Underclass', *Journal of Social Policy*, 16: 293–318.

Melucci, A. (1980) *Nomads of the Present*. Philadelphia, PA: Temple University Press.

Michels, R. (1993) 'The Iron Law of Oligarchy', in M.E. Olsen and M.N. Marger (eds), *Power in Modern Societies*. Oxford: Westview Press.

Middlemas, K. (1979) *Politics in Industrial Society*. London: André Deutsch.

Middlemas, K. (1986) *Power, Competition and the State, Volume 1: Britain in Search of Balance, 1940–61*. London: Macmillan.

Middlemas, K. (1990) *Power, Competition and the State, Volume 2: Threats to the Postwar Settlement, 1961–74*. London: Macmillan.

Middlemas, K. (1991) *Power, Competition and the State, Volume 3: The End of the Post-war Era*. London: Macmillan.

Mill, J.S. ([1869] 1983) *The Subjection of Women*. London: Virago.

Millet, K. (1977) *Sexual Politics*. London: Virago.

Milliband, R. (1969) *The State in Capitalist Society*. London: Merlin.

Milliband, R. (1970) *Parliamentary Socialism* (2nd edition). London: Merlin.

Milliband, R. (1991) *Divided Societies: Class Struggle in Contemporary Capitalism*. Oxford: Oxford University Press.

Milliband R. and Panitch, I. (eds) (1994) *Socialist Register 1994: Between Globalism and Nationalism*. London: Merlin.

Mills, C.W. (1956) *The Power Elite*. Oxford: Oxford University Press.

Mirza, H.S. (1998) 'All White Now', *The Guardian*, 2 February.

Mishra, R. (1990) *The Welfare State in Capitalist Society*. London: Harvester Wheatsheaf.

Mitchell, J. (1971) *Woman's Estate*. Harmondsworth: Penguin Books.

Mitchell, J. (1974) *Psychoanalysis and Feminism*. London: Allen Lane.

Mohan, J. (1999) *A United Kingdom? Economic, Social and Political Geographies*. London: Arnold.

Monbiot, G. (2000) *Captive State: The Corporate Takeover of Britain*. London: Pan Books.

Moran, M. (1989) *Politics and Society in Britain: An Introduction*. Basingstoke: Macmillan.

Morgan, V. (1995) *Peacemakers? Peacekeepers? – Women in Northern Ireland 1969–1995*, Professorial Lecture given at the University of Ulster, 25 October.

Morgan, V. and Fraser, G. (1995) 'Women and the Northern Ireland Conflict: Experiences and Responses', in S. Dunn (ed.), *Facets of the Conflict in Northern Ireland*. Basingstoke: Macmillan.

Mosca, G. (1939) [1896] *The Ruling Class*. Translated by A. Livingstone. New York: McGraw-Hill.

Mouffe, C. (1992) *Dimensions of Radical Democracy: Pluralism and Citizenship*. London: Verso.

Mouffe, C. (1993a) *The Return to the Political*. London: Verso.

Mouffe, C. (1993b) 'The Return of the Political', *New Times*, 27 November.

Mouffe, C. (1995) 'The End of Politics and the Rise of the Radical Right', *Dissent*, Fall: 498–502.

Mulgan, G. (1994) *Politics in an Antipolitical Age*. Cambridge: Polity Press.

Mulgan, G. (ed.) (1997) *Life after Politics: New Thinking for the Twenty-First Century*. London: Fontana.

Murray, C. (1984) *Losing Ground: American Social Policy 1950–1980*. New York: Basic Books.

Murray, C. (1989) 'Underclass', *Sunday Times Magazine*, 26 November.

Murray, C. (1990) *The Emerging British Underclass*. London: Institute of Economic Affairs.

Murray, C. (1994a) 'Underclass: The Crisis Deepens', *Sunday Times*, 22 May.

Murray, C. (1994b) 'The New Victorians and the New Rabble', *Sunday Times*, 29 May.

Murray, C. (2000) 'Baby Beware', *Sunday Times*, 13 February.

Murray, R. (1989) 'Fordism and Post-Fordism', in S. Hall and M. Jacques (eds), *New Times: The Changing Face of Politics in the 1990s*. London: Lawrence and Wishart, pp. 38–53.

Nairn, T. (1997) *Faces of Nationalism: Janus Revisited*. London: Verso.

Nairn, T. (2000) 'Ukania under Blair', *New Left Review*, January/February: 69–103.

Nash, K. (2000) *Contemporary Political Sociology: Globalization, Politics and Power*. Oxford: Basil Blackwell.

Neocleous, M. (1997) *Fascism*. Buckingham: Open University Press.

Netanyahu, B. (1979) *Terrorism: How the West Can Win*. New York: Farrar, Straus, Giroux.

Nicholson, J. (1994) 'Poorest 10pc no better off than in 1967', *The Guardian*, 3 June.

Nordhaus, W.D. (1975) 'The Political Business Cycle', *Review of Economic Studies*, 42: 169–90.

Novak, M. (1998) *Is There a Third Way? Essays on the Changing Direction of Socialist Thought*. London: Institute of Economic Affairs, Health and Welfare Unit.

O'Brien, M. and Penna, S. (1998) *Theorising Welfare Enlightenment and Modern Society*. London: Sage.

O'Connor, J. (1973) *The Fiscal Crisis of the State*. New York: St Martin's Press.

O'Connor, J. (1987) *The Meaning of Crisis*. Oxford: Blackwell.

Offe, C. (1982) 'Some Contradictions of the Modern Welfare State', *Critical Social Policy*, 2 (2): 7–16.

Offe, C. (1984) *Contradictions of the Welfare State*. Ed. J. Keane. London: Hutchinson.

Offe, C. (1985) *Disorganized Capitalism*. Cambridge: Polity Press.

Offe, C. (1987) 'Challenging the Boundaries of Institutional Politics: Social Movements since the 1960s', in Charles S. Maier (ed.), *Challenging the Boundaries of the Political*. Cambridge: Cambridge University Press.

Office of National Statistics (2000) *Britain: An Official Handbook*. London: HMSO.

Oppenheim, C. (1994a) 'Poverty: The Facts', in *Social Problems and Social Welfare*,

Block 4, D211, *Readings, Reconstructing Welfare*. Milton Keynes: Open University Press.

Oppenheim, C. (1994b) 'The Causes of Poverty', in *Social Problems and Social Welfare*, Block 4, D211, *Readings, Reconstructing Welfare*. Milton Keynes: Open University Press.

Overbeek, H. (1990) *Global Capitalism and National Decline: The Thatcher Decade in Perspective*. London: Unwin Hyman.

Pahl, R.A. and Winkler, P. (1974) 'The Coming Corporatism', *New Society*, 30 (627): 10.

Pakulski, J. (1990) *Social Movements: The Politics of Protest*. Melbourne: Longman.

Panitch, L. (1976) *Social Democracy and Industrial Militancy*. Cambridge: Cambridge University Press.

Panitch, L. (1980) 'Recent Theorisation of Corporatism', *British Journal of Sociology*, 31 (2): 159–87.

Panitch, L. (1985) *Working Class Politics in Crisis*. London: Verso.

Panitch, L. and Leys, C. (1997) *The End of Parliamentary Socialism: From New Left to New Labour*. London: Verso.

Parekh, B. (2000) 'Changing What it Means to be British', *The Daily Telegraph*, 18 October.

Pateman, C. (1989) 'The Patriarchal Welfare State', in A. Gutman (ed.), *Democracy and the Welfare State*. Princeton, NJ: Princeton University Press.

Paxman, J. (1999) *The English: A Portrait of a People*. London: Penguin.

Perryman, M. (ed.) (1996) *The Blair Agenda*. London: Lawrence and Wishart.

Petras, J. and Veltmeyer, H. (2001) *Globalization Unmasked: Imperialism in the 21st Century*. London: Zed Books.

Philips, A. (1991) *Engendering Democracy*. Cambridge: Polity Press.

Philips, A. (1993) *Democracy and Difference*. Cambridge: Polity Press.

Pickering, M. (2001) *Stereotyping: The Politics of Representation*. Basingstoke: Palgrave.

Pilger, J. (2002) *The New Rulers of the World*. London: Verso.

Pimlott, P. (1989) 'Is the Postwar Consensus a Myth?', *Contemporary Record*, 2 (6): 12–14.

Poggi, G. (1990) *The State*. Cambridge: Polity Press.

Pond, C. (1989) 'The Changing Distribution of Income, Wealth and Poverty', in C. Hamnett, L. McDowell and P. Sarre (eds), *The Changing Social Structure*. London: Sage.

Porter, N. (1996) *Rethinking Unionism: An Alternative Vision for Northern Ireland*. Belfast: Blackstaff Press.

Postman, N. (1983) *The Disappearance of Childhood*. London: W.H. Allen.

Poulantzas, N. (1969) 'The Problem of the Capitalist State', *New Left Review*, 58: 67–78.

Poulantzas, N. (1973) *Political Power and Social Classes*. London: New Left Books.

Poulantzas, N. (1976) *Crisis of the Dictatorships*. London: New Left Books.

Poulantzas, N. (1978) *State, Power, Socialism*. London: New Left Books.

Powell, M. (ed.) (1999) *New Labour, New Welfare State?: The 'Third Way' in British Social Policy*. Bristol: Policy Press.

Powell, M. (2000) 'New Labour and the Third Way in the British Welfare State: A New and Distinctive Approach?', *Critical Social Policy*, 20 (1): 39–60.

Preston, P.W. (1997) *Political/Cultural Identity: Citizens and Nations in a Global Era.* London: Sage.

Quest, C. (ed.) (1994) *Liberating Women . . . From Modern Feminism.* Choice in Welfare Series No. 19. London: Institute of Economic Affairs, Health and Welfare Unit.

Quinn, D. (1993) *Understanding Northern Ireland.* Manchester: Baseline Books.

Riddell, P. (1983) *The Thatcher Government.* Oxford: Martin Robertson.

Riddell, P. (1989) *The Thatcher Decade.* Oxford: Blackwell.

Riddell, P. (1991) *The Thatcher Era and Its Legacy.* Oxford: Blackwell.

Roberts, S. (1979) *Order and Dispute: An Introduction to Legal Anthropology.* Harmondsworth: Penguin.

Robson, M. (1992) *Italy: Liberalism and Fascism 1870–1945.* London: Hodder & Stoughton.

Roediger, D.R. (1991) *The Wages of Whiteness: Race and the Making of the American Working Class.* London: Verso.

Roemer, J. (1982) *A General Theory of Exploitation and Class.* Cambridge, MA: Harvard University Press.

Roiphe, K. (1994) *The Morning After: Sex, Fear and Feminism.* London: Hamish Hamilton.

Rooney, E. (1992) 'Women, Community and Politics in Northern Ireland – Isms in Action', *Journal of Gender Studies*, 1 (4): 475–91.

Rooney, E. (2000) 'Women in Northern Irish Politics: Difference Matters', in C. Roulston and C. Davies (eds), *Gender, Democracy and Inclusion in Northern Ireland.* Basingstoke: Palgrave.

Rowbotham, S. (1972a) *Women, Resistance and Revolution.* London: Allen Lane.

Rowbotham, S. (1972b) *Womens Consciousness Mans World.* Harmondsworth: Penguin.

Rowbotham, S. (1973) *Hidden from History.* London: Pluto Press.

Rowbotham, S. (1990) *The Past Is Before Us: Feminism in Action since the 1960s.* London: Penguin.

Rowbotham, S. (1993) 'Feminism in the Nineties', *New Times*, 6 March.

Rowbotham, S. (1999) *A Century of Women.* Harmondsworth: Penguin.

Joseph Rowntree Foundation (1995) *Income and Wealth.* York: JRF.

Joseph Rowntree Foundation (1996) 'Social Policy Research', *Joseph Rowntree Foundation: Findings* (June). York: JRF.

Joseph Rowntree Foundation (1999) *Monitoring Poverty and Social Exclusion.* York: JRF.

Joseph Rowntree Foundation (2000) 'Poverty and Social Exclusion in Britain', *Joseph Rowntree Foundation: Findings* (September). York: JFK.

Rowthorn, B. and Wayne, N. (1988) *Northern Ireland: The Political Economy Conflict.* Oxford: Polity Press.

Ruane, J. and Todd, J. (eds) (1999) *After the Good Friday Agreement: Analysing Political Change in Northern Ireland.* Dublin: University College Press.

Runnymede Trust (2000) *The Future of Multi-Ethnic Britain: The Parekh Report.* London: Profile Books.

Sales, R. (1997) *Women Divided: Gender, Religion and Politics in Northern Ireland*. London: Routledge.

Sardar, Z. and Davies, M.W. (2002) *Why Do People Hate America?* Cambridge: Icon Books.

Savage, S.P. (1990) 'A War on Crime? Law and Order Policies in the 1980s', in S.P. Savage and L. Robins (eds), *Public Policy Under Thatcher*. Basingstoke: Macmillan.

Savage, S.P. and Atkinson, R. (eds) (2001) *Public Policy under Blair*. Basingstoke: Palgrave.

Schedler, A. (ed.) (1997) *The End of Politics? Explorations into Modern Antipolitics*. Basingstoke: Macmillan.

Schlesinger, P., Murdock, G. and Elliott, P. (1983) *Television 'Terrorism': Political Violence in Political Culture*. London: Comedia Publishing Group.

Schmitter, P.C. (1974) 'Still the Century of Corporatism?', *Review of Politics*, 36: 85–131.

Schmitter, P.C. (1979) 'Still the Century of Corporatism', in P.C. Schmitter and G. Lehmbruch (eds), *Trends Towards Corporatist Intermediation*. London: Sage.

Scholte, J.A. (2000) *Globalisation: A Critical Introduction*. Basingstoke: Macmillan.

Schumpeter, J. (1976) *Capitalism, Socialism and Democracy*. London: Allen & Unwin.

Schwarzmantel, J. (1994) *The State in Contemporary Society*. London: Harvester Wheatsheaf.

Scott, J. (1991) *Who Rules Britain?* Cambridge: Polity Press.

Scott, J. (1994) 'Class Analysis: Back to the Future', *Sociology*, 28.

Scott, J. (ed.) (1996a) *Class*. London: Routledge.

Scott, J. (1996b) *Stratification & Power: Structures of Class, Status and Command*. Cambridge: Polity Press.

Scraton, P. (ed.) (2002) *Beyond September 11: An Anthology of Dissent*. London: Pluto Press.

Scruton, R. (1986) *Sexual Desires: A Philosophical Investigation*. London: Weidenfeld and Nicolson.

Scruton, R. (1990) 'In Defence of the Nation', in J.C.D. Clark (ed.), *Ideas and Politics in Modern Britain*. London: Macmillan.

Seabrook, J. (1985) *Landscapes of Poverty*. Oxford: Blackwell.

Searchlight (2001) 'Election 2001: A Guide to Far Right Results', *Searchlight: The International Anti-Fascist Monthly*, July, 313: 4–7.

Shaw, M., et al. (1999) *The Widening Gap: Health Inequalities and Policy in Britain*. Bristol: Policy Press.

Sheridan, T. and McCombes, A. (2000) *Imagine: A Socialist Vision for the 21st Century*. Edinburgh: Rebel Inc.

Shirlow, P. (2000) 'Fear, Mobility and Living in the Ardoyne and Upper Ardoyne Communities: A Report by the Mapping the Spaces of Fear Research Team'. Coleraine: University of Ulster.

Shultz, R. (1990) 'Conceptualizing Political Terrorism', in C.W. Kegley (ed.), *International Terrorism: Characteristics, Causes, Controls*. New York: St. Martin's Press.

Smart, C. (1991) 'Securing the Family? Rhetoric and Policy in the Field of Social Security', in M. Loney, R. Bocock, J. Clarke, A. Cochrane, P. Graham and M.

Wilson (eds), *The State or the Market: Politics and Welfare in Contemporary Britain*. London: Sage.

Spivak, G. (1992) 'The Politics of Translation', in M. Barrett and A. Phillips (eds), *Destabilizing Theory: Contemporary Feminist Debates*. Cambridge: Polity Press.

Spender, D. (1983) *Women of Ideas (and What Men have Done to Them)*. London: Pandora.

Spender, D. (1985) *For the Record: The Making and Meaning of Feminist Knowledge*. London: The Women's Press.

Stewart, A.T.Q. (1977) *The Narrow Ground: Aspects of Ulster, 1609–1969*. London: Faber & Faber.

Stoker, G. (1991) *The Politics of Local Government*. Basingstoke: Macmillan.

Taylor, P. (1989) *Families At War: Voices from the Troubles*. London: BBC Books.

Taylor, P.J. (2000) 'Izations of the World: Americanization, Modernization and Globalization', in C. Hay and D. Marsh (eds), *Demystifying Globalization*. Basingstoke: Macmillan.

Thompson J.B. (1984) *Studies in the Theory of Ideology*. Cambridge: Polity Press.

Thompson, J.B. (1990) *Ideology and Modern Culture*. Oxford: Polity Press.

Thompson, J.B. (1993) 'Ideology', in J. Krieger (ed.), *The Oxford Companion to Politics of the World*. Oxford: Oxford University Press, pp. 409–10.

Thornton, P. (1989) *Civil Liberties in the Thatcher Years*. London: National Council for Civil Liberties.

Thornton, T.P. (1964) 'Terror as a Weapon of Political Agitation' in C. Eckstein (ed.), *Internal War*. London: Collier and Macmillan.

Tilly, C. (1990) *Coercion, Capital, and European States, AD 990–1990*. Oxford: Blackwell.

Tomlinson, J. (2001) *The Politics of Decline: Understanding Post-war Britain*. Harlow: Longman.

Tong, R. (1992) *Feminist Thought: A Comprehensive Introduction*. London: Routledge.

Tonge, J. (1994) 'The Anti-Poll Tax Movement: a Pressure Movement?', *Politics*, 14 (2): 93–9.

Tonge, J. (1998) *Northern Ireland: Conflict and Change*. Hemel Hempstead: Prentice Hall.

Touraine, A. (1971) *The Postindustrial Society. Tomorrow's Social History: Classes, Conflicts and Culture in the Programmed Society*. Translated by L.F.X. Mayhew. New York: Random House.

Touraine, A. (1981) *The Voice and the Eye: An Analysis of Social Movements*. Translated by A. Duff. Cambridge: Cambridge University Press.

Touraine, A. (1983) *Anti-nuclear Protest*. Cambridge: Cambridge University Press.

Touraine, A., Wieviorka, M. and Dubet, F. (1987) *The Worker's Movement*. Cambridge: Cambridge University Press.

Toynbee, P. and Walker, D. (2001) *Did Things Get Better? An Audit of Labour's Success and Failures*. London: Penguin.

Trew, K. (1992) 'Social Psychological Research on the Conflict', *The Psychologist*, (5): 342–4.

Trew, K. (1998) 'The Northern Irish Identity', in A.J. Kershen (ed.), *A Question of Identity*. Aldershot: Ashgate.

Walby, S. (1990) *Theorising Patriarchy*. Oxford: Blackwell.

Walker, A. and Walker, C. (eds) (1987) *The Growing Divide: A Social Audit 1979–1987*. London: Child Poverty Action Group.

Walker, A. and Walker, C. (1996) 'Blaming the Victims', in R. Lister (ed.), *Charles Murray and the Underclass: The Developing Debate*. London: Institute of Economic Affairs.

Walker, B. (1996) *Dancing to History's Tune: History, Myth and Politics in Ireland*. Belfast: The Institute of Irish Studies.

Walker, B. (2000) *Past and Present: History, Identity and Politics in Ireland*. Belfast: The Institute of Irish Studies.

Walker, D. (1998) 'Analysis: The Third Way – Tony's Ology for Sceptics', *The Guardian*, 22 September.

Walker, R. (1989) 'Machinery, Labour and Location', in S. Wood (ed.), *The Transformation of Work?* London: Unwin Hyman.

Weber, M. (1978) *Economy and Society*. Berkeley, CA: University of California Press.

Weedon, C. (1987) *Feminist Practice and Poststructuralist Theory*. Oxford: Blackwell.

Went, R. (2000) *Globalization, Neoliberal Challenge, Radical Responses*. London: Pluto Press.

Westergaard, J. (1977) 'Class Inequality and Corporatism', in A. Hunt (ed.), *Class and Class Structure*. London: Lawrence and Wishart.

Whyte, J. (1991) *Interpreting Northern Ireland*. Oxford: Clarendon Press.

Wichert, S. (1991) *Northern Ireland Since 1945*. Harlow: Longman.

Wilding, P. (1992) 'The British Welfare State: Thatcherism's Enduring Legacy', *Policy and Politics*, 20 (3): 201–12.

Wilford, R. (ed.) (2001) *Aspects of the Belfast Agreement*. Oxford: Oxford University Press.

Wilford, R. and Galligan, Y. (1999) 'Gender and Party Politics in Northern Ireland', in Y. Galligan, E. Ward and R. Wilford (eds), *Contesting Politics: Women in Ireland, North and South*. Oxford: Westview Press.

Wilkinson, P. (1977) *Terrorism and the Liberal State*. Basingstoke: Macmillan.

Williamson, P.J. (1989) *Corporatism in Perspective: An Introductory Guide to Corporatist Theory*. London: Sage.

Wilson, E. (1992) *A Very British Miracle: The Failure of Thatcherism*. London: Pluto Press.

Wilson, G. (1994) 'Biology, Sex Roles and Work', in C. Quest (ed.), *Liberating Women . . . From Modern Feminism*. London: Institute of Economic Affairs, Health and Welfare Unit.

Wilson, W.J. (1987) *The Truly Deprived: The Inner-City and the Underclass*. London: University of Chicago Press.

Winkler, J. (1976) 'Corporatism', *Archives Européennes de Sociologie*, XVII (1): 100–36.

Winkler, J. (1977a) 'The Coming Corporatism', in R. Skidelsky (ed.), *The End of the Keynesian Era*. London: Macmillan.

Winkler, J. (1977b) 'The Corporatist Economy: Theory and Administration', in R. Scase (ed.), *Industrial Society: Class, Cleavage and Control*. New York: St Martin's Press.

Wolf, N. (1993) *Fire With Fire: The New Female Power and How it Will Change the 21st Century*. Oxford: Blackwell.

Wollstonecraft, M. (1975) *A Vindication of the Rights of Woman*. New York: W.W. Norton.

Wright, E.O. (1978) *Class Crisis and the State*. London: Verso.

Wright, E.O. (1985) *Classes*. London: Verso.

Yearly, S. (1992) *The Green Case: A Sociology of Environmental Issues, Arguments and Politics*. London: Routledge.

Young, A. (1990) *Femininity in Dissent*. London: Routledge.

Young, H. (1993) *One of Us: A Biography of Margaret Thatcher*. London: Pan Books.

Young, H. and Sloman, A. (1986) *The Thatcher Phenomenon*. British Broadcasting Corporation.

Index

Lightning Source UK Ltd.
Milton Keynes UK
UKHW03f1448010818
326610UK00010B/483/P